The Thursday Afternoon Cooking Club's Cook Book

THE THURSDAY AFTERNOON COOKING CLUB'S COOK BOOK

INTRODUCTION TX715
.T55

The Thursday Afternoon Cooking Club of Wichita, Kansas, was organized in the Fall of 1891, by Mrs. E. R. Spangler, who was the first President. It has held a unique place among women's clubs in the West, and has received many high compliments from our Eastern guests, as being the only club composed exclusively of practical housekeepers, organized solely for the exchange of ideas in the art of cooking and domestic science. The membership is limited to twenty five, and must stand for the higher and better things in life.

The motto of the club, "Health, Strength, Happiness," indicates the high value they place on food quality as a prime factor in the making of the modern home. Extravagant receipts are not sought, but every receipt must be practical and meet the requirements of every-day experience.

Great credit for the success of the Club, in organizing and planning all work, should be given to Mrs. B. H. Campbell, who gave the best of her time, strength, and advice as President for eleven years. The love and harmony that has always been with the Club, we owe to her firm, yet gentle, advice; so much so, that we feel she was the Mother of the Club. We are now in our thirty-first year, and the only one of the Charter members left to enjoy the club is Mrs. O. D. Barnes.

For many years, the one great desire of the Club has been to have a cook book, containing our very choicest receipts, not for financial profit, but to be a guide and help to the generations that follow the earnest women who have striven for so many years to bring wholesome living into the homes.

We could not publish the book without acknowledging the deep obligation we owe to our dear departed member, Mrs. Chester I. Long, whose kindness, faithful work, and generous co-operation has made the book possible. This feeling of appreciation will find a glad echo in the hearts of all the members, and of all others who receive the book.

PAST PRESIDENTS

Mrs. E. R. Spangler,	Mrs. H. W. Lewis,
Mrs Mary C. Todd	Mrs. C. E. Potts,
Mrs. W. P. Cleveland,	Mrs. O D. Barnes,
Mrs. B. H. Campbell,	Mrs. O. A. Rorabaugh,
Mrs. G. S. Purdue,	Mrs. W. E Stanley,
Mrs. Finlay Ross,	Mrs. R. B. Campbell,

Present President: Mrs. C. L. Davidson.

NOV 28 '22
© CI A G 9 2 7 6 4

ABBREVIATIONS

t—teaspoon—leveled with sharp blade of knife.

T—Tablespoon—leveled.

C—cup.

pt.—pint.

qt.—quart.

oz.—ounce.

lb.—pound.

B. P.—Baking Powder.

B. Sugar—Brown Sugar.

Egg yolks.

Egg whites.

min.—minutes.

hr.—hour.

Egg of butter—butter size of an egg

Pinch of salt—⅛t.

When sugar is mentioned we always mean *granulated* sugar.

Water means *cold* water.

BREAD

Bread is of two kinds—fermented and unfermented.

Fermented bread is made light by rising with yeast.

Unfermented bread is made light by chemicals, or by beating in the air, or by kneading. The material must be cold and mixed quickly.

Bread is the most important article of food, and history tells of its use thousands of years before the Christian era. Many processes have been employed in making and baking; and as a result, from the first flat cake has come the perfect loaf. The study of bread making is of no slight importance, and deserves more attention than it receives.

QUICK METHOD BREAD RECEIPT

2 cakes yeast　　　　　　　1 pt sweet milk
1 pt. water　　　　　　　　1 t salt

For a family say, of four persons, dissolve two cakes of Fleishman's compressed yeast in a little luke-warm water, into an earthen bowl or milk crock, pour 1 pt. of sweet milk and add 1 pint of freshly boiled water and 1 teaspoonful of salt. Stir into this enough sifted flour to make a soft batter, and if the mixture is now cool enough to admit of holding the forefinger in it, add the dissolved yeast cakes, beat well and continue to stir in more sifted flour until the mixture is pretty stiff. Then turn it out on a floured moulding-board and knead the mass until it is smooth, adding necessary flour very gradually. Be careful not to knead in too much flour. When the kneaded dough ceases to stick to the hands and the bread board, you have used sufficient flour. It is not necessary to knead this bread longer than just enough to make the dough smoothe and free from lumps of roughness

All the dough should have been scraped clean out of the bread-bowl and kneaded with the rest so that there is no waste, and then the bowl must be greased slightly with butter or clean drippings, the dough put back into the bread bowl and greased over the top. Cover with a clean linen cloth, and set in a temperature of 75 degrees fahrenheit, to rise. Do not put near a stove or in any place where it would be too warm for one's own comfort. Notice the size of the mass of dough, and when it is light enough to mold again it will be twice its original size. If the temperature of the room is right, the bread will be risen sufficiently in three hours.

Toss out again upon the molding-board and divide into loaves, mold them smooth and firm, using little or no flour; put into greased baking pans grease lightly over the top of loaves and let them rise again to double their size The best pans for baking bread are a square cornered oblong, usually called brick loaf size. Each loaf should be in a separate pan and when the loaf is put into it, it should be barely half filled. This allows for rising till it is even with the top of the pan and so ready for the oven. In ordinary weather it will take about an hour to rise. In hot, summer weather, the rising each time will be accomplished a little quicker than during the remainder of the year. When the bread is in the moderately hot oven, it must rise but not brown for the first fifteen minutes. Then it may begin browning and at the end of forty-five minutes, tip the loaf out of the pan and if the sides look white, the loaf must be returned to the oven for another quarter of an hour, or until the whole loaf is baked a' pretty golden brown, on sides and bottom as well as top. When sufficiently baked remove from the oven and stand the loaves up to cool, leaving them so that air can circulate freely all about them. Brush them over the top with a little sweet milk, to soften the crust a little. Do not cover them with anything and when perfectly cold, put away in a freshly washed and scalded earthen jar with cover, or a sweet tin bread box. Do not wrap the loaves in a towel or cloth of any kind. The bread so treated will taste of the cloth.

Suggestions: Many persons object to the proportion here given of yeast and wetting, but scientific tests have shown that the best and most nutritious results is secured by this proportion, and the bread will not taste yeasty as it is apt to do when less yeast is used and the dough is longer in rising

Always be careful not to scald the yeast when adding it to the hot water and milk. The finger is a safe thermometer to use.

There can be no measure of flour in making bread, as flours differ in the quantity of moisture. The only safe rule is not to add more flour, when the dough ceases to stick to the hands and the bread-board.

Be careful about the yeast. A good yeast cake will be firm and will break up cleanly. Avoid yeast cakes that have become soft. Never use tin or other metal in which to make bread. A large earthen bowl is by far the best for this purpose.

Mrs. B. H. Campbell.

BREADS

NUT BREAD

4 C flour
4 t B. P.
2 eggs
¾ C sugar

1 C English walnut meats
1 C milk
1 t salt

Beat eggs. Add sugar, milk, flour in which the salt and baking powder have been mixed. Last walnuts. Mould into two loaves and let rise one half hour. Then bake slowly one-half hour.   Mrs. W. B. Buck.

OLD VIRGINIA SPOON BREAD

1 C sweet milk
2 C buttermilk
1 t lard
1 t salt

3 eggs
5 T corn meal
1 t soda

Beat eggs well. Add sweet milk, then corn meal to which salt and soda have been added. Then add fat and buttermilk. Bake in deep buttered pan from which the bread is served with a spoon.   Mrs. W. B. Buck.

POTATO SPLIT BISCUIT

1 cake compressed yeast
2 eggs
2 large potatoes
1 C lard and butter mixed

1 t salt
1 T sugar
3 pts. flour
1 C sweet milk

About 8:30 o'clock put yeast to soak in the cup of milk. Bake the potatoes so they will be well done by nine o'clock. Put thru a ricer or sieve. Into the hot potato put lard and butter previously creamed. Add salt and sugar and eggs well beaten. Then add yeast and milk and two pts of the flour. Set in a warm place for three hours, then stir in 1 qt. of flour. Let it stand until two hours before dinner, when place on molding board. Roll about one-half inch thick. Cut with large cutter. Spread one biscuit with soft butter and place another biscuit on top. Stick thru with finger. Let it rise and bake in moderate oven one-half hour. Butter, sugar and cinnamon or grated cocoanut can be added over top of these biscuits with pleasing effect.

Mrs. W. B. Buck.

SIMPLE NUT BREAD

4 C flour
4 t B. P.
¾ C granulated sugar

½ t salt
2 C milk
1 C nuts

Let rise 20 minutes, bake in moderate oven.

Mrs. J. H. Black.

SALLIE LUNN

1 pt. flour	1½ t baking powder
2 T sugar	2 T butter
1 egg	⅛ t salt
1 C milk	

Mix sugar, salt and baking powder in flour—melt butter and add to milk and beaten egg. Mix and bake.

Mrs. Julia King Vail

SOUR MILK GRIDDLE CAKES

1 t salt	1 C flour
1 t soda	1 egg
1 C sour milk	

Beat together thoroughly sour milk and egg. Mix dry ingredients and add to the milk and egg, then again beat thoroughly. This makes about 18 cakes

Mrs. W. E. Stanley.

MUFFINS CORN WITH DATES

1 C corn meal	1 T brown sugar
1 C flour	2 T butter
½ t salt	1 C milk
4 t baking powder	½ C dates (chopped)

Mix and sift corn meal, flour, salt, baking powder, and sugar. Add melted butter, milk; mix well and add chopped dates. Bake in hot oven.

Mrs. Erwin Taft.

GEMS

2 eggs	2 t baking powder
1 T of butter	2 pt. flour
1 pt. of cream	1 t salt
1 T sugar	

Melt butter Beat eggs separately. If preferred, graham flour can be used—one-third graham and two-thirds white flour.

Mrs Chester I. Long.

SPOON BREAD

2 C water	1 T fat
1 C milk	2 eggs
1 C cornmeal	2 t salt

Mix water and corn meal and boil five minutes Beat eggs, mix with milk, fat and salt. Beat all well into the mush and bake twenty-five minutes in deep buttered pan from which the bread is served with a spoon

Mrs. W. B Buck

NUT BREAD SWEET

2 C sugar
1 C sour cream
1 C butter
3 C flour

2 eggs
1 C nuts
1 t soda
⅛ t salt

Beat eggs thoroughly, chop nuts, sift soda in flour, cut butter into flour, and mix all thoroughly. Bake one hour in two small loaves.

Mrs. Warren Brown.

ROLLS POCKET BOOK

1 cake compressed yeast
3 T sugar
1 egg
1 pt. sweet milk

4 T butter, melted
1 t salt
6 C flour

Dissolve the yeast in 1½ C luke warm water—stir in 1 C flour, cover and leave in a warm place, 2 hrs. If it is light and bubbly over the top your yeast is good, add egg well-beaten; add the slightly warm milk which about 20 min. ago you brought just to the boiling point. Add the other ingredients and the flour Knead on the bread-board until it does not stick to your hands. Set aside in a warm place to rise again. Place dough on board and roll to ½ inch thickness, cut with biscuit cutter, brush butter over and fold over pressing edges together. Allow to rise, bake in a quick oven about 15 min. Set yeast at night if wanted for luncheon.

Mrs. A. O. Rorabaugh.

ROLLS IN ONE HOUR

4 cakes compressed yeast
1 T sugar
2 C warm milk

2 T lard
1 T butter
Flour

Fix yeast with sugar and fill ½ pint cup with warm milk, take 2 cups warm milk and put needed amount of flour in pan, butter, lard, make as bread.

Mrs. C. L. Davidson.

PECAN BREAD

4 C flour
1 C sugar
3 t baking powder
½ t salt

1 C pecans cut up
1 egg
2 C milk

Sift the first four ingredients. Add egg beaten light and the milk and beat hard. Let rise 30 minutes. Bake in two loaves.

Mrs. Harry Dockum.

TOAST CREAM

1 pt. milk
¼ pt. cream

4 slices toast
½ t salt

Heat milk and cream to scalding, in double boiler, add salt and pour on toast.

TOAST AMERICAN

1 egg   1 cup milk
⅛ t salt

Beat egg thoroughly, mix with milk. Dip piece of toast in mixture, moistening thoroughly, and fry on hot buttered griddle. Butter and serve hot.

CRUST CUPS

2 eggs (yolks)   ½ pt. milk
¼ lb. flour

Beat eggs, then add some milk, then flour, etc. Cook on iron.

TIMBAL IRON BATTER

¾ C flour   ½ C milk
½ t salt   1 egg
1 t sugar   1 T olive oil

Mrs. C. V. Ferguson.

BOSTON BROWN BREAD—THE REAL

1 C rye meal   1 t salt
1 C yellow corn meal   2 t soda
½ C graham flour (sifted)   2-3 C molasses
½ C white flour   2 C thick sour cream

Steam three hours.

WAFFLES

2 C flour   1 T melted butter
1 t B. P.   ½ t salt
1½ C milk   3 eggs beaten separately

Mix the flour, baking powder and salt, put the beaten egg yolks in the milk and add the flour, the melted butter, and last the white of the eggs.

Mrs. L. C. Jackson.

NUT BREAD

3½ C flour   1 C sugar
3½ t baking powder   1 C milk
1 t salt   1 egg
1 C English walnuts

Sift flour, baking powder, salt five times. Beat egg mix with milk. Mix all together. Put in 2 pans. Let rise 20 minutes. Bake one hour.

Mrs. C. E. Potts.

DROP BISCUITS

1 C flour
2 T fat
¼ C milk

2 t B. P.
½ t salt

Sift the dry ingredients, cut in the fat, then add the milk. Drop from a spoon on to a well greased pan. Bake in a quick oven

Mrs. C. L. Davidson.

BREAD OATMEAL

2 C oatmeal
1 C B sugar
1 cake compressed yeast

1 t salt
1 T lard

Pour boiling water over oatmeal, when lukewarm, add sugar, salt, lard, yeast and flour to make sponge. When light add flour to make in loaves. Let rise and bake in moderate oven.

Mrs. N. Baldwin.

BROWN BREAD STEAMED

2 C graham flour
1 C cornmeal
1 C sweet milk
1 C sour milk

1 C white flour
1 C molasses
2 t soda
1 t salt

Mix all the dry ingredients well together add sweet milk and molasses, and sour milk in which soda has been dissolved. Divide the whole into three well greased B. P. cans (grease the lids also.) Steam 2 hours in covered kettle of boiling water. Remove can covers and bake 20 or 30 minutes.

Mrs. B. H. Campbell.
by Mrs. Norton.

WAFFLES, KAFFIR

1 pt. milk
½ t salt
2 C Kaffir flour
3 t B. P.

2 T melted butter
1 T syrup
3 eggs

Break egg yolks into crock, beat, add salt, syrup, butter, and milk. Mix B. P. and flour and add   Fold in the well beaten egg whites. Bake on well greased hot waffle irons.

Mrs. A. O. Rorabaugh.

· WAFFLES CRISP

1 lb. butter
1 qt milk
4 eggs (beaten separately)

1 pt flour
4 t B. P.
1 t salt

Heat butter and milk together. When cool add rest of ingredients Beat well.

Mrs. N. Baldwin.

GEMS GRAHAM

1 C graham flour	4 t B. P.
4 T sugar	4 T butter (melted)
1 egg	1 t salt

Mix with sweet milk for rather thick batter. Salt Bake in quick oven.

Mrs C. L. Davidson.

GRAHAM GEMS

1 egg	2 C graham flour
¼ t salt	¾ C milk
2 t B. P.	1 T butter

Cream the sugar, salt and butter, add egg, alternate the milk and 1 C graham, adding in small portions, mix and beat well. It should not be very stiff nor runny. Bake in a quick oven in gem pans. This quantity makes eight.

Mrs. A. O Rorabaugh.

GRAHAM GEMS

1 C sour milk or cream	1 egg
1 t salt	1 T sugar
1 t soda	

Add graham flour and make batter stiff as for muffins. Bake in buttered hot gem pans.

Mrs. W. A. Reid

DATE BREAD

1 qt. sour milk	½ lb. dates
4 C graham flour	2 t soda
2 C wheat flour	2 t salt
1 C molasses	

Steam 2 hrs. in baking powder cans filled about 2-3 full.

Mrs W. E. Stanley.
Mrs. H W. Lewis

CORN BREAD

1 C flour	1 t B P
1 C corn meal	1 t soda
3 T butter	1 C sour milk or buttermilk
3 T sugar	1 t salt
2 eggs	

Sift together flour, sugar and salt, and corn meal, add well beaten eggs, and melted butter. Warm milk, add soda, then mix with the batter. Bake in buttered tins 20 min.

Mrs. Will Dixon.

CORN CAKES

1 C flour
2 C cornmeal
½ C melted butter
2 C sour milk
1 T sugar

3 eggs
1 t soda
3 t B. P.
1 t salt

Sift the dry ingredients, add the melted butter, beaten yolks of eggs, sour milk and then the stiffly beaten egg whites. Fry on a hot griddle.

Mrs. C. L. Davidson.

CORN BREAD

2 C corn meal
2 C flour
2 T sugar
1 t salt
3 t B. P.

3 eggs
1 T butter
2 C milk (sweet)
1 C finely chopped dates

Sift together meal, flour, sugar, salt, baking powder and rub in the butter. Add egg yolks, milk and dates. Add beaten whites of eggs last. Bake in quick oven in gem pans and serve hot at once.

Mrs. L. C. Jackson.

CORN BREAD SPOON

4 eggs
1 pt. milk
1 C corn meal

1 t salt
1 T sugar

Beat eggs separately Bring milk to a scalding point; add corn meal. Let cool a little before adding the eggs, salt and sugar.

Mrs. C L. Davidson.

CORN BREAD, SOFT

3 t baking powder
4 eggs
1 pt. corn gritts

1 pt. milk
1 pt. corn meal
1 T butter

Cook gritts, use white granulated meal. Have gritts hot, add butter, then eggs, corn meal and last of all, milk and 3 t baking powder.

Have iron skillet very hot and well greased, pour in batter, bake in quick oven. Turn bottom side up on large hot plate. Must be served immediately.

Mrs. Will Dixon.

CORN BREAD SOUTHERN

1 pt butter milk (or clabber)
1 t salt
1 pt. white corn meal (scant)

1 t soda
2 eggs
1 T melted butter (or lard)

Mix, pour into a well greased, hot, shallow pan and bake in a hot oven until brown. Nice baked in gem pans.

Mrs. C. L. Davidson.

BROWN BREAD WITH FRUIT

3½ C graham flour
2 C sour milk
1 t soda
2-3 C molasses
1 t salt

2 T melted butter
½ C currants
½ C raisins
½ C nuts

Add molasses last. Bake 45 min. in moderate oven.

Mrs Whitney.

BRAN BREAD

1 cake yeast
½ C warm water
1 T butter
2 T sugar
1 pt. milk

3 C flour
1 T salt
½ C sugar
2 T molasses
2 C bran

Soak Fleishman yeast and B sugar in luke warm water. Heat milk and add flour, lard and butter. Heat, then add yeast. Let stand and raise Knead again and add ½ C sugar, molasses and bran. If not stiff enough, add a little more white flour. Let raise again, knead again, make into loaves, raise once more and bake slowly 40 min.

Mrs. F. G. Smyth.

BOSTON BROWN BREAD (CRUMBS)

1 C crumbs
1 C meal
1½ t soda
1 C graham flour

1 C water
¾ C molasses
½ t salt

Mix ingredients, add molasses and water. Steam 2 hours

BISHOP'S BREAD

3 eggs
1 C sugar
½ C nuts

½ C raisins
2 C flour
2 t B. P

Stir into stiff batter and spread into a dripping pan, cook until brown and take from pan and cut in strips, then put back in pan to brown, strips all over

C. C.

BISCUITS, CORN MEAL

1¼ C flour
¾ C cornmeal
4 t B. P
2 t sugar
¼ t salt

2 t lard
2 T butter
1 egg
½ C milk

Mix the dry ingredients together; cut the shortening into it with a knife; add the milk into which the well-beaten egg has been mixed. Roll out on a floured board, one half inch thick, cut with cooky cutter. Put small piece of butter on each one and fold over. Will make sixteen biscuits. Bake in quick oven. Serve hot.

Mrs. H. G. Norton.

BISCUIT VIRGINIA

1 T lard
1 qt. flour
1 t salt

2-3 C milk
2-3 C water

Rub lard into flour; add salt; mix milk and water, add slowly to flour, stirring all the while. The dough must be hard—not wet. Knead the dough for fifteen minutes, then pound for fifteen minutes longer, folding constantly. Then roll very thin and cut in biscuit shapes, stick the top of each biscuit with a fork. Place in baking pan so as not to touch each other, and bake in moderate oven until crisp and brown.

Mrs. A. C. Jobes.

BISCUITS

1 C flour
2 T fat
⅜ C milk

2 t B. P.
¼ t salt

Sift dry ingredients, cut in the fat, then add the milk. Roll out. Cut in shape and bake in a quick oven. One dozen biscuits.

Mrs. C. L. Davidson.

BROWN BREAD

2 C corn meal
1½ C rye meal
1 C white flour
1 C raisins

3 C sour milk
2 t soda
1 C molasses
1 t salt

Disolve soda in little hot water. Add to molasses and the well mixed dry ingredients. Mix with milk and last molasses, after which raisins which have been cut in two and rolled in a little flour. Put in baking powder cans and steam four hours.

Mrs. W. B. Brooks.

TOASTED ENGLISH MUFFINS

1 cake compressed yeast
2 T sugar
1 C milk
1 C water

4 T lard or butter
6 C flour
1½ t salt

Dissolve yeast and sugar in milk and water, add lard or butter and three cups flour. Beat until smooth, then add gradually the other 3 cups flour and salt. Place in a well greased bowl, cover and set aside to rise; when it has risen twice as high, roll to one half inch thickness and cut into cakes. Set aside half hour, brown on both sides in hot ungreased griddle and bake ten minutes in a medium oven. When ready to serve slice. Toast and spread with butter.

Madeline Lewis.

MUFFINS BRAN

2 C bran
1 C milk

¾ C flour
3 t baking powder

Sift baking powder with flour; add milk, then bran Bake in gem tins.

Mrs Spangler.

OUR EGG MUFFINS

1 egg
2 C milk
1 T sugar

4 t B. P
2 C flour
½ t salt
2 T butter

Mix in order given. Bake in hot oven.

Pauline Brown Gillespie

BISCUITS PIN WHEEL

2 C flour
2 T sugar
4 t B. P.
½ t salt

2 T citron (finely chopped)
1-3 C raisins (finely chopped)
2-3 C milk
½ t cinnamon

Mix as for a baking powder mixture, sift sugar, salt, flour, and baking powder together; cut in the fat, then add the milk. Roll this mixture to ¼ inch in thickness. Brush with melted butter and sprinkle with fruit, sugar, and citron. Roll like a jelly roll, cut off pieces ¾ inch thick. Place on a buttered tin, bake in a hot oven fifteen minutes

Mrs. C. L. Davidson.

BREAD IN THREE HOURS

2 cakes yeast (compressed)
1 T sugar
2 T lard

1 T salt
2 C milk (blood warm)
1 C water (blood warm)

Break yeast in a ½ pt. cup, add sugar, then fill glass with blood warm water, sift flour in large pan, put a well in center, add lard, salt, warm milk and salt, then yeast, then rest of milk, continue to mix in flour till it can be handled, then roll in soft ball and leave on board for 5 minutes on flour, rub in buttered bowl and turn it over, let stand one hour till it doubles, make into loaves and let stand till it doubles, then bake This makes 3 loaves and one dozen rolls. Using no milk and no shortning makes a dry crust.   Mrs C. L. Davidson.

CORN BREAD

2 eggs
2 T melted butter
1 T sugar
1 C sweet milk

1 C flour
1 C corn meal
5 t B P.

To the well beaten eggs add milk, sugar and butter; then flour and corn meal. Beat until light, add baking powder. Turn into well greased shallow tin pan, bake 20 minutes in moderate oven.   Mrs. C. V. Ferguson.

SALADS

Almond Salad   Mrs. Harry Dockum
Alligator Pear Salad
Apple Salad (whole)   Mrs Henry Allen.
Apple and Pineapple Salad
Artichokes
Asparagus   Mrs. H. W. Lewis.
Asparagus and Califlower
Banana and. Nut
Banana
Beet Salad   C C.
Brussels Sprouts
Cabbage Salad Cold   Mrs. A. O. Rorabaugh.
Cabbage Salad Hot   Mrs. H. W. Lewis.
                                       Mrs. W. E. Stanley.
Calla Lilly Salad   Mrs. O. D. Barnes.
                                       Mrs. J. H. Aley

Cauliflower Salad
Celery Salad   Mrs. F. G. Smyth.
Chestnut and Celery
Chestnut and Turkey
Chicken Salad   Mrs. C. L Davidson.
Chicken Salad   Mrs. Chester Long
Christmas Salad   Mrs. Oak Throckmorton
Cold Slaw   Mrs. H. A. English.
Combination Salad   Mrs. Chester Long.
Crab Meat Salad   Mrs W E. Stanley.
Cucumbers Stuffed   Mrs Chester Long.
Cucumber and Pineapple   Mrs. F G. Smyth.
Cranberry Salad   Mrs. Will Dixon.

Dainty Salad (Cucumbers)   Mrs. F. G. Smyth
Dainty Salad (green pepper)   Mrs F. G Smyth.
Easter Salad
Endive Salad
Frozen Salad   Mrs. F. G. Smyth.
Fruit Salad and Dressing.   Mrs. Geo. Steel
Frozen Fruit Salad   C. C.
Frozen Tomato Salad
Frozen Vegetable Salad   Mrs. H. G. Norton.
Fruit Salad   Mrs Will Dixon.
Fruit Salad and Dressing   Mrs O. D. Barnes.
Fruit Salad   C. C
Fruit Scallop
Grapefruit Salad   Mrs Erwin Taft
Grapefruit Salad   Mrs. Chester Long.
Grapefruit Salad   Mrs M. Murdock.
Green Pea and Onion Salad   C. C.
Ham Salad   Mrs. O. D. Barnes.
Heavenly Hash   Mrs. C. L. Davidson.
Killarney Salad   Mrs. J. J. McNamara.   •
Lamb Salad   Mrs. Oak Throckmorton.
Lamb Chop and Pea Salad
Lemon Shells   Mrs W. E. Stanley.
Lobster Salad   Mrs. Will Dixon.

Log Cabin Salad
Marshmallow Salad   Mrs Warren Brown
Nut Cheese Balls
Nut and Fig Salad
Peach Salad
Pear Salad
Peas in Tomato Aspic   Mrs. Finley Ross.
Picnic Salad   •
Pimento Salad   Teresa L. Comley.
Pineapple Salad   Mrs Warren Brown.
Porcupine Salad   Mrs. W. E. Stanley.
Potato Salad   C. C.
Prune and Cheese   C. C.
Radish, Cucumber, Celery
Salmon Salad   C. C.
Scotch Woodcock Salad
Stuffed Celery
Stuffed Tomato Salad   Mrs M. Murdock.
Sunflower Salad
Suggested Salads
Sweet Bread Salad   Mrs. H. G. Norton
Tomato Salad
Tomato Jelly Salad
Waldorf Salad
Walnut and Orange Salad
White Cherry Salad   Mrs. W. E. Stanley.
White Grape Salad   Mrs. W E. Stanley.
White Salad   Mrs. O. D. Barnes
Wilted Lettuce with Bacon

SALADS

Salads are most valuable in the diet because they introduce raw or fresh material in an attractive form. And some raw food, either vegetable or fruit should be eaten daily. The salad usually derives its name from the material most used in its composition. The success of a salad depends upon the absolute coldness of the materials, and the tasty combinations of fruits or vegetables used. The dressings are very varied, each salad calling for its own particular dressing.

The dressings are only of two classes: cooked and uncooked. To insure crispness of material, place on ice, or in ice water, an hour before using and dry thoroughly to prevent the moisture thinning the dressing

There are three kinds of salad dressings:
French dressing
Mayonnaise dressing.
Cream or cooked dressing.

The French dressing is best made at the table, having all the utensils and materials cold. The secret of all fine salad making is cold materials, quick beating, and immediate service. Good oil is most important. A quantity of dressing can be made by putting the ingredients into a covered fruit jar, shake the jar energetically until a smooth emulsion is formed. The true French dressing is composed of salt, pepper, oil, and vinegar. The true Mayonnaise is composed of salt, pepper, vinegar, oil and uncooked egg-yolks. Other dressings come under the head of cooked or cream dressings.

METHOD OF MIXING FRENCH DRESSING

½ t salt	⅛ t pepper
1-16 t paprika	2 T vinegar or lemon juice
6 T oil	

An onion or garlic should be rubbed over the cold bowl in which the dressing is to be mixed. Mix the oil and condiments, mix again. Then add the vinegar or lemon juice a drop at a time, whipping constantly with a four pronged silver fork or salad fork, until all the liquid is used, and then whip 5 min. Serve at once over salad; or if mixed with salad must be tossed lightly. Some tastes require mustard added to the above. This is the English dressing. Some prefer Taragon to plain vinegar. Lemon juice makes a more delicate dressing, but does not produce a beautiful golden color.

METHOD OF SUCCESSFULLY MAKING MAYONNAISE

There is no danger of it curdling if eggs are fresh and oil added slowly and all thoroughly cold and mixed in a cool place. Beat always in one direction.

2 egg-yolks raw	2 T vinegar
1 pt. olive oil	2 T lemon juice
1-16 t paprika	½ t salt

Beat the yolks with a silver fork ½ min., add condiments and mix again. Then add 1 t vinegar and mix. When well mixed add the oil drop by drop. When too thick to beat well add 1 t lemon juice and then more oil alternating oil and acid until all are used. If desired thicker add more oil. The true mayonnaise uses all vinegar, and no lemon juice, but some tastes prefer the mixture. Vinegar makes a more golden mayonnaise. The above is the foundation of all mayonnaise. Different flavors or herbs may be added for different tastes 2 T of heavy whipped cream may be added.

A Remulade sauce is made of the cooked yolks, rubbing them to a smooth paste and proceeding as above.

BOILED SALAD DRESSING

This is the foundation of most cream dressings where mayonnaise is not used as a foundation.

4 eggs	1 t salt
4 T butter	2 C water
½ T sugar	2 T flour

Place water and butter in top of double boiler. Beat eggs separately and add flour to them stirring out all the lumps with a silver fork. Add this slowly to the water and butter, which should be boiling, stirring all the time. Boil and stir 15 min., with a split spoon. If it should lump, run through a rice presser while hot. Stir in a cool place until cold. Add sugar and salt. This foundation dressing will keep two weeks in a cold place, and whipped cream, lemon juice, or vinegar, olive oil, salt, pepper, mustard or sugar, or any flavoring or nuts, may be added. It is very stiff. A tablespoonful can be used to thicken soup, milk toast or Puree before the condiments are added. Cream added to it should be very stiff. In any salad where tomatoes are used, more salt is required.

SUGGESTIONS FOR SALAD

Salads should be handled very lightly, tossed instead of pressed into shape. The fingers of both hands spread apart, are the best salad mixers that can be used.

Green vegetables must be crisp and dry

All ingredients and materials must be cold.

Meat and foul should be marinated.

Salads should not be combined until just before serving.

In many cases the dressing is best served on top the salad

Light vegetable salads dressed with French dressings are served with dinner, while heavy meat and fish salads are for luncheons or supper, served with Mayonnaise or cream dressing.

A fruit salad is served at a luncheon or supper with thick dressing

A fruit salad with French dressing may be served at dinner with game or roast.

The right place for salad is with the game or roast.

Crisp green vegetable with French dressing or only lemon

juice is most delicious and aids as a complement to the heavy meat course.

Celery may be kept fresh by wrapping the bunches in brown paper to exclude the air, sprinkle with water, then wrap in a damp cloth and put in cool dark place.

To keep lettuce or parsley put in *cold* place in air tight bag.

To keep pimentos after opening, scald and put in a glass fruit jar with closed lid.

With fish salads serve brown bread sandwiches, also with cold fish lobster or crab salads.

With beef salad serve chopped cress or parsley sandwiches.

With chicken salad serve nut sandwiches.

Cabbage salad requires sugar in the dressing.

A little olive oil may be added to a boiled dressing for chicken or fish.

COMBINATIONS FOR SALADS

Celery and apple	Beets and beans
White grape and nut	Lettuce and Roquefort
Cheese and tomato	Spinach and egg
Beet and celery	Celery and tomato
Tomato and peppers	Cabbage and almonds

SIMPLE SALADS

The simplest fruit salads may be made by combining whatever fruit you have, and boiling:

½ pt. sugar	30 drops lemon juice
½ pt. water	¼ t salt

Boil 7 min., cool and pour over cold fruit. This is a good simple accompaniment to a heavy meat dinner.

ALMOND SALAD

1 pkg. Knox gelatine soaked in	1 medium sized can sliced pine-
½ C cold water	apple
1 C blanched almonds	8 sweet pickles

Cut these into small pieces. Then cook 1½ C sugar, ½ C vinegar, ½ C water to a thick syrup, or until it hairs well. Add pineapple juice while still hot, also gelatine and let cool. Then add pineapple and nuts, pickles, and mold. Serve with boiled mayonnaise.

Mrs Harry Dockum

Alligator pear should be served with French dressing.

APPLE SALAD (WHOLE)

8 apples	¼ pt. water
1 pt. sugar .	1 C blanched almonds

First remove the core, then peel apples. This preserves them whole Make a syrup of sugar and water; while boiling drop in apples and cook until clear, being careful not to break. Cool in syrup, fill centers with chopped nuts and serve with mayonnaise dressing.

Mrs. Henry J. Allen.

APPLE AND PINEAPPLE SALAD

1 C apple cubed	1 t sugar
1 C pineapple cubed	½ C lemon juice
1-16 t salt	

Mix apple and pineapple   Mix salt, sugar and lemon juice well, and stir into fruit. Have all very cold and salad plates cold.

ARTICHOKES

Artichokes are best served with a Tartar sauce, the leaves being broken from the artichokes with the fingers and dipped in the sauce   French people always eat lettuce with their fingers Cutting seems to take u

ASPARAGUS SALAD

Asparagus	1 hard boiled egg
Lettuce leaves	1 T pickle
½ T parsley dressing	1 T pimento
4 T olive oil	2 T lemon juice
½ t salt	⅛ t pepper

Arrange several stalks of cooked asparagus, which has been chilled, on a bed of cirsp lettuce leaves and arrange the following mixture to represent a band across the middle of the bunch.   To the white of 1 hard boiled egg finely divided or chopped, add finely chopped pickle, pimento and parsley   Pour over a dressing made of the olive oil, lemon juice, salt and pepper.

Mrs. H. W. Lewis

ASPARAGUS AND CAULIFLOWER

1 C Cauliflower (Cooked)	1 C Mayonnaise
1 C Asparagus tips (Cooked)	

Break cauliflower into flowers and surround with asparagus tips. Pour over both a Mayonnaise dressing, and sprinkle with finely sliced pimentos.

BANANA AND NUT SALAD

6 Bananas	½ c nuts (Pecans)

Chill bananas in lengthwise strips, roll in nuts and serve 2 to a person on lettuce leaves with 2 T of Mayonnaise on each plate between the 2 layers of bananas   All must be cold

BANANA SALAD

½ C sugar	4 bananas
1 T water	¼ C walnuts
½ lemon	6 candied cherries
1-16 salt	

Boil sugar, water, lemon and salt. When very cold slice bananas, chop walnuts, halvé the cherries and pour all over banana. This prevents their darkening

BEET SALAD

1 qt. cabbage
1 qt beets
1 C horseradish
1 C vinegar

2 C sugar
1 t salt
½ t pepper

Chop cabbage. Cook beets and chop. Grate horseradish and add vinegar. Mix thoroughly.   C. C.

BRUSSELS SPROUTS SALAD

1 pt sprouts
2 T onions
1 T chopped celery or celery seed

2 T capers
⅛ C olives
½ C walnuts
1 T lemon juice

Boil and drain sprouts, cool, add onions, capers, olives, walnuts and celery all chopped fine. Mix together with lemon juice and pour over all a mayonnaise dressing. Serve ice cold.

CABBAGE SALAD (COLD)

2 C cabbage
1 C onions

2 C green peppers
1 t catsup

COLD DRESSING FOR CABBAGE SALAD

Slice cabbage, peppers and onions very thin. Pour over this a rich French dressing in which you have mixed a t. of catsup and let stand in ice-box for two hours before using. Serve on lettuce leaves.

Mrs. A. O. Rorabaugh.

HOT CABBAGE SALAD AND DRESSING

½ cabbage (small head)
1 C vinegar
1 egg
2 T butter

1 t mustard
2 t sugar
1 t salt
½ t pepper

Let vinegar come to a boil. Beat together egg and other ingredients and pour over this mixture the boiling vinegar. Stir well, return to the stove and cook 2 or 3 minutes. Pour over chopped cabbage and serve hot.

Mrs. W. E. Stanley
Mrs. H W. Lewis

CALLA LILLY SALAD

Make a pie crust, not too rich, and roll thin.

To make shells, cut a circle 10 in. in diameter of glazed white paper, as heavy as will roll. Fold in quarters; cut; roll over and fasten with a pin, in the shape of a cone. Take a similar quarter, cut off the center point 1 in. and round off the outer edges, to form lilly. Use this for pattern, cut crust with

sharp pointed knife. Place on cones and press together at small end by moistening with a little water. Bake in shallow tins in moderate oven, until they slip off the cone, but not too brown. The cones may be used a second time, but the better way is to use new ones. Lay the shell on a lettuce leaf and fill with any white salad. Cover with whipped cream, and place stamen in place, made of the yolks of hard boiled eggs, moistened with mayonnaise. Make roll about an inch long. This is very attractive.   Mrs. O. D. Barnes
                                            Mrs. J. H. Aley

CAULIFLOWER SALAD

Break the cold boiled cauliflower into flowerets and serve with Tartar sauce or Mayonnaise.

CELERY SALAD

Cut ripe olives and pimentos in small pieces, mix this with neuchatel cheese, line the larger stalks of celery, tie two stalks together until the cheese is firm, then use a sharp knife and slice. Pour oil dressing over this and a dash of Mayonnaise. These, of course, are put on a large leaf of lettuce.
                                            Mrs. F. G. Smyth.

CHRISTMAS SALAD

1 cup sweet cooked mayonnaise, salt and paprika. Mix with cottage cheese until firm enough to mold in tall bowl. Place on ice. Make ring of cranberry jelly or tomato aspic. Put this on platter. Place cheese in center of ring. Around outside of jelly put more mayonnaise mixed with whipped cream and chopped almonds. Garnish with lettuce and red pimentos.
                                            Mrs. Oak Throckmorton

CHESTNUT AND CELERY

Cut chestnuts in half, add small pieces of celery and Maraschino cherries. Serve with a French dressing over all.

CHESTNUT AND TURKEY SALAD

1 C cooked chestnuts (hulled)
2 C Turkey (dark and light meat)

Cut chestnuts in half and Turkey in cubes. Dip the meat in olive oil and drain. Mix with the chestnuts and serve with Mayonnaise.

CHICKEN SALAD

1 chicken	7 egg-yoks
3 stalks celery	1 egg-white
1¼ C vinegar	1 t mustard
1 t salt	½ t white pepper
1 C whipped cream	1 t flour or starch

Boil vinegar, pour over yolks, then boil till thick. Add mustard and flour or starch, salt and pepper. Cook till very thick, then cool thoroughly. Add cup of whipped cream.
                                            Mrs. C. L. Davidson.

CHICKEN SALAD

2 C cold chicken (white meat   ½ C pecans
   preferred)   ½ t salt
1 C celery   ¼ t pepper
1 C Mayonnaise

Cut the celery and chicken in ½ in. cubes, Marinate the chicken, drain, add the nuts and celery and mix with a stiff mayonnaise. The celery must be kept on ice until crisp and thoroughly dry.

Mrs Chester I. Long

CRAB MEAT SALAD

2 Stalks Celery   4 Cans (medium sized) Crab Meat
1 Cup Blanched Almonds   One half dozen hard boiled eggs
Olive Oil Mayonnaise

Serve on head lettuce leaves and at last minute mix thru some shredded lettuce. Will serve 16.

Mrs. W. E. Stanley.

COLD SLAW

Shred cabbage very fine on slaw cutter.

Dressing for Slaw
2 T sweet cream (Whipped)   4 T vinegar
2 T sugar   ½ t salt

Cover the slaw with this dressing and serve.

Mrs. N. A English.

COMBINATION SALAD

½ C radishes   ½ C onion
1 C cucumber   ½ head lettuce
1 C tomato   1 T parsley
½ C celery

Slice cucumbers, onions and radishes in ring. Cut tomatoes in square dices. Mince parsley, cut celery in in. sticks. Mix all together and serve with French Dressing All must be cold. Do not let stand.

Mrs. C. I Long.

STUFFED CUCUMBER SALAD

6 cucumbers   2 T celery
2 tomatoes

Pear a cucumber, cut in half lengthwise, remove seeds and stand on ice 1 hr Chop tomato using just the hard part; chop celery fine, mix with 3 T of Mayonnaise and fill cucumber shells.

Mrs. Chester Long.

CRANBERRY SALAD

1 qt. cranberries	2½ T gelatin
2 C boiling water	1 C diced celery
2 C sugar	1-3 C walnut meats

Cook cranberries and water together for 20 min. Run thru sieve, stir in sugar and cook 5 min. Add gelatin dissolved in a little cold water. Just before this begins to set pour half of the mixture into a shallow enameled pan which has been rinsed in cold water. Allow to set keeping the remainder warm from becoming stiff. Over the first half sprinkle celery and nuts, pour remainder of gelatin mixture over this and allow to set. Serve as a salad on crisp lettuce leaves.

Mrs. Will Dixon.

CUCUMBER AND PINEAPPLE

1 pt. can pineapple, cut in fine pieces	1½ packages gelatine
	½ t vanilla
1 good sized cucumber sliced fine	juice from 6 lemons
	1 C sugar

Heat the lemon and pineapple juices adding sugar and Knox's gelatine dissolved in 1 C cold water. When dissolved, add to the heated mixture on the stove Boil 2 min. Strain, and pour over pineapple and cucumber, mix together and let set in a shallow granite pan. Cut in squares, serve on a lettuce leaf. Serve with Mayonnaise dressing with cream.

Mrs. F. G. Smyth.

DAINTY SALAD (CUCUMBER)

Pare cucumber, scoop out part of inside and stuff with a cream cheese (In jars). Let set in refrigerator until ice cold. Slice and serve with head lettuce or tomatoes with thousand island dressing.

Mrs F. G. Smyth.

DAINTY SALAD (GREEN PEPPERS)

Scoop out the inside of pepper, fill with soft cream cheese, let it stand in ice box until very cold, then slice and serve with any dressing desired, on lettuce leaves.

Mrs. F. G. Smyth.

EASTER SALAD (LILLIES)

6 hard boiled eggs	2 T Mayonnaise
6 lettuce leaves	

Cut the egg whites into pointed petal-like strips. Reserve the yolks of 3. Mash the other yolks. Mix with Mayonnaise and fill the calex of the petals with the mixture Put the 3 yolks through a ricer, dropping over the petals to give the appearance of pollen. Cut lettuce leaves in fine points to simulate the outer green. Served on glass dishes to resemble water.

ENDIVE SALAD

Endive is kept on ice and served cold with a French dressing. Lettuce the same. Cucumbers are best served ice cold with a French dressing made with lemon juice instead of vinegar.

FROZEN SALAD

Make a rich mayonnaise, then add white cherries, nuts, grapes or anything you care to add as a fruit salad, pack in baking powder cans and pack in salt and ice for 4 hrs. Serve on a lettuce leaf with a dash of whipped cream.

Mrs. F. G. Smyth.

FRUIT SALAD AND DRESSING

½ C cream, whipped   4 T sugar
3 T lemon juice   salt

Put in lemon juice, drop by drop the same as oil. The fruit for salad, even quantities of oranges, pineapples, ½ as much apple, grapes, dates, and nuts.

Mrs. Geo. Steel.

FROZEN FRUIT SALAD

½ envelope Knox gelatine   ⅛ t cayenne
2 T cold water   2-3 C milk
1 T butter   1-3 C vinegar
2 eggs (yolks)   2 T canned pineapple juice
3 T sugar   1 C prepared fruit
1 t salt   1 C heavy cream
1-3 t paprika   lettuce

Soak gelatin in cold water five minutes. Melt butter, and add yolks of eggs, well beaten, sugar, salt, paprika, and cayenne. Remove from fire and add gradually milk, vinegar, and pineapple juice. Cook in double boiler, stirring constantly until mixture thickens, and add soaked gelatin. Remove from range, and beat 2 minutes. Cool, stirring occasionally, and when beginning to set, add prepared fruit, using Maraschino cherries, cut in small pieces and strained, orange pulp, canned sliced pineapple, cut in small pieces, and cream, beaten until stiff, being careful that the fruit does not settle to the bottom. Pack in a wet brick mold, having mixture overflow the mold, adjust cover, and pack in finely crushed ice and rock salt, using 2 parts ice to 1 part salt, and let stand 2 hrs. Remove to bed of crisp lettuce leaves, and cut in slices, crosswise, for serving. Accompany with Mayonnaise dressing.

C. C.

FROZEN TOMATO SALAD

Pack a can of tomatoes in ice. Let stand 4 hrs. and serve with Mayonnaise dressing.

FROZEN VEGETABLE SALAD

5 Blue Label cheese	1 C mayonnaise
2 green peppers	1 C cream (whipped)
1 C nuts	1 can pimentos

Mash the cheese, grind the peppers and pimentos, cut the nuts fine, and add the salad dressing and whipped cream, pack in baking powder cans, in equal parts of salt and ice and let stand 3 hrs., serve in slices on lettuce. Will serve 18 or 20.

Mrs. H. G. Norton.

FRUIT SALAD

¾ box gelatine	10 nuts
6 figs	2 C sugar
2 oranges	½ pt. boiling water
9 dates	½ pt cold water
2 lemons	

Soak gelatin in cold water 20 min, dissolve in hot water. Add juice of lemons and sugar. Strain and let stand until it begins to thicken. Stir in all the fruit cut into small pieces and let harden. Serve with Mayonnaise.

Mrs. Will Dixon.

FRUIT SALAD AND DRESSING

1 can white cherries	1 can pineapple
1 C water	½ lb almonds
1 pt. Mayonnaise	1 pt. whipped cream
1 package gelatine	

Dissolve gelatine in water Scald the juice of cherries and pineapple, and add gelatine. When cool stir in the mayonnaise and whipped cream. When it begins to set, add the cherries, pineapple and blanched almonds, cut fine. Fill individual molds or platter. Chill. Serve with whipped cream or French dressing.

DRESSING

Juice 1 lemon; juice 1 orange; 1 T olive oil, 1 T juice Maraschino cherries. Put in glass can, cover and shake until well blended.

Mrs. O D. Barnes

FRUIT SALAD

1 can pineapple	juice of 1 lemon
3 oranges	2 C water
6 bananas (sliced)	2 C sugar
½ box gelatine	

Omit lemon juice if berries are used. It may be served in orange shells.

Slice pineapple, oranges and bananas. Dissolve gelatine in water, add all together with sugar.

C. C.

FRUIT SCALLOP

1 C pineapple	1 T sugar
1 C oranges	1 C apple
2 C walnut meats	1 C seeded grapes
1 banana	1 C strawberries
1 C lemon juice	1 C cherries
½ t salt	

Alternate layers of nuts and fruit and pour over all lemon juice, salt and sugar mixed well.

GRAPEFRUIT SALAD

1-3 C sugar	1½ T gelatine
1-3 C water	1 T lemon juice
½ C grapefruit juice	⅛ t salt

Dissolve gelatine in water, add other ingredients. Put in indvidual molds. Serve with Neufchatel cheese on mold and mayonnaise on top.

Mrs. Erwin Taft.

GRAPEFRUIT SALAD

3 grapefruit	1 t paprika
½ C French dressing	

Chill the grapefruit, cut in halves crosswise, take out the pulp and cover with cold French dressing. A strip of pimento may be used on each as an ornament. Sprinkle with paprika.

Mrs C. I. Long

' GRAPEFRUIT SALAD

2 C grapefruit juice and pulp	½ cake chili cheese
2-3 C boiling water	cream
2-3 C sugar	Few chopped nuts
Mix	1 package of gelatin
1 tinfoil of cream cheese	

Dissolve gelatin in hot water, add sugar, add to grapefruit pulp, put small amount in individual mold, add layed of cheese mixed with cream and nuts, then put layer of grapefruit gelatin on top. This makes six individual portions. Serve with oil mayonnaise.

Mrs. M. Murdock.

GREEN PEA AND ONION SALAD

1 can peas	1 T. onion

Drain and chill peas and onion. Chop onion very fine. Mix peas and onion. Marinate thoroughly with cold French Dressing. Serve very cold on crisp cold lettuce leaves.

C. C.

HAM SALAD

1 C cold chopped boiled ham	1 bay leaf
1 C stock of ham	2 small red peppers
1 T onion	1 T gelatine
½ C water	

Chop onion, add with spices to stock. Cook 10 min., dissolve gelatine in water, add and strain and when it begins to set, stir in ham. Fill molds, serve on lettuce leaf with mayonnaise dressing.   Mrs. O. D Barnes.

HEAVENLY HASH SALAD

1 C chopped marshmallows	1 C chopped cabbage
1 C pineapple	1 C sliced almonds

Mix all together and then fold in cream mayonnaise dressing.
Mrs. C. L. Davidson.

KILLARNEY SALAD

½ pt mayonnaise	2-3 C milk
½ pt. whipped cream	3 T apple juice
2 eggs	1-3 C pineapple juice
2 T sugar	1 T lemon juice
1-3 C vinegar	½ C pecans, broken
1 T flour	½ C cherries, cut
½ t salt	½ t paprika
1 T butter	

Boil milk, add flour, butter and paprika, beaten eggs, sugar and salt. Then cool and add fruit juices, nuts and cherries Freeze 3 hrs. Serves 8 people.
Mrs J. J McNamara.

LAMB CHOP AND PEA SALAD

6 French Lamb Chops   1 small can peas.

Bake chops and cut from bone chopping into fine bits. Cool and mix with cold peas. Cover with French dressing and sprinkle 1 T finely minced mint leaves over all. If these are not procurable add 1 T mint sauce to the Dressing
Mrs. C. Long.

LEMON SHELLS

Lemon shells iced, stuffed with cucumbers and bits of lemon pulp, mixed with mayonnaise.
Mrs. W. E. Stanley

LOBSTER SALAD

1 can lobster	1 small onion
5 lettuce leaves	6 tomatoes

Chop lobster meat coarsely. Prepare in same way the onion and lettuce leaves. Season to taste. Hollow out the tomatoes and fill with salad. Any cold meat may be added to the lobster. Serve with mayonnaise dressing
Mrs. Will Dixon.

LAMB SALAD

½ pound cold cooked lamb   1 teaspoon mint juice
1 cucumber cut fine   1 cup mayonnaise oil
½ can of peas

                      Mrs. Oak Trockmorton.

LOG CABIN SALAD

½ C grated cheese   ½ C butter
1 C flour   1 t paprika
¼ t cinnamon

Rub together all ingredients. Mix with ice water. Roll very thin, cut in straws. Bake in quick oven. When cool pile in log cabin style on a large platter and leave a space inside in which pile some good fruit salad or vegetable salad mixed with French dressing and a ½ C of mayonnaise piled on top.

MARSHMALLOW SALAD

1 C sour whipped cream   1 small can diced pineapple
1 C sweet whipped cream   ½ juice of lemon in sour cream
1 C pecans   Salad dressing on top.
½ lb. Marshmallows, cut fine

                      Mrs. Warren Brown.

NUT-CHEESE BALLS

½ C cream cheese   ¼ C celery
¼ C pecans   ¼ C olives

Chop pecans, celery and olives fine, mix celery and olives with cream cheese. Make into balls and roll in nuts. Place molded currant or blackberry jelly in center of plate and surround with the nut balls.

NUTS AND FIG SALAD

Serve well mixed, divided nuts and figs with French dressing.

PEAS IN TOMATO ASPIC

½ box gelatine   ⅛ t pepper
3 C tomato liquor cooked   ⅛ t salt
1 bay leaf   2 C green peas, canned or
1 small stalk celery   cooked
1 slice onion

Soak the gelatine in cold water, heat to boiling the tomato liquor which has been cooked for 15 min. with a slice of onion, the celery, bay-leaf and strain. Stir the gelatine into the tomato liquor, strain again and season to taste with salt and pepper and put aside to cool. When it begins to stiffen stir into it the peas, first rinsing them off in cold water and draining them dry. Turn into small cups rinsed out in cold water and set on ice to form. Serve on lettuce leaf with a good dressing.

                      Mrs. Finley Ross.

PEACH SALAD

Cut ripe peaches lengthwise into small pieces. Make a dressing as follows:

(6 large peaches)	2 T sugar
4 T almond butter	½ t salt
1 T cream	3 drops lemon juice

Rub almond butter smooth in cream, add sugar and salt. Cook 3 min., add lemon juice and cover peaches. Cream may be omitted.

PEAR SALAD

1 can pears	¼ lb pecans
¼ lb. grapes	½ C mayonnaise

Drain juice from pears and fill center with grapes and pecans mixed with mayonnaise Then add a t. of mayonnaise on top of each pear and a maraschino cherry. .

PICNIC SALAD

1 lb. dates	½ C grated cheese
2 oranges	½ C pecans
½ C orange juice	

Stuff dates with nuts which have been chopped and mixed with cheese, roll in lemon juice. Peel oranges and cut in slices. Place dates on top of slices of oranges. Cover all with French dressing

PIMENTO SALAD

1 C boiling water	1 C pecans
1 pkg. gelatine dissolved in ½	1 small can pimentos
C cold water	½ C pearl onions
¼ C vinegar	3 sweet pickles
When cold add	When it commences to jell add
5 hard boiled eggs, chopped fine	1 C of mayonnaise
	serve with mayonnaise on top.

Teresa L Comley.

PINEAPPLE SALAD

1 can diced pineapple	1 C English walnuts
1 C white seeded grapes	1 C diced celery

Let stand in pineapple juice 30 min., drain, add 3 t lemon Mayonnaise and 1 pt. heavy whipped cream.

Mrs. Warren Brown.

PORCUPINE SALAD

Place ½ of large sized pear on lettuce leaf, flat side of pear down. Take blanched almonds slice in thin pieces, and stick thickly over the pear. In small end of the pear stick small piece or red pepper or pimento for tongue. Serve with French salad dressing made with lemon instead of vinegar

Mrs W. E. Stanley.

POTATO SALAD

1 cucumber
2 onions
2 eggs

6 potatoes
½ lb. English walnuts

Hard boil the eggs, either dice or slice cucumbers, onions, eggs and potatoes. Chop English walnuts. Mix lightly with French Dressing.

C. C.

PRUNE AND CHEESE SALAD

1 lb prunes

½ lb. cheese

Plump some prunes by letting them soak for a time in hot water. Remove the stones and fill with cream cheese. Serve on crisp lettuce leaves with mayonnaise dressing with whipped cream on top.

C. C.

RADISH, CUCUMBER SALAD

Equal parts of radishes, cucumbers, celery, watercress and green peppers. 1 T grated onion, and 1 T chives. Slice and mix and serve in lettuce cups with French dressing.

SALMON SALAD

1 can of salmon
4 eggs
½ small head cabbage or
6 stalks celery
1 large sour pickle

¼ t mustard
1 t salt
1 cup nuts
½ C vinegar

Hard boil eggs, chop nuts. Mix all ingredients together and serve on lettuce leaves. Can be used for bread sandwiches. Vinegar etc, can be used to taste.

C. C.

SCOTCH WOODCOCK SALAD

1 C English Walnut Meats
½ C celery
6 large olives
Cut fine, and turn over in the
   following dressing:
1 T butter

1 T flour
1 C hot milk
⅛ t paprika
1 C cheese cut fine
½ t parsley, chopped
¼ t salt

Put butter in dish over hot water. When melted stir in flour, then add hot milk, paprika, parsley and salt. Stir until smooth, add cheese. Stir until dissolved.

STUFFED CELERY SALAD

Mix cream cheese with Mayonnaise dressing, until paste is formed. Stir in chopped nuts. Fill the concave side of celery with the mixture. Serve cold on lettuce leaf.

STUFFED TOMATO SALAD

Tomatoes   Small amount of onion
1 tinfoil of Cream Cheese   oil mayonnaise
Small amount of cucumber

Peel tomatoes and put on ice to cool. Add to cream cheese a little oil mayonnaise, then cucumber and onion chopped fine, and stuff into tomatoes. Put oil mayonnaise on top. Serve on lettuce leaf.

Mrs. M Murdock

SUNFLOWER SALAD

Press the yolks and whites of hard boiled eggs separately thru a ricer. Pile the yolks in the center of salad plate, and the whites in circle outside of it. Outside of egg-whites arrange shredded lettuce. Serve with Mayonnaise dressing.

SUGGESTED SALADS

Tomatoes stuffed with olives. French dressing
A head of lettuce, cut in quarters, and served with French dressing.
Lettuce sliced across the grain in rings, and grated cheese piled on the mayonnaise.
Celery and apples cut in thin strips. Mayonnaise Dressing.
Heart of lettuce stuffed with orange and pear Cream added to Mayonnaise.
Salmon and shredded lettuce and hard boiled egg tossed in French dressing.
Cheese and cucumber with Mayonnaise.

SWEETBREAD SALAD

1 pair sweetbreads   Mayonnaise true
1 cucumber, large

Boil sweetbreads 30 min., blanch 5 min. in cold running water, separate the meat from the connecting membrane, add to a cucumber which has been peeled and cubed and bind together with mayonnaise.

Mrs. H. G. Norton.

Chopped celery and peppers Add cheese and use cream dressing.
Cucumber and new onions sliced. French Dressing.
Cucumbers on lettuce with oil and lemon juice.
Apple and pineapple, 2 parts apple to 1 of pineapple. Serve with lemon juice.
Cauliflower, string beans and beets
Lettuce, asparagus and sliced radishes.
Grape fruit juice may be used instead of lemon in Fruit Salad.
Lime juice may be used on pear salad.

TOMATO SALAD

1 can tomatoes	2 T gelatine
1 t salt	¼ C water
½ t paprika	

Cook tomatoes, salt and paprika 10 min. Dissolve gelatine in cold water, strain the tomato mixture and add the mixture to the gelatine. Pour into molds and when cold and firmly set, serve with mayonnaise dressing.

TOMATO JELLY SALAD

1 qt. tomatoes	½ C lemon juice
3 bay leaves	1 t salt
1 T onion chopped fine	2 T celery minced
1½ T sugar	2 T gelatine

Boil tomatoes, onion, bay leaf, sugar and celery 10 minutes. Prepare gelatine according to directions on package. Run tomato preparation thru sieve, add to gelatine. Let cool. Serve with mayonnaise or French dressing on lettuce leaf, pour in molds.

WALDORF SALAD

½ C English walnuts	1 C celery
1 apple	

Cut apple and celery into fine long strips. Cut nuts in half. Mix with French Dressing. Oranges may also be added and use a cream dressing.

WALNUT AND ORANGE SALAD

Prepare walnuts, slice oranges and mix with prepared white grapes. Serve with French Dressing.

WHITE CHERRY SALAD

Seed and fill cherries with cream cheese made smooth with a little pimento thru it. Serve with Grape Fruit cut in rather large pieces. Over this put a T of cooked Mayonnaise. Also fill cherries with nuts, filberts, preferred, as they fill the space of cherry seed nicely.

Mrs. W. E. Stanley.

WHITE GRAPE SALAD

Peel white grapes, remove the seeds and insert small strips of pimento. Pile on sliced pineapple with cooked mayonnaise on top.

Mrs. W. E. Stanley.

WHITE SALAD

2 C celery	2 C apples
4 slices pineapple	1 lb. white grapes
1 t salt	

Cut celery fine; seed and half grapes; dice apples, drain pineapple and cut in small pieces. Mix with mayonnaise.

Mrs. O D. Barnes.

WILTED LETTUCE WITH BACON

¼ C vinegar	¼ lb. bacon
2 heads lettuce	½ t salt
1 t sugar	⅛ t pepper

Chop bacon fine. Cut lettuce with scissors into small shreds. Fry bacon crisp. Mix fat with vinegar, salt, sugar and pepper. Have very hot and pour over lettuce. Cover dish and let set to steam 5 min. Serve hot. The bits of bacon can be poured on top.

Salad Dressing

Biltmore Sauce	
Boiled Dressing	Mrs. H. W. Lewis
Cooked Dressing	Mrs. W. E. Stanley
Cooked Dressing	Mrs. O. D. Barnes
Creamed Dressing	Brooklyn Institute
Fruit Salad Dressing	Mrs. Henry Lassen
Fruit Dressing	Mrs. W. E. Stanley
Fruit Dressing	C. C.
Golden Dressing	C. C.
Hollandaise Sauce	Mrs. A. C. Jobes
Jellied Cheese Salad	Mrs. O. G. Hutchinson
Pineapple Dressing for Fruit Salad	Mrs. Henry Lassen
Roquefort Dressing	
Russian Salad Dressing	Mrs. Warren Brown
Sour Cream Dressing for Cabbage Salad	Mrs. W. E. Stanley
Tartar Sauce	Mrs. C. L. Davidson
Tartar Sauce	Mrs. Chester Long
Thousand Island Dressing	Mrs. Finley Ross
Thousand Island Dressing	
Tomato Salad Dressing	Mrs. Spangler

BILTMORE SAUCE

½ C Mayonnaise
½ C lemon juice
1 T Worcestershire Sauce

2 T Chili Sauce
2 T chopped olives
1 t minced pickles

Have plate iced. Into it squeeze lemon juice and add other ingredients beating thoroughly.

BOILED DRESSING

1 T butter
2 T flour
1 t salt
3 egg-yolks
1 C milk

½ C vinegar
1 t mustard
2 t sugar
Few grains red pepper

Cream butter and flour, add condiments, mix, then beaten yolks, milk and then add vinegar slowly. Cook in double boiler beating constantly.

Mrs. H. W. Lewis.

COOKED DRESSING

4 eggs
1½ T sugar
¼ C milk
½ t salt

½ t celery seed
½ t mustard
1 T flour
2 T butter

Mix flour, sugar, salt, celery seed, and mustard. Add eggs, one at a time, beating thoroughly each one as put in Add milk. Heat vinegar and add to the above stirring constantly. Take from the fire and add butter, then beat, beat, beat, until perfectly smooth. Then set away in a cool place. When required for a salad, take the above dressing and mix with whipped cream. This if kept in a cool place, will keep for a week or more, and may be used on many different salad combinations.

Mrs. W E. Stanley.

COOKED DRESSING

6 egg-yolks
1 t salt
1 t flour
½ C vinegar

½ C water
1 t mustard
1 T butter
1 t sugar

To cold vinegar and water, add the beaten yolks and dry ingredients mixed with butter. Cook in double boiler, until thick, add whipped cream just before serving.

Mrs. O. D. Barnes.

CREAM DRESSING

3 T Oil
1 T lemon juice
¼ t paprika

¼ t salt
⅛ t pepper
½ of a cream cheese

Mash cheese with fork, add French dressing until it is a thick dressing. Put over lettuce or tomato. Must be rebeaten if not used at once.

Brooklyn Ins't.

FRUIT SALAD DRESSING

Beat one egg until smooth, add one-third cup sugar, one-third cup pineapple juice, one-third cup lemon juice. Cook over hot water till thick. Add whipped cream when cool. Use with fruit and marshmallows.

Mrs. Henry Lassen.

FRUIT DRESSING

2 egg-whites	$\frac{1}{4}$ C lemon juice
$\frac{1}{4}$ t salt	$\frac{1}{2}$ C pineapple juice
2 T butter	$\frac{1}{2}$ C cold water
$\frac{1}{4}$ C sugar	$\frac{1}{2}$ C cream whipped
5 T flour	

Cook. Add whipped cream, one C.

Mrs. W. E. Stanley.

FRUIT DRESSING

$\frac{1}{2}$ C cream whipped	4 T sugar
3 T lemon juice	$\frac{1}{4}$ t salt

Put lemon juice in drop by drop. To be used on fruit salad, composed of oranges, pineapple, grapes, dates and nuts, other fruits can be used as you like.

C. C.

GOLDEN DRESSING

$\frac{1}{4}$ C pineapple juice	2 eggs
$\frac{1}{4}$ C orange juice	$\frac{1}{2}$ C sugar
$\frac{1}{4}$ C lemon juice	$\frac{1}{2}$ C heavy cream

Heat the fruit juices in double boiler, beat eggs light, gradually adding the sugar. Combine with the hot juice and cook like a custard. When cold fold in the cream, whipped stiff. This dressing is suitable to serve with any fruit salad.

C. C.

HOLLANDAISE SAUCE

$1\frac{1}{2}$ T boiling water	$\frac{1}{2}$ T olives
2 T butter	$\frac{1}{4}$ t paprika
$\frac{1}{4}$ t salt	1 egg-yolk
$\frac{1}{2}$ T pickles	$\frac{1}{2}$ t lemon juice

Melt butter in boiling water in a bowl. Place bowl in pan of hot water, add other ingredients, beat constantly with dover egg-beater. Add finely-chopped pickles and olives. Beat until thick, not any longer as it will curdle. Cool and serve with fish, although it is good with all meats.

Mrs. A. C. Jobes.

—48—

JELLIED CHEESE SALAD

1 T gelatin	1 C whipped cream
1 scant cup water	¼ t salt
½ C rich grated cheese	⅛ t pepper

Dissolve gelatin in the cold water. To the grated cheese add the whipped cream, salt and pepper Then add the dissolved gelatin. Fill small molds, when it begins to congeal, sprinkle with grated cheese. Serve in lettuce nests with cream mayonnaise.

Mrs. Henry Lassen.

PINEAPPLE DRESSING FOR FRUIT SALAD

4 T sugar	1 t salt
2 T flour	1 egg

Three-fourths cup pineapple juice, add juice of one lemon, fill up cup with water, put this in double boiler to heat. Beat egg and gradually beat in dry ingredients. Add warm juice a little at a time, put back in double boiler and cook until smooth, when cold add one cup cream, whipped.

Mrs. O. G. Hutchinson.

ROQUEFORT DRESSING

4 T oil	1 t salt
½ C Roquefort cheese	

Rub cheese and oil together slowly five minutes, add salt and pepper if desired

RUSSIAN SALAD DRESSING

½ bottle chili sauce	1 small bottle stuffed olives
½ bottle capers	(grind olives and pickles)
½ doz. small sour pickles	

Mix with oil mayonnaise.

Mrs. Warren Brown.

SOUR CREAM DRESSING FOR CABBAGE SALAD

½ head cabbage (chopped fine)	2 t sugar
1 C sour cream	½ t salt
1 t celery seed	

Mrs W. E Stanley.

TARTAR SAUCE

1 T minced sour pickles	1 hard boiled egg (chopped)
1 T onions	¼ t salt
1 T capers	1/16 t pepper
1 T parsley	1 lemon
2 T mayonnaise	

Wet with the lemon juice and mix with mayonnaise.

Mrs. C. L. Davidson.

TARTAR SAUCE

4 T true mayonnaise	1 T capers
1 t mustard	1 T dill pickle
1 t onion juice	1 t sugar

Chop capers very fine. Mince dill pickles and mix all ingredients with the mayonnaise. Good with fish, tongue, boiled meat or asparagus.

Mrs Chester Long.

THOUSAND ISLAND DRESSING

3 T mayonnaise	1 T olive oil
3 t chili sauce	1 T cream
3 t tomato catsup	1 T chopped sweet pickle

Mrs. Finlay Ross.

THOUSAND ISLAND DRESSING

½ C olive	1 t Worcestershire Sauce
½ orange	⅛ t paprika
½ lemon	⅛ t celery seed
2 sprigs of parsley	or chopped celery
1 t onion	

Use the juice only of the lemon and orange. Chop parsley very fine, grate onion, and put all in a bottle or fruit jar. Shake quickly and place in ice chest until ready to serve; then shake again.

TOMATO SALAD DRESSING

1-3 C mayonnaise	1-3 C Blue Label Chili Sauce
1-3 C whipped cream	

Mix thoroughly. Is very good over head lettuce.

Mrs. Spangler.

❦ SOUP ❦

SOUP—WHAT IT IS

Soup is always started with cold water.

Stock is the foundation of all soups except those which have no meat in them

Stock will keep for several days, in winter a week.

If no vegetables are used in making the stock it will keep longer. Many prefer to add vegetables and seasoning when making the soup.

Soups are served as appetizers.

The seasoning is the making of the soup.

An important item in soup making is slow warming at first, and then a steady, slow fire.

Stock must be cooled quickly but not on ice.

Every particle of fat must be removed from stock for a clear soup. This can be done easily when the stock becomes cold, it becomes cold and settles on the top.

The white and broken shell of an egg can be used to clarify the soup. It can also be strained through a muslin bag

Soup may be thickened by egg, or egg and cream.

In passing vegetables through a fine sieve, if they are kept moistened by some of the liquid to be used in the soup, it will be easier.

Soups are divided into 2 classes:

Stock soup and soup without stock.

The divisions are:

White Stock—made from veal or poultry.

Brown Stock—made from beef marrow, bone and fat.

Bouillon—made from lean beef only.

Consomme—made from beef and veal.

Lamb or Mutton Stock—

Purees and Bisques—made from vegetables, or fish and milk.

Cream Soups with milk or cream as a foundation, and vegetables

Bouillon is used for luncheon or supper rather than dinner, served in Bouillon cups.

Consomme for dinner and served clear.

Cream soups and purees are not served with a course dinner.

A stock pot may be kept covered and trimmings of meat and scraps can be put in boiled and thus keep a stock always on hand. A slightly tainted piece of meat will spoil the whole pot.

The foundation of all cream soups is made from the following sauce

| 4 T flour | 2 C milk |
| 4 T butter | 1 t salt |

Rub butter and flour together and boil, adding milk, stirring constantly to prevent lumps. Add salt last.

To this white sauce may be added cooked celery strained for celery soup.

Cooked corn strained for corn soup.
Cooked potato strained for potato soup.
Cooked rice strained for rice soup.
Cooked asparagus strained for asparagus soup.
Cooked peas strained for pea soup.
Cooked beans strained for bean soup.
Cooked spinach strained for spinach soup.

The quantity of vegetable and water should equal one pint, added to the cream sauce.

SUGGESTIONS FOR SOUP

Rice, squash, peas, cucumber, celery, asparagus, potato, cauliflower, tomato, mushrooms, barley, carrots, onion, peanuts, chestnuts, spaghetti and okra, all may be made into delicious cream soups.

Raspberry, strawberry, cherry, apricot, peach, blackberry, pear, loganberry and orange, all make good iced soups for hot weather. Lemon juice should be added to sweet fruits.

Any vegetable puree may be made by taking the cream sauce recipe omitting, the flour and adding the soup stock to the desired vegetable.

A soup bunch consists of onions, carrots, tomatoes, celery, parsnips, cabbage and parsley.

In warm weather fruit soups and purees are sometimes served, instead of hot soups and a thick puree.

Parsley and celery may be dried to advantage and used as flavoring.

Thyme, bay leaf, and onion juice each add much to the distinctive taste of the soup and can be used best to suit the taste of the user. Cream soups are fattening and nourishing.

Soups may be served with crisp crackers, cheese sticks, croutons, meat balls, noodles, grated cheese—A T to each service, is good on soup. Cheese sticks are made by buttering thin, long slices of bread, and spreading grated cheese on top, then brown in oven

Crackers or wafers should be crisped in hot oven and served at once.

Soups are appetizers and may be made most nourishing.

The flavoring is important, often the soup is made or marred by too much or not enough.

ALMOND SOUP, CREAM OF

¼ C rice

½ lb. blanched almonds

1 t sugar

2 qts. hot milk

1 qt. boiling water

1 C cold water

1½ t salt

Cook rice and add to hot milk, cook forty-five minutes, pulverize almonds adding the cold water as they are mashed. When the almonds form a smooth paste add to the rice and milk. Then add sugar and salt.

APPLE SOUP (ICED)

6 apples

Rind ¼ lemon

½ C sugar

¼ t ginger

Slice and core apples, add lemon and boil until tender. Run through colander, add flavor and water. Serve with shaved ice. Cinnamon or any desired flavor may be added.

APRICOT PUREE (ICED)

1 can apricots

Run through colander and serve in sherbet cups iced. Any sweetened fruit can be served in this way.

ASPARAGUS PUREE

1 C cooked asparagus

1 t chopped onion

1 qt white stock

Run asparagus through colander, add onion and stock. Cook till thick. The puree is thickened with the strained vegetable instead of flour.

ASPARAGUS SOUP

1 C celery

1 C asparagus

3 C water

1 t salt

½ t pepper

1 C cream sauce

Put celery and asparagus in cold water, gradually heating and let simmer twenty minutes, strain through colander. Reheat and add 1 C cream sauce, salt, and pepper.

BLACK SOUP

1 hock of veal

1 hock of beef

1 onion

Small stalk of celery

1 C cabbage

1 t cloves

2 potatoes

1 small can tomatoes

1 turnip

2 carrots

1 t allspice

2 bayleaves

Cook on back of stove, let simmer all day, strain, let stand in open crock. When cool take off grease. Heat, add 2 T catsup, 1 t salt, ½ t pepper, strain through cheese cloth and serve.

Mrs. P. C. Lewis.

BEEF TEA

Beef Tea or essence may be made by placing one pound of juicy rump steak (no fat) in a closely closed jar in a moderate oven, or a boiling kettle of water three hours. For beef tea add boiling water to the juice when done.

BOUILLON

1 lb. meat	1 piece celery
3 eggs	1 turnip
½ doz. cloves	1 onion
1 doz. allspice	1 carrot (chopped fine)
1 doz. peppers	1 gal. soup stock
Parsley stems	

Cut meat fine, add eggs (shells also), cloves, allspice, peppers, celery, turnip, onion, parsley, carrot, soup stock. Stir gently to keep from sticking, check back several times with cold water, boil several hours as it will be stronger. Strain.

BOUILLON

6 lbs. round steak (no bone)	1 T salt
½ onion (large)	1 stick cinnamon
1 slice of carrot	1 T parsley
1 slice turnip	2 bay leaves
3 cloves	1 t sage
2 egg-whites	2 stalks celery
1 t pepper	

Remove all fat from meat. Cut 5 lbs. into small pieces, cover with water, heat slowly, simmer 5 hrs. Then add seasoning, tie all the vegetables in cheesecloth bag. Simmer 2 hrs and cool quickly but not on ice. Let stand 12 hrs, then chop fine the other 1 lb. of meat, put in soup, beat egg-whites, breaking shells and adding both eggs and shells to the cold soup. Then set over fire, heating slowly and simmer 2 hrs, adding salt last, and strain, skimming fat, if any.

BROWN STOCK

5 lb. shin beef	1 T Thyme
½ C diced celery	½ bay leaf
¼ C diced turnip	½ doz. cloves
½ C diced onion	1 T salt
½ C diced celery	3 qts. cold water
1 T parsley	2 T butter

Cube meat, remove marrow, break bones. Place butter and marrow in soup kettle, fry meat in this; bones and fat. Over these pour the water and allow to stand for 1 hr. that the juices may be drawn from the meat. Then bring slowly to the boiling point, add vegetables and seasonings and let simmer 6 hrs. If a clear stock is desired pour in 1 cup of cold water and skim the top. Be sure to simmer and not boil.

CAULIFLOWER CREAM

1 qt. chicken stock	2 egg-yolks
1 C cooked cauliflower	½ pt. cream
1 C mushrooms	

Rub cauliflower through fine sieve, add to boiling stock. Season, add cream and egg mixed and well beaten. Place the mushrooms at the bottom of the bowl and pour soup over them.

CELERY CREAM

1 C celery	2/3 t salt
2-3 C milk	2 T cream sauce
1 T butter	

Cook celery, mash through sieve and add to hot milk and butter. Add salt and cream sauce. Cook

CHESTNUT SOUP, CREAM OF

2 C mashed chestnuts	4 T flour
4 T butter	6 C milk
1½ t salt	

Boil chestnuts ten minutes, then quickly remove hull and skin with sharp thin-bladed knife. Mash through colander, add to white sauce.

CONSOMME

3 lb. round steak	1 T butter
3 lb. knuckle of veal	1 T salt
1-3 C diced carrots	1 t pepper
1-3 C turnips	1 t mayonnaise
1-3 C celery	1 t parsley
1-3 C onions	6 cloves
1 lb. marrow bone	2 T marrow
1 T lemon juice	

Cut meats into 1 inch pieces, take ½ lb. of beef, and brown in marrow. Put 4 qts. cold water in soup kettle, add veal, with marrow, bone, and the browned steak. Let stand 1 hr., then gradually heat, and simmer 4 hrs, removing skum. Brown the vegetables in butter, and add to soup other ingredients Cook 2 hrs. more, strain, remove fat, and clear by pouring in ½ C of cold water.

CORN AND POTATO SOUP

2 medium potatoes	1 T tomato
1½ C water	1 C corn
½ small onion	1 C milk
1 t salt	1 C cream

Slice onion and cook with potato in boiling salted water. When tender add tomato and corn and bring to boiling point. Heat cream and milk and vegetables just before serving. Mix.

CREAM CORN SOUP

1 can corn	1 t onion
2 C water	3 T butter
2 C milk	2 T flour
1 t salt	1/10 t pepper

Cook onion, corn and water ten minutes, rub through sieve, scald milk and thicken with flour and butter rubbed together. Cook five minutes, add salt and pepper when done.

CROUTONS

Cut bread in cubes, and bake to a golden brown in a quick oven.

FISH CHOWDER

5 lb. fish	1 qt. water
½ lb. pork	1 pt. milk
½ C onions	2 T flour
1 qt. sliced potato	1 t salt
6 crackers	½ t pepper

Remove fish bones and cook the bones in one quart water ten minutes. Cook the fish, fry the pork, then add onions sliced, cover and cook five minutes, add flour and cook five minutes longer, stirring. Strain on this the water in which the fish bones have been cooked and boil five minutes, then strain on the fish and potato. Salt, pepper and simmer fifteen minutes. Add milk and crackers that have soaked in the milk five minutes. Let it boil up once and serve. Tomato may be preferred to milk in this.

FRAPPE FRUIT CUP

1 pt. pitted cherries	1 pt. peaches, diced
1 pt. strawberries	2 oranges
1 pt. shredded pineapple	4 C sugar

Put all into saucepan, simmer ten minutes, chill and serve.

FRUIT SOUP I

1½ C strawberry juice	2 t lemon juice
1½ C pineapple	2 t sugar
½ C water	2 t orange juice

FRUIT SOUP II

4 oranges	1 lemon
1 pt. pineapple	½ C sugar

Run oranges and pineapple through presser, add lemon juice and sugar, chill and serve in glass cups.

LIMA BEAN SOUP, CREAM OF

1 C beans
1 pt. milk
1 T butter
½ T flour

½ t salt
½ t pepper
1 t onion juice

Soak beans and cook till soft, and rub through a strainer, there should be about one pint of pulp, scaled milk, thicken with butter and flour rubbed together, add the bean pulp and season to taste with salt, pepper, and onion juice.

Mrs. H. W. Lewis.

LENTIL PUREE

½ pt. lentils
1 carrot
1 onion
3 leeks

1 celery heart
2 T butter
2 qt. water

Wash and cook lentils well. Put into sauce-pan with cold water, carrot, onion, leeks and celery. Set over slow fire and add butter, bring to boiling point, stir well and serve hot.

Mrs. Geo. Whitney.

MEAT AND VEGETABLE SOUP

4 lbs. soup bone and meat
½ C carrots
1 C potato
1 onion
½ C celery
3 T tomatoes
1 T parsley

2 T butter
½ bay leaf
½ C rice and barley mixed
2 qts. water
2 t salt
1 t pepper

Dice potato, chop onion, celery and parsley fine. Slice tomato, add all together with cold water, pour over soup bone and boil forty-five minutes, then place in fireless cooker and leave twelve hours at least. When done skim off grease, reheat on stove, cut the meat into small dices, and serve in soup bowl with soup, which makes a meal of itself. Serve piping hot.

Mrs. Chester Long.

NOODLES

1 egg
¼ C flour

½ t salt

Beat egg, add flour and salt, and cut in thin slices. Boil in soup.

ONION SOUP

1 Spanish Onion
2 T butter
½ t salt
¼ t paprika

2 T flour
1 qt boiling water
5 bouillon cubes

Wash and peal onion, cut into slices, melt butter, add onion and salt. Cover and cook until onion is tender. Add flour and bouillon cubes dissolved in boiling water. Place crisp croutons in dish. Pour soup over and serve.

Mrs. Willard Brooks.

ORANGE SOUP, ICED

2 C orange juice   ½ C sugar
1 t corn starch   1 C lemon juice

Cook juices, sugar and corn starch until clear, place on ice and serve ice cold.

PEA SOUP

One can peas, mashed, added to one C milk, 2 T cream sauce, 1 t salt and ½ t pepper.

POTATO SOUP

1 gal. water   3 T butter
6 large potatoes   1 T flour
1 C rice   1 C sweet cream

Chop potatoes and add to water and rice. Work butter and flour together, add cream just before taking from fire. Boil one hour.

RICE AND CELERY SOUP, CREAM OF

2 T cooked rice   1 t salt
1½ C milk   ½ t pepper
½ C celery   2 T cream sauce

Mash and strain celery (cooked), use rice whole or mashed, add 2 T cream sauce and milk. Add salt and pepper. Cook.

SOUP BALLS

3 eggs   1 C cracker crumbs
2 t butter

Beat eggs, melt butter, and roll together in cracker crumbs, drop in soup and cook.

STRAWBERRY PUREE

1 qt. fresh strawberries   ½ C water
2 C sugar   Juice of 1 lemon

Mash the berries fine. Add sugar and water and let stand three hours Rub through sieve and add lemon juice. Serve in sherbet glasses with cracked ice.

TOMATO BISQUE

1 pt. water   ¼ t cinnamon
1 qt. can tomato   ½ C lemon juice
1½ t salt   1 T butter
1 T sugar   3 T flour
1 C cream   ¼ t onion juice

Cook the tomato in the water and salt, sugar, cinnamon, and lemon fifteen minutes. Run through colander and after mixing butter and flour add to this, and let boil five minutes. Add hot cream and serve at once

TOMATO SOUP, CREAM OF

1 pt. strained tomatoes	2 T butter
1 sliced onion	2 T flour
½ bay leaf	¼ t soda
1 piece of mace	½ t salt
1 qt milk	⅛ t pepper

Put tomatoes, onion, bay leaf, and mace in sauce pan, cover and cook five minutes Put milk into a double boiler. Rub together butter and flour; add to milk and stir until thick and smooth. Strain tomatoes into a soup tureen, add soda, season with salt and pepper, stir, and while this is frothing, add hastily the thickened milk, stir just enough to mix and serve. There is not the slightest danger of this curdling if the milk is added quickly. This soup cannot be reheated If necessary to keep warm any length of time, keep the materials in separate vessels, mixing at the last moment.

C. C.

TUTTI FRUITI CUP

1 C lemon juice	½ C grapefruit pulp
1 C orange pulp	½ C apples chopped
1 banana	1 C sugar
½ C water	

Cut orange pulp in cubes, chop apples fine, cut grape fruit in one inch cubes. Slice oranges and cut each slice in two. Mix lightly. Let stand four hours on ice, put cracked ice in sherbert cup and serve.

WHITE CREAM SOUP

3 pt. milk	3 T parsley
3 T butter	Blade of mace
3 T flour	3 t salt
3 T onions	1/3 t pepper
3 T celery	1 C cream
3 T carrot	4 egg-yolks
1 bay leaf	

Cook vegetables and butter in stewpan slowly twenty minutes. Heat milk in double boiler with herbs and spices. When vegetables have cooked twenty minutes (not browned) add flour and stir until frothy, then gradually add the hot milk, stirring constantly Cook five minutes, then turn into double boiler and cook twenty minutes Beat the yolks well, add the cream to them. Stir this into soup. Cook one minute, stirring constantly. Serve immediately.

Mrs. B. H. Campbell.

WHITE STOCK (chicken)

1 old chicken	3 qts. water
3 T rice	1 T salt
1 T onion	1 t pepper
1 T celery	

Cut chicken from bones, break bones and add cold water, rice which has been washed and picked over, onion minced, celery minced, salt and pepper Simmer for 4 hours. This can be used as a basis for cream soups, and white sauces.

WHITE STOCK (veal)

6 lb. knuckle of veal	4 cloves
2 lb skin of beef (lean)	1 T salt
2 onions	1 t pepper
2 turnips	1 T butter
2 carrots	6 qts. water

Cut the meat in cubes, crack the bones, slice the veg. and add 3 qts. of water, bring to a boil slowly, simmer for 1 hr , take off scum as it rises. Add other 3 qts. of water, simmer very slowly five hrs, strain.

YACHT CLUB OYSTER SOUP

1 pt. milk	1 t celery chopped fine
1 pt. cream	1/4 t onion juice
1 t salt	1/2 C powdered crackers
1/2 t pepper	1 T butter
1 qt. oysters	

Wash oysters Boil milk, celery and onion in double boiler twenty minutes. Then strain, add butter, crackers, and when boiling hard add oysters and let boil, stirring with split spoon until the edges of oysters begin to curl. Add salt and pepper. Do not use oyster water.

FISH

FISH

Anchovy Canapes	
Bake, To,	C. C.
Catfish, Fried	C. C.
Camp Fish,	C. C.
Codfish Roll,	C. C.
Croquettes,	C. C.
Dressing for Fish	
Deviled Crabs	Mrs. P. C. Lewis.
Deviled Shrimp	Mrs. R. B. Campbell
Fish and Eggs,	C. C.
Fried Fish,	C. C
Halibut a la Flaneade	Mrs. J. H. Black.
Loaf Fish,	C. C.
Lobster a la Newburg,	C. C.
Lobster Chops	Mrs. Rebecca Cooper Round.
Lobster Cocktail,	C. C.
Mock Oysters	Mrs. J. H. Black

OYSTERS

Boston Fried,	C. C.
Broiled,	C. C.
Creamed,	C. C.
Chicken with	C. C.
Croquettes	Mrs. E. Taft.
Cutlets	Mrs. Geo. Pratt.
Deviled,	C. C.
Entres,	C. C.
Fried,	C. C.
Fricassee, of Oysters,	C. C.
Loaf	Mrs. Chester I. Long.
Maryland,	C. C.
New Orleans,	C. C.
Panned,	C. C.
Pates,	C. C.
Pigs in Blankets	C. C.
Rabbit and Oysters	C. C.
Shell, In,	C. C.
Oyster Soup	C. C.
Pie Fish	Mrs. J. H. Black.
Planked Shad	Mrs. Chester Long.
Salmon Cutlet	Mrs. H. W. Lewis.
Salmon with Peas,	C. C.
Salmon Fritters,	C. C.
Salmon Loaf	Mrs. J. H. Black.
Salmon Puff	Mrs. Ermie Taft.
Salmon Pudding with Sauce	Mrs. J. H. Aley.
Salmon Scollop	Mrs. J. H. Black.
Salmon Souffle	Mrs. R. Millison.
Shad Roe Croquettes,	C. C.
Tuna Chops with Whipped Cream Sauce	Mrs. W. E. Stanley.
Molded Tuna or Salmon	Mrs. Geo. Steel.
Fish Mousse,	C. C.

A CHAPTER ON FISH

If the eye of a fish is sunken the fish is stale, also if the fish is flabby. The gills should be red and the scales bright in a fresh fish.

Do not leave fish in a warm place.

Turn a lobster on its back and straighten out its tail, if when released it springs back to its normal curve, you may be sure it is fresh

Medium size fish are the sweetest, salt fish require much soaking, if very salty, soak 36 hrs , changing the water several times during the process.

The best roes come from shad   All roes must be parboiled 10 or 15 min. in boiling salt water to which 1 T vinegar has been added, then let them cool in the liquid in which they were cooked. This prevents sputtering when cooking   When cool, wipe dry and dip in melted butter, or olive oil, and boil, or dip in equal parts meal and flour, 1 t salt, ½ t pepper, and fry in hot lard; serve with lemon and sauce Tartare.

Roes may also be baked after parboiling.   Bake about 20 min. with equal parts butter and water, salt and pepper.   Serve with Maitre d'hotel sauce.

TO CLEAN A FISH

Remove the scales by scraping with a dull knife from the tail toward the head.   The head and tail may be removed or not. The entrails may be removed by splitting half way down the under side of the fish and removing the contents, washing good and scraping, then salt and pepper the insides.   Mix the salt and pepper, 2-3 salt, 1-3 pepper before rubbing on fish.

WATER TO BOIL FISH

2 qts. water	1 bay leaf
½ C vinegar	1 slice lemon
6 cloves	1 t salt and ¼ t pepper

Mrs C. L. Davidson.

ANCHOVY CANAPES

6 anchovies	¼ t salt
2 hard boiled eggs	½ t lemon juice
4 T butter	6 croutes of bread
1-32 t cayenne	

Wash and bone Anchovies   Pound them to a paste with egg-yolk, butter and season.   Cut toast into ¼ in. slices round, dust with butter and brown in oven. Spread with the above paste and sprinkle over them the egg-whites riced fine.   Serve in place of Oysters at dinner or luncheon, either hot or cold.

BAKE, TO

Fish	Bits of butter
Salt	Bits of lemon
Pepper	Bits of parsley

Bone fish and lay on tin, salt, pepper, bits of butter, lemon, parsley (cut bits of stem in pan) dredge with flour, bake in hot oven 20 or 30 min.

CATFISH FRIED

Soak in cold water ½ hr. to draw out the blood and any bad taste, scrape outside and clean inside, then mix meal and flour equal parts, 1 t salt, and ½ t pepper, and dip the fish into this, rubbing pepper and salt inside the fish. Fry in bacon fat or lard with 1 T butter—must be hot.

CAMP FISH

Build hot fire and when it is reduced to coals, rub fish outside and inside with salt and pepper mixed, proportions of ¼ t of pepper to 1 t of salt, grease wire toaster and lay fish on wires close together, lay very close to coals turning until done—Butter when done, serve at once.

CODFISH ROLL

1 C Codfish	⅛ t pepper
1 C potatoes	2 eggs
1 T butter	4 slices fat pork

Pare and quarter potatoes. Shred soaked codfish. Cover both with boiling water and cook until potatoes are done. Drain and mash, add butter and beat until light. Add eggs and beat until all is creamy. Fry pork, put fish mixture on top and cook slowly until it is brown. Turn over and repeat until it is done. Slip knife under one side and turn out on hot buttered platter. Serve with mint sauce.

CROQUETTES FISH

1 can salmon or any fish same amount	1 egg
	1 1-3 C cracker crumbs
4 T milk	½ t salt, ¼ t pepper
4 T butter	

Mash fish fine. Add beaten egg, melted butter and bread crumbs, milk, make into round or cone shape and roll in egg and cracker crumbs. Fry in hot deep lard.

DRESSING FOR FISH

1 C bread (or crackers)	1 t onion
1-3 C butter	1 t parsley
Salt and pepper	1 t capers
Soup stock (or water, warm)	1 t pickles

Moisten with soup stock or warm water.

DEVILED CRABS

1 can crabs
1 pt. bread crumbs
2 T butter
1 t salt, 1-16 t pepper

1-32 t cloves
1 can tomatoes
2 T flour

Crabs, bread crumbs, butter, salt, red pepper. Put in shells or dishes and serve with tomato sauce

Mrs. P. C. Lewis

DEVILED SHRIMPS

1 can shrimps
2 T butter
2 T flour

½ t salt
2 C milk
3 hard boiled eggs

Make white sauce of butter, flour, salt and milk, cook until smooth. Remove veni from shrimps, break in small pieces, add to the sauce, chop the eggs add these and a T chopped parsley, a few drops of onion juice Season with paprika. Put mixture in ramekins, cover with buttered bread crumbs and brown.

Mrs. R. B. Campbell.

FISH AND EGGS

Warm left over fish in enough milk to moisten, turn out on platter, keep hot, poach egg and place on top of fish. Mix parsley, salt and melted butter, pour over eggs and serve hot.

1 C fish
½ C milk
3 eggs

1 T parsley
½ t salt
2 T butter

FRIED FISH

For large fish, clean and cut into spuares 4 in. square, or split down the back and fry in halves. Small fish fry whole.

Have skillet hot, and enough fat to cover bottom ¼ in. deep, ¼ as much butter as lard. Roll fish in meal and flour half and half, salted and peppered, ¼ as much pepper as salt, and place in the boiling fat, fry on one side until brown, then turn over and fry until the other side is brown. Serve at once. Any kind of fish may be fried in this way.

HALIBUT A LA FLAMADE

2 T onion (minced)
2 T celery
2 T parsley
½ t mace

2 T butter
2 T flour
1 pt tomatoes
½ t white pepper

Cover bottom of baking dish with onion, celery and parsley minced fine. Place good sized piece of fish on this after dusting with salt and pepper and brushing with melted butter. Bake in a quick oven. Put butter and flour in a pan and mix, add 1 pt. of cooked strained tomatoes and stir until boiling, add mace and white pepper. Stain this around fish, serve with boiled potato-balls basted with melted butter and dusted with parsley.

Mrs. J. H. Black.

LOBSTER A LA NEWBURG

2 lobsters (large)	3 egg-yolks
1 T butter	1 C cream
½ T flour	¼ t pepper
½ t salt	½ t ground mace

Cut lobster meat in large pieces, cut the claw into 3 and tail into 6, rub flour into butter, mash the hard boiled egg-yolks add the cream slowly while mashing, add butter and flour, salt pepper and mace, and lastly the lobster. Served hot.

LOBSTER CHOPS

2 C boiled lobster or 2 cans	¼ t nutmeg
3 T flour	3 egg-yolks
1 T chopped parsley	¼ t salt
1 C cream or milk	⅛ t cayenne
1 T butter	

Add all the seasoning to the lobster. Put the cream or milk on to boil. Rub butter and flour together and add to the cream or milk when boiling. Now add the beaten yolks and cook 2 min. Take from fire and add to lobster. Mix well and turn out on a dish to cool. When cool form in chop, roll first in beaten egg then in bread crumbs. Put in a frying basket and fry in boiling oil or dripping until nice brown. If you wish put the end of a small claw in each chop to represent the mutton bone Garnish with parsley and serve with cream or tartare sauce. One can make these chops the day before.

TARTARE SAUCE

½ pt. of oil mayonnaise dress-ing	1 gherkin
3 olives	1 T of capers

Chop all these fine and add them to dressing.

Rebecca Cooper Rounds.

LOBSTER COCKTAIL

1 C lobster meat	½ t catsup
2 T Worcestershire sauce	¼ C lemon juice
½ T tobasco sauce	½ t salt

Mix, chill thoroughly and serve in cocktail glasses.

MOCK OYSTERS

1 C cooked and mashed pars-nips	½ t salt
1 egg	⅛ t pepper
4 soda crackers rolled fine	1 t Worcestershire or catsup

Add liquids and seasoning to parsnips, then egg and crackers. Let stand 30 minutes, form into oyster-shaped patties, dip in slightly-beaten egg diluted with a ¼ C of water to each egg, then in dry bread crumbs Fry in deep fat—like oysters. Serve with catsup and cold slaw. Left over creamed parsnips may be used by omitting the cream in list of ingredients.

Mrs J. H. Black.

BOSTON FRIED OYSTERS

12 large oysters   2 C grated bread crumbs
1 egg   1 C grated cheese
Wash and dry oysters—dip in beaten egg; roll in cheese. Dip again in egg, then roll in bread crumbs. Fry in deep fat, or skellet with 1 C lard and ¼ C butter. Get platter hot. Cover the bottom with good tomato catsup, on this, place the oysters and garnish with parsley.

OYSTERS BROILED

1 doz large oysters   2 T butter
Use the largest oysters dipped in melted butter, and place in broiler buttered under gas flame, or over clear coals. Turn and when done serve on hot buttered toast, and lemons cut in eighths.

CREAMED OYSTERS

Make rich cream sauce by formula given, and drain oysters, put in sauce and let come to boil, until oysters begin to curl on edges. Add paprika and serve on toast. Can be served in Patty shells.

OYSTERS WITH CHICKEN

25 oysters   ½ chicken stock
1 chicken (white meat)   2 T flour
½ C oyster liquor   1½ T butter
½ C cream   1 t salt
Wash and drain oysters, cook until the bills curl, then chop fine. Cut white meat of chicken into blocks, make a sauce from oyster liquor, cream and chicken stock. Melt butter, add flour; add liquor and stir until it boils. Add chicken and oyster and salt.   C. C.

OYSTER CROQUETTES

2 eggs (beaten)   Flour
1½ C milk   1 pt. oysters
½ t salt and pepper
Chop oysters, make thin batter, add salt and pepper. Drop in hot lard.

                                    Mrs. Erwin Taft.

OYSTER CUTLETS

1-3 C macaroni   ½ C oyster liquor
1 pt. oysters   ¼ t red pepper
2½ T butter   ½ t salt
1-3 C flour   1-32 t mace or nutmeg
½ C milk   2 eggs
Break macaroni in small pieces and boil until very tender. Cook oysters in their own liquor. Drain and chop fine. Salt oysters while cooking. Mix all together; cook. After it is cool mold, dip in crumbs, eggs, crumbs and fry. This will serve ten.
                                  Mrs. Geo Pratt.

DEVILED OYSTERS

1 pt. oysters
1 t Worcestershire sauce

1 T butter, ⅛ t curry
¼ t salt

Put butter in pan, when melted add 1 pt. of the oyster liquor, when boiling add oysters and cook until plump. Add seasonings, put in all cracker crumbs with butter on top, and bake until brown.

ENTREES OF OYSTERS

Oyster fritters are one of the best oyster entres. To make them, drain 2 doz good-sized oysters and chop them fine. Beat 2 eggs light, add cupful of milk and cupful and about seven-eights —a scant two cupfuls of flour sifted with half a teaspoonful of baking powder. Beat this batter smooth, and season it with salt and pepper. Add the oysters, and drop the mixture by tablespoonsful into smoking hot fat. Cook them carefully until light brown.

OYSTERS, FRIED

1 qt. oysters
2 eggs
½ C bread crumbs

1 T butter
2 T lard

Wash and dry oysters. Dip in beaten egg and then in cracker crumbs. Repeat this once, fry in boiling butter and lard. Serve hot at once.

FRICASSEE OF OYSTERS

1 pt. rich milk or cream
2 T flour
2 doz. oysters

1-16 t mace
1-32 t cayenne
1 t salt

Make a thick white sauce from milk, flour; season with mace, cayenne and salt; add chopped oysters, cook a minute or two and serve on toast. C. C.

OYSTER LOAF

1 large loaf bread
1 qt. oysters
8 strips bacon
2 T butter

1 pt. cream sauce
½ t salt
¼ t pepper

Cut crust off top of loaf of bread, cut out all of the inside of loaf making a square box-like case of the crust. Mix the oysters with the cream sauce made by formula No. 1 and salt and pepper. Break the inside of bread into small crumbs butter and toast in oven, until crisp. Put layer of crumbs in bottom of loaf, then layer of oysters and sauce, with dots of butter, repeating this until the bread loaf is full, on top spread layers of bacon, and put on lid cooking 30 minutes.

Mrs. Chester I. Long.

MARYLAND OYSTERS

¾ pt. corn meal	1 qt. boiling water
1 t salt	

Boil half hour, drain 1 pt oysters, stir until mush, cook 10 minutes, pour all into square mold wet in cold water, cut in slices and fry.

NEW ORLEANS OYSTERS

2 T butter	1 C canned tomatoes
1 T flour	¼ t pepper
1 T sliced onion	1 T parsley
1 pt. oysters	1 T celery
½ t salt	

Melt butter, add onion and cook until brown, add flour and brown, then add tomatoes, when thick add the drained oysters and cook until the edges burn. Add salt and pepper.

PANNED OYSTERS

Place 1 doz. large oysters in hot pan, greased, on top of stove and turn as soon as cooked on one side Do not let brown, salt and pepper and butter. Serve on buttered toast.

OYSTER PATES

Chop a quart of oysters fine with a sharp sliver knife. Melt two tablespoonfuls of butter, add the same amount of flour, cook, and then add a cupful of rich milk. Season with red and black pepper and salt. Add the minced oysters to the cream sauce and cook for five minutes. Have the pate shells hot, fill them with the oyster mixture, and set in the oven for a minute before serving, very hot.

PIGS IN BLANKETS

12 large oysters	12 slices of toast
12 strips bacon	Mash oysters

Roll each oyster in slice of bacon and pin with wooden tooth picks Put in pan in oven and bake 10 or 15 minutes. Serve at once.

OYSTERS AND RABBITS "Spanish"

1 rabbit	1½ doz. oysters
2 bay leaves	1 t parsley, ½ t salt
1 t sage	⅛ t mace
1 C cauliflower	1 C onions
1 C carrots	½ C green peppers

Cook rabbit 1¼ hours in 1½ qt boiling water into which the bay leaves, sage, parsley, mace and salt have been added. Ten minutes before it is done add oysters, when done put rabbit and oysters on large platter, garnishing with the vegetables which must all be cooked in the same water Thicken the liquid in pot with milk and flour and pour over all.

OYSTER IN SHELL

Oysters in shell should be cooked in hot oven or in steamer until shells open. Always place the round shell down to retain the juice, serve melted butter and lemons with them.

OYSTER SOUP

Oyster soup is a good luncheon soup, especially satisfactory for school children. There are several ways of varying it to make it tempting.

The first requisite for good oyster soup of any sort is to cook the oysters only long enough to make them plump. Longer cooking toughens them.

Wash a quart of oysters and strain in the liquid in which they came, through a piece of cheesecloth. Then boil it, skim it, and add the oysters to it. When the oysters are fuffled and plump take it from the fire, add a pint of hot milk, well seasoned with salt and pepper, and a T butter, and serve immediately.

Vary this soup by adding 2 T of chopped celery to the hot milk, or 1 T of chopped onion or parsley, or 1 T of finely grated cheese. Sometimes thicken it with 1 T of butter and 1 T of flour rubbed together. Sometimes add a few oyster crackers when you mix the oysters and hot milk.

FISH PIE

Any good firm cold fish (boned) covered with thin white sauce, place in baking dish, then cover all with layer of mashed potatoes, dotted with butter, and bake in quick oven. (English Dish).

Mrs. J. H. Black.

SHAD PLANKED

3 large shad	1 t salt
4 T butter	⅛ t pepper
2 T catsup	1 lemon juice

To prepare a new plank fish board. Procure a plank board, oak is best, that will just fit into the oven, grease this all over with olive oil and heat slowly in a slow oven the day before it is to be used for the first time. When ready to use, heat well, then grease on the top side with the above mixture of butter, catsup and lemon, then, after cleaning fish, split them down the back and lay on board, with inside of fish up. Baste every 10 minutes.

Do not have oven hot enough to burn board. Serve on board on tray at table, garnished with lemon slices. Never wash your plank shad board, and never use it for anything but fish, scrape clean and brush off with tissue paper. Then wrap carefully in oiled paper, and brown paper over this, the older the plank the better the fish.

Mrs. Chester I. Long.

EGG DRESSING FOR PLANK SHAD

½ lb. butter   4 eggs
½ C flour   1 pt. milk
½ t salt   ½ t pepper

Heat butter in stew pan, stir in flour until dissolved, then add milk stirring constantly. Add to this the 4 eggs which have been hard boiled and chopped very fine. Serve hot.

Mrs. Chester I. Long.

SALMON CUTLETS

1 pt. cooked salmon sauce   1 t salt
4 T butter   ⅛ t pepper
6 T flour   ½ t lemon juice
1 C milk

Make sauce, stirring flour in the butter. Add milk and seasonings. Flake salmon, mince, bread and fry in hot grease. Turn on soft paper and garnish with lemon, pickled beets or jelly. Oysters, shrimps, lobsters or any cooked fish may be substituted.

Mrs. H. W. Lewis.

SALMON CUTLETS WITH PEAS

1 lb. salmon   ½ C bread crumbs
1 C cream sauce   ½ t salt
4 eggs   ¼ t paprika

Chop salmon, beat 3 eggs, add cream sauce and boil all together for 5 min. Then mold into cutlets, dip in beaten egg with salt and pepper and then in bread crumbs, fry in 2-3 lard and 1-3 butter.

SALMON FRITTERS

2 eggs   Pinch salt
½ C milk   1 C salmon
1 t B. P.   ½ C flour

Have mixture just so it will drop from the spoon, have fat hot, stir well together and drop large spoonfuls into the fat. Serve hot.

Shredded codfish may be used or any kind of fish left over.

SALMON LOAF

1 can salmon   4 T butter
½ C fine bread crumbs   ¼ t salt
2 eggs (well beaten)   1 t poultry seasoning
1 t parsley   ½ C milk

Melt butter, cut parsley fine. Remove oil and cut salmon fine, add bread crumbs, egg-yolks, butter, salt, seasoning and parsley, egg-whites well whipped. Steam in mold 1 hr. Serve hot or cold. If eaten hot, serve with following sauce:

1 C milk   2 T butter
1 T corn starch   1 t catsup
1 egg   ⅛ t cayenne pepper

Cook over hot water until it thickens.

Mrs. J. H. Black.

SALMON PUFF

1 lb. can salmon	½ lemon (juice)
3 eggs (beaten)	½ t salt
1 T melted butter	⅛ t pepper

Bake 15 min. in well greased gem pans. Will serve 6.

Mrs. Erwin Taft.

SALMON PUDDING WITH SAUCE

1 large can salmon	3 eggs
5 T melted butter	½ t salt
½ C bread crumbs	⅛ t pepper

Mince the salmon, save the liquor for sauce, add bread crumbs cut fine, then add butter and well beaten eggs and salt and pepper. Put in a well buttered mold, set in pan of hot water, cover and steam in the oven for 1 hr.

Sauce:	1 T butter
1 C milk	1 egg
1½ T corn starch	½ lemon

Heat milk to boiling, thicken with cornstarch wet in cold water. Add salmon liquor and beaten egg. Cook 5 min. then add lemon juice and pour on the pudding and serve.

Mrs. J. H. Aley.

FISH SCALLOP

Use either Tuna or Salmon, alternate layers of fish and hard boiled eggs, cover with white sauce and bread crumbs. Bake in quick oven.

Mrs. J. H. Black.

SALMON SOUFFLE

1 lb. can salmon	2 T flour
1 t chopped parsley	1 C milk
1 t salt	3 eggs
4 T butter	

Break up the flakes of salmon fine and mix with chopped parsley and salt. 1-16 t cayenne. Mix butter with flour in a sauce pan over fire Have 1 C of milk heated in another vessel to which add thickening and stir until smooth. Then pour it over the salmon and add the beaten egg-yolks to the mixture. At last add the stifly beaten whites lightly. Drop into individual dishes and bake about 15 minutes.

Mrs. R Millison.

SHAD ROE CROQUETTES

To 4 shad roe boiled 15 min. in salt water, and then drained and mashed. Allow 2 C sauce and seasoning to taste. Shape and fry.

TUNA CHOPS

1 25 cent Tuna	1 t mustard
1 ½ C cold rice	1 t red pepper
6 egg-whites	1 t salt
2 eggs	1 T lemon jam
1 T parsley	

Chop egg-yolks coarse, add cold boiled rice and thick white sauce, beat well 2 eggs and add to Tuna and other ingredients. Mold into chops, adding cracker crumbs if to moist, then roll in egg and cracker crumbs and fry in oven.

Mrs. W. E. Stanley.

WHIPPED CREAM SAUCE

Whipped cream makes a dainty fish sauce appealing to the eye and the palate. Whip the cream, which should be cold and 24 hrs. old, to a thick substance, far beyond froth, yet not turned to butter, remembering that it doubles in bulk by this operation. Add 4 drops of anchovy sauce and serve cold.

Mrs. W. E. Stanley.

MOLDED TUNA OR SALMON

1 small can Tuna	½ box gelatine
2 eggs	½ C water
½ C celery	1 T salad dressing

Mince the fish, chop the hard boiled eggs, add salt and pepper and salad dressing. Soak gelatine in cold water, add enough boiling water to dissolve it. Mix with fish and mold.

Mrs. Geo. Steel.

FISH MOUSSE

2 T gelatine	2 T butter
2 T water	1 t salt
1½ t lemon juice	½ t mustard
1 egg	¼ t paprika
1 T olive oil	¾ C milk
2 C canned or fresh fish	

Soak gelatine in cold water and lemon juice, heat milk in double boiler, add butter, olive oil, egg beaten and paprika. Stir continually with a split spoon or egg beater. When thickened add gelatine, fish and salt. Remove from fire and cool. Serve cold with Tartar Sauce.

MEATS

WHAT IS WHAT IN MEAT

Rib 1st cut are best for roasts.

Rib 2nd cut for roasts.

Shoulder for pot roasts.

Neck used for stews, mince and soup.

Brisket for stews, corning and braises.

The round for steak, lean soup meat, and dried.

Tenderloin for steaks.

Porterhouse, those next the tenderloin are best for broiling.

Sirloin for steak.

Tenderloin most expensive.

Porterhouse and sirloin next, round, rib roast and rump steak next, shank, flank and shoulder next. Brisket and chuck cheapest.

Flank for stews and curing—the flank steak is considered by some the juciest meat there is.

Shank for soup—solid meat.

FACTS ABOUT COOKING MEATS

Meats roasted should be put into a hot oven to set the juice, then cooled down after 15 min. Meats broiled should be as close to the gas flame or coals as possible. Meats boiled should be plunged in hot water. Meats should boil gently to be tender. Soup meats should be put in cold water gradually brought to boil then simmer.

Soaked meat in vinegar 20 min. is said to make it tender.

Meat cooked too rapidly becomes tough.

If salt is put in flour before it is wet, lumps will be avoided in mixing batter.

Extract of beef added to gravy improves the flavor, ½ T to a 6 lb. roast.

The foundation of most of the sauces is either soup stock or cream sauce, with the vegetable or article added from which the sauce will take its name.

When lard becomes stale, try frying a potato in it to sweeten it.

To keep ham—slice and pack in glass jar and cover with vinegar and pepper, will keep for weeks.

C. C.

Blanquette—A sort of fricasse.

Bouilli—Boiled beef.

Braise—Cooked in covered stew pan with vegetables and flavorings.

Carmelon—Rolled stuffed meat.

En Casserole—Cooked in casserole.

Compote—A stew of pigeons or birds.

Flamber—To singe game or fowl.

Fricasse—Foul or meat cut in pieces in a white sauce with herbs.

Pate—A small pie.

Ragout—A brown stew with herbs or vegetables and mushrooms.

Salmi—Game stewed, which has been half roasted.

Vabau-vent—A rich crust of puff paste which is filled with stews or fricasses of meat, chicken or fish.

Piece de Resistance—Is the main course of the dinner or the dish around which the dinner is built.

MEATS, FISH AND GAME AND THEIR RELISHES

Porter house steak—Maitre de Hotel.
Roast beef—Horse radish, brown gravy.
Roast pork—Apple sauce.
Roast veal—Tomato or mushroom sauce.
Roast mutton—Currant jelly or celery sauce.
Boiled Mutton—Caper sauce.
Boiled chicken—Bread sauce or tart jelly.
Roast lamb—Mint sauce.
Roast turkey—Cranberry sauce and chestnut sauce.
Boiled turkey—Oyster sauce.
Boiled bluefish—White cream sauce.
Fried chicken—Blackberry jelly or loganberry jelly.
Shad—Boiled rice and egg sauce.
Compote of pigeons—Mushroom sauce.
Fresh salmon—Green peas, cream sauce.
Roast goose—Apple sauce.
Venison or wild duck—Black currant jelly.
Broiled fresh mackerel—Sauce of stewed gooseberries.
Catfish—Parsley sauce.
Pickles are good with all meat. Lemon is an addition to all fish.

C. C.

FOR FRYING PURPOSES

1 lb. butter   1 lb. suet

Clarify butter, fry out suet and mix.

C. C.

Cover beef suet with milk, boil until all milk is gone, then use for frying.

Use 1-3 as much beef suet as leaf lard, cut in small chunks and place in pan in oven, and when all is rendered, place in a jar and salt and use the same as lard.

MAKING FRYING COMPOUND

Suet at the present time is 10c. a lb. Lard is 28c. From 1 lb. can be obtained 14 oz. of fat at 12c. a lb. To this can be added 1 part of oil to 2 parts of suet, cottonseed oil or corn oil, can be used at 21c. a lb. Making the frying compound 15c. a lb., or suet has harder consistency and the oil reduces it to the consistency of lard.

1 part beef suet and 2 parts leaf lard—pork—makes a fine frying mixture.

ACCIDENT SCALLOP

4 slices bacon	1 T parsley
1 C cold meat	1 T butter
1 C cold potatoes	1 T celery
1 small onion	1 bay leaf
4 slices tomato	

Salt, pepper, paprika, chop meat and onion very fine, dice cold boiled potato fine, mince parsley and celery, break bay leaf into little bits, grease bottom of small baking dish, cover with meat then vegetables, adding bits of butter and then meat and vegetables again until all is used, cover this with the bacon and tomato, bake 20 min.

Mrs. Chester Long

BACON PUFFED

6 large strips	4 T cracker crumbs
1 egg	4 T butter
1 T water	

Beat egg, add water, cut bacon strips in two, dip in crumbs then in egg then in crumbs and fry in butter.

DOUBLE BOILED BEEF

In order to make tough meat tender, it is advisable to put the roast in a double boiler. Have the water in the outer vessel boiling and when the inner vessel is hot put in the steak which has been well buttered and salted, this can safely cook five or six hours. The juices coming out of the meat can be used to bake it with and make an excellent brown gravy. Be sure the water in outer boiler does not boil dry.

TO CORN BEEF

25 lb. beef	2 lb. salt
1 gal. water	¾ lb. B sugar
¾ oz. saltpetre	½ oz. Saleratus

Boil ingredients, skim and set away to cool. When cold add the beef and put weights on the meat to keep it under the brine.

CANULON OF BEEF

2 lb. lean beef, ground	2 T melted butter
½ lemon, grated rind	¼ t nutmeg
1 T chopped parsley	¼ t salt
1 egg	¼ t pepper
½ T onion juice	

Shape in loaf, wrap in buttered paper, bake 30 min. in hot oven. Baste every ten min. with melted butter. Make sauce of the butter left in pan.

Mrs. C. V. Ferguson

BEEF STEAK BROILED

1 t salt	½ t pepper
1 lb. porter house	

Grease broiler and have live coals in stove. Place meat over coals and in 2 min. turn repeating the process until meat is done, salt and pepper, serve with Maitre de Hotel sauce. If a gas stove is used, turn on top burner in oven until very hot, place meat in broiler under flame, and turn first one side and then the other until done. It is well to rim off all fat in broiling as it catches the flame and burns.

BEEF A LA MODE

6 lb. rump roast	1 t celery
1 lb. salt pork	1 slice lemon
2 T lard or butter	2 bay leaves
1 T onion	6 cloves
1 t carrot	6 allspice
¼ lb. bits of pork	6 whole peppers
1 t parsley	1 t salt

Select rump roast, use salt pork for larding, cut slits in beef and put in this strips, salt and pepper, put fat in the frying pan, also slice of lemon, onion, carrot, bits of pork, parsley, celery. Sear beef, add bay leaves, cloves, allspice, whole peppers. When brown put into a kettle of boiling water with ingredients in frying pan, add salt. Boil 3 hrs.

C. C.

BEEF LOAF

2½ lb. round steak ground	½ t pepper
½ lb. fresh pork, ground	2 T water
½ C bread crumbs	1 t salt
2 eggs	1 T butter

Beat egg, mix altogether. Have oven hot and after the loaf has been in long enough to brown a little, pour over it 1 C of boiling water and add butter on top.

C. C.

BEEF'S HEART

1 lb. veal	1 t salt
½ C dry bread crumbs	¼ t pepper
1 t grated onion	1 egg
1 t sage	1 T butter

Soak heart in cold water 3 hrs. Remove tubes from inside and every particle of blood. Chop veal, mix well with all other ingredients and stuff into heart, sew the heart in a cloth and put in sauce pan with point down, cover with boiling water simmer 3 hrs. Then bake 1 hr., serve cold.

Mrs. Geo. Whitney

BEEF HASH FRIED

1 lb. cold cooked beef	1 T butter
1 C potato cooked	1 t salt
1 T onion	1 t pepper
1 t parsley	1 t celery chopped

Chop beef very fine, also potato and onions, mix all together with melted butter, salt, pepper, celery and parsley, make into small flat cakes and fry until brown in hot grease, equal parts lard and butter. This is also good baked.

ROUND STEAK FRIED

Select tender round steak, cut in slices ½ in. thick and 3 or 4 in. square, chop with large dull knife on both sides, dip in equal parts meal and flour, salted and fry in very hot fat 1-3 butter and 2-3 lard. When quite brown on one side turn and brown the other side. Do not put in too much at once it cools the fat. Be sure the fat is very hot all the time. Make gravy.

FILLET OF BEEF

3 lb. beef fillet	1 t salt
¼ lb. bacon	½ t pepper

Cover beef with strip of bacon, salt and pepper, put in bake pan covered, without water. Bake in hot oven first 15 min., then reduce heat, cook 45 min. Serve with parsley sauce or Maitre de Hotel.

BROILED CHICKEN

If cooked in gas range, turn on top burner, have oven very hot. Place broiler in broiler rack after splitting them down the back. Dust flour over them, salt and 1 T butter to each half of chicken, add 1 C water. Do not place them on top of each other. Cook 25 min. on one side and 15 min. on the other. If rather large chickens cook longer. Baste often. Serve at once, on toast, moisten the toast with the sauce in the pan.

CHICKEN A LA KING

1 C chicken, white meat	2 chopped pimolas
2 T butter	2 egg-yolks
½ t salt	1 C cream
¼ t pepper	

Heat the chicken in the butter, season, add the pimolas and vinegar, cook 5 min., then add the eggs well beaten in the cream. Stir until the mixture thickens slightly, serve at once or it will curdle. Serve on small squares of toast or in patty shells.

Mrs. Ralph L. Millison

CHICKEN A LA KING

½ green pepper cut in small   1 t onion chopped fine
   pieces

Fry together in batter but *do not brown.* Stir in 3 table-spoons flour. Cook with ½ pt. of rich chicken stock until frothy. Place in double boiler and add 1 pt. cream. Salt and paprika. When thickened lay in white meat of chicken cut in large slices, 1 can of asparagus tips and ½ pound of fresh mushrooms saute in butter or 1 small can mushrooms. *Do not stir after adding last ingredients.*

Mrs. Oak Throckmorton

CHICKEN A LA KING

4 T butter	1 C mushrooms cut in halves
½ green pepper chopped fine	2 C cooked chicken cut in strips
2 T flour	¼ t paprika
½ t salt	Pimentos
1 pt. cream or part cream and part stock	

Melt the butter in a chafing dish, add the green pepper and cook 3 or 4 min. without browning. Add the flour and salt and cook till frothy. Then add cream or cream and stock, and stir till sauce thickens. Add the mushrooms, chicken and pimentos. Serve on strips of toast. If necessary to keep warm before serving place in double boiler for if allowed to cook too long, it will curdle.

Elsie Fitch Buck

CHICKEN A LA BALTIMORE

2 spring chickens	1 t salt
2 eggs	½ t pepper
½ C butter	1 C dry bread crumbs

Split chicken down the back, season, dip into beaten eggs then into crumbs, then into eggs and crumbs again. Lay in a well buttered pan, place the inside of chicken up, pour melted butter over them and bake 30 min Basting and turning outside up for browning for the last 10 min. Make cream sauce from the drippings and garnish with strips of bacon and parsley. Cove oysters are usually served with this.

12 ears of corn	3 T flour
4 egg-yolks	½ t salt
½ t paprika	

Grate corn from cob, add flour, eggs, salt and paprika, mix well. Have piping hot equal parts of lard and butter, dip 1 T of the batter into the boiling fat and brown until all is used.

ROAST BEEF

Sirloin or rib makes the best roast. Place roast covered with butter in covered self basting pan, in very hot oven, which should remain same temperature 15 min., then lower temperature and cook very slowly, allowing 10 min. for each pound of steak after the first 15 min. It has been found the slower a roast is cooked after the first 15 min. the more tender it becomes. If a self-baster is not used, 4 T butter and 1 C water must be added, and roast must be basted in this every 15 min

CHICKEN WITH DUMPLINGS

Cover 1 three lb. chicken with boiling water, cut as for frying, boil 3 hrs. if tough, or cook in fireless cooker 10 hrs. When done remove the chicken from the liquid, and when boiling drop in dumplings made of biscuit dough recipes, add parsley, celery, and onion, cover kettle and boil without removing lid 20 min. The dumplings should be flavored well and not allowed to touch each other when placed in kettle. The flour from the dumplings will thicken the liquid, making the gravy, adding more salt and pour all in large platter over chicken.

Formula:

1 3 lb. chicken	½ t onion
1 T chopped parsley	1½ t salt
1 T chopped celery	½ t pepper

Mrs. Chester I. Long

CHICKEN AND CORN PIE

1 chicken	3 T butter
2 C corn	1 t salt
1 C milk	½ t pepper

Cut chicken as for frying, put alternate layers of chicken and corn, salt and pepper in buttered dish. Cover with butter, steam ¾ hr. and then pour over all 1 C sweet milk and steam 20 min. more. Select tender chicken, steam longer if larger chicken.

CHICKEN IN CASEROLE

Equal parts of diced cold chicken and boiled rice, put in layers. Pour over it, tomato sauce, cover with buttered crumbs, bake until brown.

Tomato sauce:

½ can tomatoes	1 T butter
1 small onion	2 T flour
1 bay leaf	

Stew tomatoes, onion, bay leaf for 10 min. Cook butter and flour, add strained tomatoes gradually, season well.

Mrs. E. Taft

CHICKEN IN CASSEROLE

Fry a 2½ or 3 lb. hen and make gravy according to recipe for fried chicken, place chicken in Casserole and pour over it the gravy made with water—rather thin, not made with milk as the milk may curdle—and cook very slowly in casserole at the lowest temperature, 4 hrs., change the pieces on top to the bottom occasionally. This is a good way to make tough chicken tender. Parsley and celery chopped, add to the flavor, 1 t of each.

Mrs. Chester I. Long

SMOOTHERED CHICKEN

Cut spring broilers in half, place in large covered bake dish, in hot oven, after rolling in flour which has been salted and peppered. Dot with butter allowing 1 T to each one half of chicken, change the top pieces to the bottom of pan when they become brown. Allow 30 min. at least for 1 chicken.

CHICKEN LOAF

1 3½ lb. chicken	½ C almonds
½ C bread crumbs	½ t salt
1-5 t pepper	½ C celery
½ C milk	2 eggs

Cook chicken until tender, brind meat, cut the celery and nuts, mix all the ingredients together adding a few T of the chicken fat rising on the broth. Make into a loaf and bake in a steam boiler ½ hr. This will serve 12 or more portions.

Mrs. Rorabaugh.

Chicken loaf or beef loaf is improved by putting strips of bacon in the bottom and top of the pan.

FRIED CHICKEN

1 spring chicken	2 T milk
1 C fine cracker crumbs	½ C lard
1 C meal or flour mixed half	¼ C butter
and half	½ t salt
1 egg	¼ t pepper

Dress and singe chicken, cut off legs, wings, thigh, 2 breast neck, back, liver and gizzard, making in all 12 pieces, dip each piece in well beaten egg to which milk has been added, then dip in cracker crumbs or bread crumbs or bread and flour to which salt and pepper have been added, then place in hot lard and butter in skillet, putting in the largest pieces first, cover with lid and turn over when brown, cooking about 30 min. Watch carefully to not burn, and remove to hot platter.

GRAVY FOR FRIED CHICKEN

Gravy for fried chicken, allow the grease to brown in which the chicken was cooked, add enough browned flour to thicken, stirring constantly and then add boiling water or hot milk stirring constantly until the consistency required for gravy. Flour is browned by putting in bake pan in oven 5 min. or longer if required a deeper brown. Watch carefully and stir to prevent burning and to get an even brown.

CHOP SUEY

3 pounds chicken, full weight	2 green peppers
1 C Japanese brown sauce	1 small onion
1 can mushrooms	2 t salt
6 large bamboo sprouts	2 C chicken stock
1 large or two small bunches	1 t pepper
celery	1 T sugar
3 t cornstarch	

Boil chickens tender, also celery, onions and green peppers separately. Mix dry ingredients with rich chicken stock in which some of the fat is retained. To this add brown sauce. Then add chicken and other ingredients. Place all in a large kettle on a low burner where it will simmer for an hour or more before serving. Serve with steamed rice. Mrs. W. B. Buck

CHICKEN ROLLS

1 chicken	1 C stock from chicken
1 C oysters	1 t salt
2 t parsley	½ t pepper
2 T butter	1 C cream
2 T flour	

Melt butter. Add flour, salt, pepper and then cream. Stir until smooth and well cooked. Then add parsley, chicken and oysters, chicken and oysters first having been cut into not too small pieces. Turn mixture into shallow pan to cool. When thoroly chilled and firm, have ready good rich puff paste. Cut chicken mixture into slices four by two inches. Envelope in the puff paste and fry in croquet basket in deep hot fat, first having dipped the rolls in beaten egg and then in cracker crumbs. Mrs. W. B. Buck.

CHICKEN PIE CRUST

2 C flour   ½ t salt
2 t B. P.   1 egg
2 T lard   1 C milk

Sift together the flour, B. P. and salt, cut the lard thru it with a knife, and moisten with the milk which the egg, well beaten, has been added. Spread the mixture over the top of the pan of chicken meat, and gravy, which has been previously heated, and bake immediately.

Mrs. Robt. B. Campbell.

CHICKEN PIE

Stew chicken, remove bones   1 C milk
Make rich gravy of broth   2 t B P.
Place chicken in casserole   1 t salt
Cover with gravy   1 egg well beaten
Place following crust on top 2 T melted butter
2 C flour

Mrs. H. W. Horn.

CREAM SAUCE FOR CROQUETTES

2 T butter   1 t salt
2 T flour   1 C milk

Put butter in hot sauce pan, rub in flour and add milk, stirring constantly, salt. Tomato sauce may be made by using tomato instead of milk. Drop croquettes in vermicelle crushed with a rolling pin, after being dipped in egg and fry. Add ½ t onion juice to each egg

CORNED BEEF AND CABBAGE

Soak beef over night in cold water if very salty. If not, wash and boil 30 min., then in fireless cooker all day. Place in cabbage, cut in quarters, boil 10 min. in beef kettle and boil 2½ hrs. longer with beef.

CHICKEN WITH VEGETABLES IN FIRELESS COOKER

Put chicken in cooker with boiling water, salt, onions, parsley, potato, boil 20 min. Put in cooker 12 hrs Just before serving remove chicken and vegetables and thicken gravy with 4 T each of butter and flour cooked together, season with salt and pepper and pour over chicken, garnish with cress or parsley.

FORMULA

3 lb. chicken   8 potatoes
3 C boiling water   ½ t pepper
1 t salt   1 t parsley
8 small onions

Mrs. Chester I. Long

CHICKEN TURBOT

1 4-lb chicken	3 T flour
1 pt. milk	½ C cracker crumbs
1 C bread crumbs	1-3 t pepper
1 t salt	1 can mushrooms
1 C celery	4 T butter

Cook chicken, cut the meat in small pieces with scissors. Melt 2 t butter and rub in the flour. Add 3 T milk. Add the rest of the milk: boil until nicely thickened. Add ½ C chicken broth. Heat mushrooms, stir into chicken. Now place in buttered bake dishes a layer of chicken, a sprinkle of celery, cream sauce, cracker and bread crumbs, dotting with bits of butter and making two layers of each with crumbs on top, dotted with butter. Bake ½ hour. This will serve 12.

Mrs. Rorabaugh.

CHICKEN PIE

Joint and cook chicken tender, put chicken and liquid into deep uncovered bake dish, add parsley and celery, onion, salt and pepper, have hot and make a biscuit dough rolled about ½ in thick and cover the top of the pie with this, having first sprinkle some flour over the top of the chicken and the liquid cook until dough is done and brown on top 30 min.

1 3-lb. chicken	1 T chopped celery
1 T chopped parsley ·	½ t onion
1½ t salt	½ t pepper

CHILI

1-3 lb. ground suet	3 T Dye's Chili Mixture
1 large onion (ground fine)	1 section garlic
3 lbs. round steak (ground)	1 qt. water
2 medium sized cans tomatoes	2 cans medium sized chili
1 T salt	beans

Fry suet quite brown then add onion and round steak and brown. Add tomatoes, salt, Dye's Chili Mixture, garlic and water. Boil 2 hours, then add kidney beans and cook 1 hour longer.

Mrs. Gilbert Tucker.

CROQUETTES

Save bills of war times.

Potato, rice, vegetables, cereals, bread, meat, fish, fowl or game and bind together with an egg—add cracker crumbs for a good economical croquette.

CROQUETTE MEAT

2 T minced onion	1 C grated bread crumbs
2 eggs	1 C cream sauce
1 C chopped meat of any kind	

Add onion, bread crumbs, meat and beaten eggs to cream sauce, mold any desired shape, and roll in eggs and bread crumbs and fry in deep fat.

CROQUETTES CHICKEN

1 pt white sauce	1 t celery salt
½ lb. chicken	½ t salt
1 t fine parsley	1 egg

Mince chicken, add to sauce, add parsley, salt, and beaten egg, mold, dip in beaten egg and 1 T water, roll in bread crumbs and fry in deep fat.

The foundation of all croquettes is cream sauce, mixed with meat, fish, fowl, vegetables or cereals and shaped into round, pyramidial or cylindrical shapes, in shaping croquettes use 1 T of the mixture, press into shape desired, roll in bread or cracker crumbs, then into egg beaten, and again into crumbs, then fry in deep fat. Do not put too many croquettes into the fat at once, it will lower the temperature and the croquettes will become grease soaked and will not brown—they should be a golden brown .

DUCKLINGS

Young ducks are called ducklings: young geese, green geese or goslings An old goose is strong and unpalatable. One of the choice dishes among German-American people is goose stuffed with sauerkraut. The sauerkraut is washed thoroughly and soaked over night in cold water, then stuffed into the goose, the goose trussed and cooked slowly.

DRIED BEEF CANNED

1½ T butter	1 C milk
½ lb. chipped beef	1 T flavor

If beef is salty boil in fresh water 10 min Pour off water. Brown butter in frying pan, add minced beef. Dissolve flour in milk, and stir into minced beef and butter. Serve hot on toast or crackers.

STUFFED FLANK STEAK

2 flank steaks	6 strips bacon
1½ C dressing	

Have 2 flank steaks pounded well on both sides, salted and peppered and place sauce dressing between them as made for stuffing chicken. Put in covered bake pan and cover meat with strips of bacon and bake 1 hr slowly after the first 15 min Serve with tomato sauce   Mrs. Chester I. Long

FLANK, NEW ORLEANS STYLE

Select a thick flank steak: Have it scored: Sprinkle lightly with salt, put in a baking pan, cover with a layer of sliced onion, ½ t salt and chile pepper, a thick layer of sliced raw potatoes, pour over all ¼ can seasoned tomatoes, put in a slow oven, bake 2½ hrs. adding a small quantity of hot water from time to time. ½ hr. before steak is done, spread over the top a layer of cooked rice, put in the oven again until brown. Slice thru like short cake   Mrs. H. Lassen

FLANK STEAK

Trim off all fat, rub in all flour possible; brown on both sides in butter or nice drippings. Do not have skillet too hot: then pour on a little water and cover and let cook slowly on back of stove for two hrs., adding water so as to have nice brown sauce when ready to serve.

Mrs. Geo. Whitney.

DUCK AND GOOSE ROAST

Turn ducks with head down and pour boiling water over. Then roll them in newspaper for 20 min. and let steam. Then feathers will come off easily.   C. C.

To be prime, ducks must be fat and young, lower part of the legs and webbing of the feet soft, and the under bill sufficiently soft to break easily. The usual rules for roasting and baking will apply to ducks and geese. They contain more fat than either turkeys or chickens. this, melting while they are roasting may be saved for frying purposes and used in place of butter. Instead of using breadcrumbs as dressing for ducks or geese, use potato. For a medium sized duck, allow four good sized potatoes or two cupfuls of mashed potatoes. While potatoes are hot add one C chopped English walnuts, a t of salt, half a cup of chopped celery and a salt spoon of pepper. When thoroughly mixed put the dressing into the duck or goose, sew up the vent, and it is ready to roast. The peculiar flavor imparted by the celery in the roasting gives a tame duck much the flavor of a wild one.

BAKED HAM

Cover ham with cold water and simmer gently, just long enough to loosen the skin so it will peal off, two or three hours, according to the size of the ham when skinned put it in a pan in the oven, pour over it, one teacup of vinegar, and a little water, in which dissolve one teaspoonful of mustard. Bake slowly 2 hours, basting with the liquid. Then cover ham all over one inch thick with brown sugar pressed down firmly and do not baste again. Let it remain in the oven one hour after covering with sugar, until it forms a rich crust and becomes a rich brown. When done drain the liquor and put on a platter to cool Press by turning another flat dish on top with weight. The pressing makes it especially nice and firm for sandwiches.

Mrs G. M. Lowry.

STUFFED, BAKED HAM

Boil the ham ten min. to the pound.

DRESSING

1 pt. bread crumbs	Saltspn. cinnamon
little cream	" cloves
2 eggs beat up	" spice
1 t melted butter	" ginger
1 t sugar	" mustard
1 grated nutmeg	" celery salt

Take out ham and skin, slash and fill with the dressing. Rub the whole ham with the white of eggs and bread crumbs, then put in the oven and bake. Better cold than hot.

Mrs. A. C. Jobes.

BAKED HAM

Soak ham over night if salty. Boil 10 min. to the lb. Skin and stick with cloves.

Bast with	1 C B. sugar
½ C vinegar	Bake 20 min. to lb.
1 C water	Mrs. G. M. Dickson
	Mrs. Finlay Ross.

FRIED MEAT AND VEGETABLES

1 C chopped meat—cooked	1 t celery
1 C potato	1 t onion
1 t parsley	½ C bacon chopped
¼ t pepper	½ t salt

Fry all together 10 min., stirring occasionally, then turn over the mixture 1 C of boiling water and let cook 10 or 15 min. longer.

FLANK STEAK AND VEGETABLES

1 flank steak	1 turnip
4 C bread crumbs	1 carrot
1 t salt	1 onion
½ C celery	½ t pepper

Wipe steak clean, remove skin and fat, fry fat, spread bread crumbs on steak moistened with fat fryings, slice vegetables and lay on bottom of pan, roll meat and place on top of vegetables, pour in stock or water to cover 1 inch of pan, cover and bake 3 hrs.

Mrs. Chester I. Long.

HAM AND NOODLES

Cook Noodles 15 min., in salted water, drain, blanch and retreat in white sauce. Place chopped cooked ham in bottom of baking dish, alternate with noodles, cover with buttered bread crumbs and bake ½ hr. in quick oven.

1 Pkg. egg noodles	1 C bread crumbs
1 C white sauce	Mrs. Black.

MINCED HAM AND EGGS

Mince equal parts of ham and bread crumbs and break eggs over the top. Bake in oven until eggs are set.

Mrs. J. H. Aley

HAM COUAPE'S

1 C ham minced   1 t parsley chopped
2 t butter   Mix and spread.

WASHINGTON BAKED HAM

Soak ham in cold water 24 hrs., drain and put in fresh cold water and boil slowly for 2 hrs. Pour off the water, skin the ham, cover again with boiling water and cook slowly one more hr. Again drain the ham and pour over it liquid. Stick cloves in ham. Cook another hr., then cool in liquid, and drain and trim ham, mix spices and sugar and bread crumbs together and place on top side of ham and bake another two hours—bake slowly.

LIQUID

4 quarts cider   2 T whole cloves
2 quarts water   1 C crumbs
1 T allspice   1 t black pepper
1 T cinnamon   1 C B. sugar
1 T cloves

Liquid can be saved and kept in cool place and used another time by adding water.   Mrs. Chester I. Long.

MEAT CASSEROLE

2 C chopped meat   1 egg
Juice of 1 lemon   1 t chopped onion
1 sprig parsley   ½ t salt
½ C cracker crumbs

Fill a bowl ½ in. thick with rice, fill with meat and steam 40 min. Serve with tomato sauce.   Helen Brooks Hall.

LIVER AND BACON

6 slices bacon   6 pieces liver
½ C flour and meal

Fry out bacon. Put to one side of pan, dip liver into flour and meal mixed and salted, fry until nicely brown, serve with bacon, or calf's liver and but ½ in. thick.

LANCASHIRE PIE

1 C cold veal chopped   2 t butter
1 C cold potatoes   1 t mint leaves
1 t parsley

Grease bake dish, put in alternate layers of meat and potato, dotting each layer with butter, parsley and mint leaves, bake until a nice brown covered.

ITALIAN HASH

1 lb. round steak   ½ t pepper
6 cabbage leaves—firm   2 C soup stock or
½ T onion juice   4 T butter
1 t salt   2 C water

Chop meat very fine, add onion juice, salt and pepper, spread the mixture inside cabbage leaf, roll and tie with piece of string. Place close together in bake dish, cover with liquid, bake 1 hr., covered, thicken the liquor, and serve on toast or with vegetable garnish.

HAM SWEET

3 lb. ham   1 T cloves
6 T B sugar

Cut ham in 3 in. slices, place ham in casserole, cover each slice with sugar and cloves then cover all with water and bake slowly 1 hr.

C. C.

HAM AND POTATOES BAKED

1 slice ham ¾ in. thick   ½ t salt
1¼ C milk   ½ t pepper
1 qt. sliced raw potatoes

Season potatoes with salt and pepper. Put a layer of potatoes in bottom of casserole or closed baking dish, then ham, then potatoes, add milk, put on close fitting cover, bake slowly 1 hr. Potatoes and ham should absorb the milk Will serve 6.

Mrs C. V. Ferguson

SAUSAGE

5 lb. fat pork   15 t salt
10 lb. lean pork   5 t sage
1 T parsley sifted fine   5 t pepper

Grind pork, add flavoring, mix well and fry in ½ in. slices until brown.

SCHNITZEL BULGARIAN

1½ lb. round steak   3 T butter
1 large onion   Sauce for kettle
2 eggs   1 qt. canned tomato
2 light rolls   1 T butter
1 t salt   1 onion
½ t paprika

Beat eggs, run meat through grinder and put into a bowl eggs and two light rolls, that have soaked until crust is soft, add meat, salt and pepper and the chopped onion and butter, mix all together and form into 2 rolls.

Put in iron kettle tomatoes, butter, chopped onion and put in meat, let it cook slowly ½ hr. covered, then turn over and cook another half hr.

Mrs. Chester I. Long

QUICK LUNCH

Trimbal cases or rosettes can be kept on hand and filled with creamed fish, chipped beef, creamed rice, creamed potato, chicken, seasoned with parsley or celery Fresh fruit and iced drink make a quick lunch

PORK LOAF

3½ lb. lean fresh pork
½ lb. fat fresh pork
6 crackers, rolled
1 T salt
1 T paprika
1 T onion juice

½ onion, chopped fine
2 T butter
1 T powdered sweet herbs
2 T pickles
3 eggs
1-3 C tomato puree

Chop pork fine, add crackers, rolled fine, salt, paprika, onion juice, or onion chopped fine, and cooked in butter until yellowed a little, powdered sweet herbs, fine chopped pickles, capers or nasturtium seeds, eggs well beaten, and tomato puree. Mix all together very thoroughly, the shape of a long loaf. Roll into fine cracker crumbs and bake about 3 hrs. in moderate oven. Baste occasionally with bacon fat of the fat in pan. Use less of tomato puree if the mixture seems moist Serve hot or cold, cut in thin slices.

Mrs. P. C. Lewis

POCKET ROAST

A round or rump steak cut 2 in.
  thick with pocket.
1 C mashed potatoes
1 C buttered bread crumbs

1 t salt
¼ t sage
1 t minced onion
¼ t pepper

Mix and stuff pocket. Sew up the opening. Bake in double roaster 1½ hr.

Mrs. Barnes

MOCK DUCK

1 calf's liver
4 strips of bacon
2 onions

1 T flour
1 t salt
½ t pepper

Lard 1 calf's liver, scald, then rub with flour, salt and pepper. Put strips of bacon in double roaster, liver on top of bacon, cover with ground onions. Bake slowly. This is fine.

Mrs. F. G. Smyth

MEAT BREAD

Use ½ cup of cold corned beef minced fine, mixed in a biscuit dough. Bake in hot oven for 15 min. Split and spread with butter Serve in folded napkin.

MEAT GEMS

1 C meat
1 C milk
2 eggs

1 T flour
2 T butter

Chop the meat fine, mix the milk, butter, flour, salt and pepper, add the beaten egg-yolks, then the meat and beaten egg-whites. Bake 20 min , in well buttered gem tins.

Mrs. Barnes

BAKED SWEET BREADS

2 lb. sweet breads   Strips of bacon

Boil sweet breads until tender, salt and pepper. Cut the size wanted and wrap each in strip of bacon, secure with a tooth pick and place in oven, baking until brown. When ready, serve with button mushrooms.

C. C.

ROLLED STUFFED STEAK

Round steak 1½ thick   1 C bread crumb dressing
½ t salt   2 T butter
½ t pepper

Score and butter steak. Spread dressing on top and season. Roll into loaf and spread strips of bacon on top and bits of suet or fat, steam and cook 1½ hr. or bake 45 min in first very hot oven and then moderate.

SQUAB

Squab to be tender must be used before they begin to fly. The dry dressing is good for squab and all small birds Place birds when stuffed in bake dish, breast down with 1 T butter to each bird. When ½ done turn breast side up and put strip of bacon on each bird, finish cooking and serve at once. Place in hot oven first 5 min. then medium Cook 30 to 45 min.

Mrs. Chester I. Long

SPANISH MEAT LOAF WITH TOMATO SAUCE

2 lb. round steak   2 T parsley
1 lb. fresh pork   2 eggs
2 medium onions   2½ T salt
3 green peppers   1 T pepper
12 soda crackers

Grind all, mix well, add eggs well beaten, then ground parsley, form into a loaf, roll in cracker crumbs. Put loaf in baking pan, pour around it 1 pt. fresh milk. Bake 1¾ hrs. slowly after first quarter hour., basting often Will serve 14.

Mrs. C V. Ferguson

SCOUSE

1 C cold roast beef   1 t salt
1 onion   ½ t pepper
2 potatoes

Peel and slice potatoes thin, slice roast beef and onion in baking dish, put in a layer of potatoes then a layer of meat then onions, salt and pepper, alternate layers until pan is full. Sprinkle flour over top add any left over gravy and bake until brown.

Mrs. Steel

TURKEY TAMALE

1 C corn meal	1 C cooked turkey, chopped fine
1 T butter	½ C stoned olives
1 T onion juice	4 T catsup
1 C tomatoes	¼ t cayenne pepper
3 T oil	½ t salt

Scald corn meal with ¾ C boiling water, add other ingredients in order given. Put in a buttered dish and bake ½ hr.

Mrs. Henry Lassen

STUFFED TOMATOES

14 tomatoes, medium sized	Thick white sauce
1 chicken	7 slices bacon
1 small can mushrooms	

Hallow out tomatoes, do not peel. Stew chicken until well done, remove from bones and cut in cubes. To thick white sauce add the chicken and mushrooms and liquid in which chicken was cooked. This mixture should be very thick. When boiling hot fill tomatoes with chicken. The mushrooms may be omitted. Serve tomatoes on lettuce leaf and top with a ½ slice of crisp bacon. Bacon grease may be added as seasoning.

Mrs. Williard Brooks

TAMALE PIE

2 C corn meal	2 C tomatoes
6 C water	1 lb. hamburger steak
1 T fat	1½ t salt
1 onion	

Make a mush by stirring the corn meal and salt into boiling water. Cook 45 min. Brown onion in fat, add hamburger and stir until red color disappears Add salt, pepper and tomato. A sweet pepper is an addition. Grease baking dish, put in layer of corn meal mush, add seasoned meat, and cover with mush. Bake ½ hr Serves 12.

Katherine Lewis Mechem

TURKEY GRAVY

Use the fat in baking pan, set on stove, when smoking hot, stir in 2 T flour or more to use up all the fat, let flour brown, then add boiling water, 1 qt. or more salt and pepper if more is desired and add 1 T kitchen bouquet.

STUFFING FOR BONED TURKEY

12 oz. bread	6 eggs
½ lb. butter	1 T herbs
1 lb. veal, finely ground	1 t salt
¾ lb. pork, finely ground	¼ t pepper

If a little too soft, add cracker meal, this makes a good meat loaf. After turkey is boned lay in a thin layer of dressing, 3 rows thin strips of ham, mushrooms, apples, oysters, or chestnuts between.

Mrs C L. Davidson

TURKEY OR CHICKEN CREAM HASH

Chop cold meat fine, use a thick white sauce or cream. Use butter and season   Cook half an onion in sauce, then lift it out, add chopped meat. Serve on toast with poached eggs on top

Mrs Millison

SWISS ROAST

2 lb. round steak	½ can tomatoes
2 T butter	2 onions

Steak cut in in slices, fry 5 min. in very hot butter, then cover with tomatoes and onions grated.   Simmer 2 hrs.

SWEET BREADS AND MUSHROOMS

6 eggs	⅛ t onion
1 can mushrooms	1-16 t nutmeg
3 lbs. sweet breads	2 C white sauce

Hard boil eggs, chop and mix all together with white sauce. serve in patties or ramekins or on toast.

VEAL BALLS WITH TOMATAO SAUCE

1½ lb. neck of veal	¼ lb. salt pork or bacon
1 C dry bread crumbs,	. 2 t salt
1 t grated onion	1 t table sauce
¼ t nutmeg	1 t poultry seasoning

Grind raw meat and pork, add bread crumbs and seasoning mix well and roll into 8 balls.   Brown quickly in a little hot drippings or oil, place in earthenware serving dish.   Cover with strained tomato sauce and bake for 45 min. Serve in the casserole

BUTTERNUT AND POTATO DRESSING

1 qt. mashed potato	1 t salt
1 qt. fine bread crumbs	½ C cream
1½ C butternut meats	1 egg
1 t mixed herb seasoning	½ t pepper

All mixed together used to stuff turkey.

CELERY STUFFING

1 C celery finely cut, with dry turkey dressing.

CHESTNUT DRESSING

1 C cooked chestnuts split, added to dry turkey dressing.

DRY TURKEY DRESSING

1½ qt. stale bread finely crumbled	1 t sage
	1 T minced celery
2 t salt	1 t minced onion
1 t pepper	¾ C butter
2 t minced parsley	

Rub the butter through the bread crumbs, add seasoning mix all thoroughly, and cover with damp cold cloth and set in cool place over night. This dressing flavors the turkey and in turn becomes moist from the turkey juices.

OYSTER DRESSING

1 C oysters added to dry turkey dressing.

TURKEY TO ROAST

Wash and singe, salt the turkey inside and out and fill with preferred dressing. Draw the thighs close to the body and tie with twine. Cross the legs over the tail. Turn the tips of the wings back and tie close to the body. Lay the fowl breast down in baker. Put in very hot oven for 5 min. then reduce the heat, and add any fat which may have been inside the turkey, or ½ C butter and 1 C water. If browning too fast, cover with oiled paper. Baste every 15 min., turn breast up to brown last 15 min. Do not stick a fork into the meat, it prevents the juices to escape. 8 lb. turkey requires 2½ or 3 hrs. slow baking, 15 min. to each lb. more. Make brown gravy of fat. Chopped giblets may be added to the gravy if desired, or any preferred sauce may be served.

VEAL CUTLETS—PAPINOTTE

6 cutlets	¼ t pepper
½ C toasted bread crumbs	¼ t nutmeg
2 T finely cut parsley	½ t salt
1 T finely chopped onion	4 slices bacon

Trim cutlets—with ground trimmings—mix bread crumbs and seasonings to make a dressing. Salt cutlets and put small pat of dressing on each side, topped with 1-3 slice of bacon. Wrap cutlet in oiled paper, oiled in olive oil. Put in greased pan with square of butter on top each cutlet. Bake 2 hrs. Baste frequently.

Gaby Gouldner Powell

VEAL LOAF

3 lb. ground veal   2 T salt
¼ lb. ground pickled pork   1¼ t pepper
2 egg   1 t sage
6 rolled crackers

Mix well in the order given. Form into a loaf, roll in a few cracker crumbs. Put in a buttered pan. Set the pan in hot water. Bake 3 hrs., basting frequently.

Mrs. C. E. Potts

JELLIED VEAL

1 knuckle veal   Several whole peppers
½ C vinegar   Several whole allspices
1 medium sized onion sliced   1 lemon sliced
2 bay leaves   ¼ t salt

A good sized knuckle of veal well broken. Boil with ½ C vinegar and have knuckle covered with water about 1½ qts. Add onion, bay leaves, spices. When meat is almost done, slice 1 lemon and add salt. Remove meat and cut into cubes. Boil liquid down until there remains about 1½ pts. Serve with oil mayonnaise.

Mrs. Harry Dockum

RIBBON VEAL

Knuckle of veal, 3 or 4 lbs.   1 lemon
7 eggs   1 t salt
1 small can pimentos   1 t pepper

There will be approximately 2 lb. meat, end of bone often discarded may, also, be used to advantage, as stock from bone fills easily. Boil meat until tender, remove from bone, put through grinder. Put layer of veal in mold over this, sprinkle salt, pepper and few drops lemon juice, pour over this some of the stock then layer of pimentos, then eggs, hard boiled, then pimentos, then salt and pepper, then the other half of veal. Pour stock over all, set in ice-box to chill. Serve with oil mayonnaise. Will serve 15 or 18 people.

Harriet Stanley

WILD DUCKS WITH JELLY

Let the ducks lie in strong salt water for several hrs. Wipe dry and rub thoroughly with soft butter, salt and pepper. Then with a tart jelly both inside and out. Place them in a casserole with several spoonsful of butter and jelly inside each duck and around in the dish. Add sufficient water for frequent basting, cover and bake slowly for 2 hrs., or until the birds are tender. Remove the ducks to a hot platter and thicken the gravy to use as with any other roast meat.

Mrs. L. C. Jackson

VEGETABLES SCALLOPED WITH MEAT

1 lb. lamb, beef or lean pork	2 t salt
2 C boiled rice	2 t grated onion
2 T drippings	⅛ t pepper
1 C fresh or canned peas	

Wash, boil and drain the rice but do not blanch. Put the meat on to boil in the rice stock, when tender, remove and cut into thin pieces. Brush a baking dish with drippings and put in a third of rice, then a layer of meat, then seasonings to thickened stock, pour over meat, bake in a moderate oven 40 min.

VEAL STEAMED

3 lb. veal, round steak	1 egg
1 T water	½ C bread crumbs

Pound well, then cut in pieces for serving. Beat egg, add water, dip meat into this and roll in bread crumbs. Fry in butter to a delicate brown.

Mrs. Will Dixon

SAUCE FOR STEAMED VEAL

2 T butter	1 pt. milk
2 T flour	Salt and pepper

Melt butter, add flour, mix thoroughly, add milk, season with salt and pepper. Cook until thick. Place meat in a double boiler, cover with the sauce. Steam 2 or 3 hr.

Mrs. Will Dixon

VEAL BIRDS

1½ lb. veal cutlets	1 t salt
1 C dry turkey dressing	½ t pepper
8 slices bacon	3 T butter

Cut cutlets 4 in. square, salt and pepper, fill each with stuffing, bring together in round shape of bird, skewer with tooth picks and put strips of bacon on top of each. Put in casserole with butter, cover and cook 30 min. Make gravy of fat in casserole.

Meat Sauces

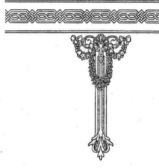

SAUCES FOR MEATS, ETC.

Apple Sauce—Mashed.
Apple Sauce—Quartered.
Asparagus (sauce for).
Bechamel Sauce.
Bread Sauce
Brown Gravy.
Caper Sauce.
Celery Sauce.
Chestnut Sauce.
Crab Meat Cocktail.   Mrs. Oak Throckmorton
Drawn Butter Sauce.
Fish (sauce for)   C. C
Gooseberry Sauce
Hollandaise Sauce.
Horseradish Sauce.   C. C.
Horseradish Hollandaise Sauce
Lemon Sauce.
Maitre D'Hotel Sauce.   Mrs. Chester Long.
Melted Butter Sauce.
Mint Jelly.
Mint Sauce.
Mushroom Sauce.
Mushroom Sauce.
Oyster Sauce .
Oyster Cocktail Sauce.   Mrs. Warren Brown.
Remolade Sauce.
Tomato Sauce.   Mrs. Oak Throckmorton
Tomato Sauce.   Mrs. C. V. Ferguson.
Tomato Sauce.   Mrs. G. M. Lowry.
Tomato Sauce.   Mrs. Warren Brown.
Tuna Sauce for Molded Tuna. Mrs. Geo. Steel.
White Sauce.   C. C.

APPLE SAUCE—MASHED

6 apples   1 C sugar
1 pt water   ¼ lemon rind

Wash and core apple, cut and add water. Cook When very soft run through colander, add sugar and lemon and boil 5 min. More water may be used or more sugar.

APPLE SAUCE—QUARTERED

6 apples   1 C water
2 C sugar

Pare, core and quarter apples. Pour over them a syrup of sugar and water. Boil slowly until apples are soft but not broken.

ASPARAGUS (SAUCE FOR)

2 egg-yolks   ⅛ t nutmeg
4 T butter   ¼ t salt
1 T lemon juice   ⅛ t pepper
2 T boiling water

Season hot water, add egg-yolks. Do not boil. Melt the butter and beat all until creamy. Add lemon juice last.

BEACHAMEL SAUCE

1 pt milk   ½ t minced parsley
3 T butter   1 T minced onion
4 T flour   ¾ C minced celery
1 t salt   ½ t pepper

Heat celery and onion, add to flour and butter melted in sauce pan. Cook slowly and carefully 12 min. Add salt and pepper and parsley when done.

BREAD SAUCE

2 C milk   ¼ t pepper
1 C grated bread crumbs   ½ t onion minced
½ t salt   1 T butter

Boil milk, add onion and bread crumbs, simmer 20 min., add butter, salt and pepper. Serve hot.

BROWN GRAVY

½ C fat in which beef was   1 t butter
    roasted   ½ t pepper
4 T browned flour   1 t salt

Brown fat, stir in flour and add 1 qt. boiling water stirring constantly. Let cook 5 min. 1 T chopped celery improves the gravy.

CAPER SAUCE

4 T butter
2 T flour
1 pt. hot water
½ t salt

¼ t pepper
4 T capers
1 T lemon juice
1 T vinegar

Melt 2 T butter, stir in flour, add water, salt and pepper, stir constantly. Add remainder of butter, lemon juice, vinegar and capers.

CELERY SAUCE

Add minced celery to cream or White Sauce.

CHESTNUT SAUCE

½ t catsup
1 pt. chestnuts
1 T flour
½ t pepper

4 T browned butter
1 qt. water
1 t celery salt
1 t salt

Shell, scald and remove chestnut skins. Break in halves and cook in salted water. Mash fine in the cooking water, mix the flour with the melted butter and add to mashed chestnuts. Add pepper, celery salt and catsup.

DRESSING CRAB MEAT COCKTAIL

1-3 pt. oil mayonnaise
3 T Heinz chili sauce

1 T chopped chow chow
1 t Worcestershire sauce

1 pinch chopped tarragon, parsley, and shallots. Salt and pepper.

Mrs. Oak Throckmorton.

DRAWN BUTTER SAUCE

¼ C butter
¼ t salt
⅛ t pepper

1 C boiling water
2 T flour

Melt the butter, add the flour mixed with seasonings, and stir well. Pour on water 1-3 at a time, stirring until well mixed. Do not scorch or burn.

SAUCE FOR FISH

2½ oz. butter
3 T flour
1 pt. white broth or stock

3 eggs
½ lemon (juice)

Melt 2 ozs. butter in saucepan on slow fire, add flour. Stir well, do not let it brown, moisten with white broth, beat constantly, cook 10 min.

Beat yolks and whites separately, mix, pour sauce over eggs a little at a time, then strain. Add remainder of butter, and lemon juice.

C. C.

GOOSEBERRY SAUCE

½ pt. gooseberries   ½ pt. stock
1 T sugar   1 t butter
½ t parsley

Cook berries, run through colander. Put in pan, add sugar and butter; boil, add stock and parsley minced fine.

HOLLANDAISE SAUCE

½ C butter   1 T lemon juice
2 egg-yolks   ½ t salt
¼ t pepper   1-3 C boiling water

Beat egg-yolks, add lemon juice and 1-3 of butter Set pan in hot water and stir until butter melts. Then add another 1-3 of butter beating while adding. When this melts, add remainder of butter, then boiling water, stirring constantly. Cook 1 min., add salt and serve hot.

HORSERADISH SAUCE FOR MEAT COURSE

½ C grated horseradish .   Little minced parsley
4 T vinegar   ¼ t salt
1 pt. stiffly whipped cream 1-16 t white pepper

Let horseradish stand in vinegar over night, squeeze through cheese cloth then add stiffly whipped cream, a little minced parsley, salt and white pepper.

C. C.

HORSERADISH HOLLANDAISE SAUCE

Add 4 T grated horseradish to Hollandaise Sauce.

LEMON SAUCE

1 lemon (juice)   2 egg-yolks
1 C melted butter   1 T parsley

Add butter to lemon, simmer. Beat until thick, add egg yolks stiffly beaten and serve at once.

MAITRE D'HOTEL SAUCE

4 T butter   1 T parsley
½ t salt   1 T lemon juice
1-32 t pepper

Cream butter, add salt, pepper and parsley chopped very fine. Add lemon juice very slowly. Cool. Fine for hot broiled porterhouse.

Mrs. Chester Long.

MELTED BUTTER SAUCE

2 egg-yolks
1-3 lb. butter

½ t salt
¼ t pepper

Put ¼ of butter in hot saucepan, season, add eggs and stir until eggs begin to thicken. Take pan off fire and add other ¼ butter. When mixed set on fire again and mix, then remove once more repeating the process until butter is used. Pour into dish and add ¼ t lemon or ¼ t vinegar tarragon

MINT JELLY

1 C vinegar
1 C sugar
1 t gelatine

¼ t salt—paprika
¾ C mint chopped fine and
    pressed down in cup

Boil vinegar and sugar 5 min. after it starts to boil, soften gelatine in cold water, stir into vinegar, add salt, mint and paprika. Put in bowl, set on ice and stir until it thickens; then put in mold on ice.

Mrs. Erwin Taft.

MINT SAUCE

½ C lemon juice or vinegar
1 t sugar

½ C mint leaves, chopped fine

Combine acid, mint and sugar. Serve cold over lamb.

MUSHROOM SAUCE

¼ lb. mushrooms
2 T butter
1 C milk gravy or stock

1 t lemon juice
½ t salt

Slice mushrooms, cook in the butter until brown, add flour, gravy or stock and lemon juice. Add salt.

MUSHROOM SAUCE

1 pt cream sauce
½ pt. mushrooms

1 t celery seed

Chop mushrooms, warm and add to hot cream sauce and celery seed.

OYSTER SAUCE

1 pt. cream sauce
1 T butter

1 C oysters
1 T celery

Add chopped oysters to hot sauce, butter and finely minced celery.

OYSTER COCKTAIL SAUCE

6 T catsup
2 T grated horseradish

½ juice of lemon
⅛ t salt

Mrs Warren Brown.

REMONLADE SAUCE

3 egg-yolks	½ t mustard
2 T oil	½ t salt
1 T vinegar	1 t minced parsley

Rub hard boiled eggs into oil, vinegar, mustard, salt and parsley. Set on ice. Serve with meat or fish.

TOMATO SAUCE

35 tomatoes	4 C vinegar
8 large onions	20 T B. sugar
4 red peppers .	5 t salt

Chop all of above and cook until tender, and then add vinegar, sugar, salt—cook 3 hours.

Mrs. Oak Throckmorton.

TOMATO SAUCE

½ can tomatoes	1 small onion
1 green pepper	4 T butter
3 T flour	¾ C water

Cook tomatoes, then strain, add pepper and onion ground. Cook 8 min. Put flour in hot pan with butter. Stir, add tomato mixture and water. Boil 2 min.

Mrs. C. V. Ferguson.

TOMATO SAUCE

1 pt. tomatoes	1 bay leaf
1 T flour	1 sprig parsley
3 level t butter	1 blade of mace
1 small onion	Salt and pepper to taste

Put tomatoes on the fire with the onion, bay leaf, parsley, and mace. Simmer slowly for ten minutes. Melt the butter, add the flour and mix smooth Press the tomatoes through a sieve, add the butter and flour, stir constantly until it boils. Add salt and pepper and it is ready for use. Serve with chops, fillet or broiled steak.

Mrs G M. Lowry.

TOMATO SAUCE FOR MEATS

½ can tomatoes	1 spray parsley
1 bay leaf	1 stalk celery

Cook 10 min., remove and press through seive, then add 1 t melted butter.

1 T flour	⅓ t pepper
1 t salt	Serve hot

Mrs. Warren Brown.

SAUCE FOR MOLDED TUNA OR SALMON

1 T chopped parsley
1 T chopped olives
Juice of 1 lemon

1 C salad dressing
1 t chopped onion

Mrs. Geo. Steel.

WHITE SAUCE

1 T butter
3 T flour

½ t salt
1 C milk

Melt the butter and stir in the flour. Then gradually add the milk.

C. C.

Vegetables

VEGETABLES

Apple, Tomato, Sweet Potato   Mrs. F. G. Smyth.
Artichokes
Asparagus
Asparagus, French
Asparagus and Peas

Bananas, Baked
Bananas, Creamed
Bananas, Fried
Banana Fritters
Beans, Baked   Mrs. Harry Dockum.
Beans, Baked   Mrs. W. E. Stanley.
Bean Rarebit, Baked
Bean Polenta
Beets, Boiled
Boquet of Sweet Herbs
Brussel Sprouts
Bryn Mawr Corn Cake

Canned Vegetables
Carrots
Cauliflower
Celery au gratin
Celery Curled
Celery Scalloped   Mrs. Ralph Millison.
Chestnuts, Casseroled
Corn, Boiled on Ear
Corn, Boiled in Milk
Corn and Cheese
Corn Chowder
Corn Croquettes   Mrs. Charles Cohn.
Corn Fritters
Corn, Nantucket
Corn Pudding   Mrs. J H. Black.
Corn Pudding   Mrs. Chester Long.
Corn Pudding   Mrs. Ralph Millison.
Cucumbers   Mrs. O. D. Barnes.

Egg Plant, Fried
Egg Plant, Stuffed   Mrs. A. O. Rorabaugh.
Egg Plant, Diced   Mrs. Henry Lassen

Green Peppers with Asparagus
  Tips   Mrs. Cohn.
Green Peppers, Stuffed   Mrs. L. C. Jackson.

Halibut Potato

Hominy and Cheese
Hominy Croquettes
Italian Vegetables   Mrs. Chester Long.

Lettice Roll
Lima Beans

Macaroni Loaf
Macaroni Spanish   Mrs. Erwin Taft.
Mushrooms and Asparagus
Mushrooms and Tomato   Mrs. Warren Brown.
Mushroom Test

Onion Juice
Onions and Potatoes, Fried
Onions, Stuffed

Parsnip Croquettes   Mrs. English.
Parsnip Fritters·   Mrs. G. M. Dickson.
Peas (Washington)
Pecans and Celery   Mrs. Chester Long.
Potato Balls
Potato Balls, Curried
Potato Balls in Parsley   Mrs. Chester Long.
Potato Eggs
Potato with Cheese   Mrs. P. C. Lewis.
Potato, Creamed with Cheese
Potato and Corn
Pineapple and Sweet Potato   Mrs. F. G. Smyth.
Delmonico Potatoes
Duchess Potatoes
Escalloped Potatoes
French Fried Potatoes
King's Potatoes
Marble Potatoes   Mrs. Chester Long.
Potato Nests
New Potatoes
Parsley New Potatoes
Potato Puffs
Souffled Potatoes
Popcorn Balls

Radishes, Fried

Spaghetti, Plain Boiled
Spaghetti and Cheese
Spaghetti and Tomato
Spinach   Mrs. A. O Rorabaugh.
Spinach, Stuffed
Squash, Summer
Succotash
Succotash
Suggestions for Vegetables
Sweet Corn
Sweet Potato   Mrs. Ralph Millison.
Sweet Potato Croquettes
Sweet Potato, Georgia   Mrs. Chester I. Long

Sweet Potato with Marsh-
    mallow   Mrs. O. D. Barnes.
Sweet Potato and Nut
    Croquettes   Mrs. Ralph Millison
Sweet Potato, Stuffed

Tomatoes, Baked and Stuffed
Tomatoes, Mexican
Tomatoes, Green, Fried
Tomatoes, Scalloped
Tomatoes, Stuffed
Vegetable Cutlets
Wartime Hash

SUGGESTION FOR VEGETABLES

Meat supplies mainly protein Peas, beans, and lentils take the place of meat in supplying protein. Nuts are meat substitutes but should be thoroughly chewed until perfectly creamy

Combinations of vegetables to bake: Peas and asparagus, peas and mint—a sprig of mint added to peas when cooking, peas and potatoes, peas and celery, peas and rice, potatoes and celery.

Maitre D'Hotel sauce is good on potato balls as well as on meat.

Peeling Tomatoes—Hold the tomato with long fork over gas flame a few seconds. The heat bursts the skin which will then come off easily.

Canned beans, peas and asparagus should be rinsed before serving. This takes away the can taste. Serve with ¼ lb butter melted to each qt. of hot vegetable

Pimentos can be fried in butter.

FOR BREADED DISHES

Beat ¼ t B. P. into egg before dipping things to be fried into it. This makes the egg thicker and more foamy and holds more crumbs. Also put ¼ t B. P. into flour and meal before dipping chicken into it for frying.

Instead of taking a tonic in the spring for spring lassitude, the best of all tonics is to be found in fresh fruits and vegetables —spinach, lettuce and dandelion.

A well beaten white of egg added to mashed potatoes, whipping the potatoes hard before serving, will add to the looks and taste of the dish.

If a vegetable or cereal burns plunge the vessel containing the burned mass into cold water and allow it to remain for a few minutes before pouring the contents into another pan. This will do away almost entirely with the burned taste which is so disagreeable.

To preserve the color of green vegetables, put them to cook in boiling water with a pinch of soda or keep the cover off the kettle while boiling them.

If potatoes are boiled in salted water for 10 minutes, then put into the oven they will bake more quickly. The boiling water will heat them through more rapidly than if they were placed in the oven cold

Vegetables may be rendered crisp by standing in ice water with a t of lemon juice added.

Always cook vegetables grown above the ground in salted water, those which grow beneath the surface in fresh water.

Onions, squash, turnips, beets, carrots, parsnips, cabbage, potato, keep in sand in cool place.

Beets plunged in cold water after boiling, makes the skins easily removable.

APPLE, TOMATO, SWEET POTATO

Slice tomato across, core and slice apples across, sweet potatoes partly cooked, slice the same thickness.

Put a slice of tomato in bake pan, then a slice of sweet potato, lastly the apple; hold together with a tooth pick and pour over it a syrup of cooked sugar and water. Bake in the oven until apple is soft and baked.

Mrs. F. G. Smyth.

ARTICHOKES

Peel and wash artichokes. Boil until tender and serve with cream or tartar sauce, picking the leaf from the choke with the finger and dipping in the sauce.

ASPARAGUS

Immerse bunches in boiling water leaving tips out of water. Boil 20 min., drain and serve with melted butter, or cream sauce. Salt.

ASPARAGUS, FRENCH

3 bundles of asparagus   ½ t salt
3 small onions   3 egg-yolks

Boil asparagus 20 min., mince the tender parts with onion, add salt and pepper and well beaten egg. Stir until hot and pour over toast.

ASPARAGUS AND PEAS

6 bunches asparagus   2 T butter
2 C peas   1 t salt

Cook asparagus and peas separately. When done and hot serve peas on asparagus. Salt, and pour over both melted butter.

BAKED BANANAS

6 bananas   ½ lemon
6 t butter

Slice bananas and place in earthenware dish, cover with butter and squeeze 1 drop of lemon juice on each slice. Bake 25 min.

BANANAS CREAMED

2 C whipped cream   5 eggs
1 C bananas   ½ C sugar

Whip cream, beat egg together, chop fine bananas, stir fruit and cream together lightly, add eggs and sugar. Butter ramekins and fill ½ full of mixture and bake until puffed and light brown. Serve at once or they will fall when cool. Cinnamon may be sprinkled on top.

BANANAS FRIED

6 bananas   1 T powdered sugar
2 T butter

Peel and split the fruit. Put butter in pan, add fruit and when brown on both sides place on platter and sprinkle with powdered sugar. Serve very hot.

BOSTON BAKED BEANS, PORTLAND, MAINE

2 qt. small navy beans   Salt, pepper
½ lb. salt pork   2 T New Orleans molasses
Hot water

Put beans to soak over night. In the morning boil 20 min. Plunge into cold water. Rinse and place alternately in bean pot with salt pork which has been cut into slices ½ in. thick. Salt and pepper and cover with boiling water. Last use the molasses on top. Bake in a covered earthen bean pot for 10 hours, replenishing water when needed with water brought to the boiling point. Then your beans will not break in cooking.

Mrs. W. B. Buck.

. EXCELLENT BAKED BEANS

One and one-half lbs. of beans soaked over night. Next morning add ½ t soda and bring to a boil. Pour off, then boil in clear water a few min. Place a layer of beans in a bean pot, add salt and pepper and a sprinkle of mustard, 3 slices of onion, medium size, 2 slices of salt pork (you use ½ lb of salt pork for the 1½ lbs of beans) then another layer of beans, etc., until the top layer, then add to this 3 iron spoonfuls of molasses. Cover well with water and cook in a slow oven all day.

Mrs. Harry Dockum

BANANA FRITTERS

1 T lemon juice   1 T sugar
6 bananas   1½ C flour
2 eggs   1 t B. P.
1 T butter

Mash bananas, beat eggs, melt butter, add B. P. to flour and mix all together. Have deep fat boiling and drop this mixture into it by the spoonful, not putting enough in at one time to cool the fat.

BAKED BEANS

2 C navy beans   ⅛ t pepper
¼ lb. salt pork   1 t mustard
6 T brown sugar   ¼ lb. butter
½ t salt

Pick over and thoroughly wash the beans, cover with water and soak over night with ⅛ t soda Cook until skins begin to break then drain off the water, saving enough of this to cover beans in the baking pan. Put beans in baking pan with all the above ingredients and bake in moderate oven for 4 hrs.

Mrs. W. E. Stanley

BAKED BEAN RAREBIT

2 T butter
½ t salt
¼ t paprika
1 C cold baked beans

½ C hot milk
1 C soft cheese
1 T Worcestershire Sauce

Put butter in saucepan, add salt and paprika, then the beans which have been put through a vegetable press. Heat thoroughly and then stir in the hot milk, mix thoroughly, and add the cheese chipped fine and the Worcestershire Sauce. Continue to stir until cheese melts, then pour over thin slices of soft toast and serve quickly.

BEAN POLENTA

1 pt. common white or brown beans
2 T molasses
1 t salt
1 t mustard

1 T vinegar
1 T olive oil or melted butter
½ t pepper
Cayenne

Pick over, wash and soak the beans overnight. In the morning put them in 2 qts. cold water and boil them slowly until soft and mealy, about 3 hrs. Add 2 T molasses, salt, mustard, olive oil or melted butter, pepper, cayenne and vinegar, stir and cook for 10 min. The beans should be quite dry when done.

BOILED BEETS

Beets must not be cut down too closely or they bleed and become pale and lose flavor. Boil until tender 2 or 3 hrs. Rub off skins while hot and serve with melted butter and sugar, or sliced in vinegar and sugar.

6 beets
2 T butter

1 t sugar

BOUQUET OF SWEET HERBS

Tie together 4 sprigs of parsley, 4 bay leaves, 4 sprigs of thyme, 4 leaves of sage. Dry and use for soups or stew.

BRUSSELS SPROUTS

Lay sprouts 15 min. in salted water. Drain well and cook in plenty of boiling water 20 min. Drain colander and serve with Bechamel or Hollandaise Sauce.

BRYN MAWR CORN CAKE

1 pt. grated corn
½ C flour
¼ C milk

2 eggs
1 T melted butter
1 t salt

Beat the eggs, yolks and whites separately. Add the yolks to the corn, then the milk, flour, butter, and the salt. Beat well, then fold in lightly the stiffly whipped whites of the eggs and bake in a hot and well greased griddle.

CANNED VEGETABLES

Canned vegetables can be served by emptying the contents of can; using the liquid or not. If liquid is used, heat vegetable in liquid, add 1 T butter, salt and pepper To beets add 1 T sugar. If the liquid is not used, use ½ C cream to a can, salt, pepper and 1 T butter or use cream sauce All these must be served hot Never let canned goods stand in the can, empty as soon as opened and cover.

CARROTS

Peel and boil 2 hrs. Mash.

Or, peel and boil and cut in cubes and serve with sweetened butter, salt and pepper.

Or, peel and prepare as above and bake in covered dish with milk

Carrots may be creamed with peas.

CAULIFLOWER

Trim off outside leaves and lay blossoms down in cold salted water 20 min Shake in water causing insects to drop out. Tie in a piece of cheese cloth and cook in boiling salted water gently 30 min Drain and serve with cream sauce or Hollandaise Sauce or with melted butter poured over while hot. Serve hot.

CELERY AU GRATIN

3 C diced celery
1½ C white sauce

½ C grated cheese
½ C dry bread crumbs

Boil celery until tender in salted water allowing it to cook dry. Butter a baking dish and put in a layer of celery, then one of white sauce, alternating till all is used. Cover top with bread crumbs and cheese and bake 20 min in moderate oven.

CELERY CURLED

Cut stalks of white thick celery into 2 in. lengths. With a sharp knife make parallel cuts on each end then cut at right angles. Throw into a pan of ice water for a couple of hours to curl. Drain, shake dry and arrange on a low dish.

CELERY SCALLOPED

2 bunches celery
1 C bread crumbs
1 C milk

3 T butter
1 C grated cream cheese

Cut celery in small pieces and boil in salt water until tender. Make a white sauce of the milk, butter and flour. Butter a baking pan, put in a layer of celery, salt and pepper, then a layer of the cheese. Repeat until the pan is filled and on top and last a layer of cheese, bake in a moderate oven ½ hr.

Mrs. Ralph Millison

CHESTNUTS CASSEROLED

3 C chestnuts	3 C chicken stock
2 T butter	1½ T flour

Shell chestnuts, put in casserole and pour over it chicken stock. Cover and cook slowly 3 hrs. Then thicken with flour and butter cooked together. Serve in casserole.

CORN BOILED ON EAR

Strip down the husks of the corn, and test its freshness by pressing the thumb nail in one or two of the kernels. If the milk flows freely the corn is in good condition. Strip off the outer husks leaving the tender inside ones on, but turning them back. Remove every thread of silk, rubbing it off with the hands. Now turn the inner husks back, tie with an outside husk and place in a kettle. Cover the corn over with a layer of the outside husks then pour on cold water to the depth of the corn. Put on the kettle lid and set over a quick fire. Watch carefully and when the water has boiled five minutes from the time it reaches the boiling point, it is done. Serve at once leaving the inside husks on, or not, as preferred. Boiling water may be used in the place of the cold and the corn boiled exactly 8 min. from the time the boiling point is reached, but it will not be quite so delicious as with the cold water process.

CORN BOILED IN MILK

Husk the corn and drop into the boiling milk. Cook just 5 min from the time it begins to boil. Keep covered closely while cooking, and serve as soon as done.

CORN AND CHEESE

1 C samp(coarsely ground	or	1 qt. water
cracked corn)		1¼ t salt

Boil the samp in the salted water until tender. Drain and combine with the following sauce:

1 C skim milk	2 T flour
1 C finely cut cheese	1 t salt
¼ t mustard	Paprika

Mix the seasonings with the dry flour. Add enough milk to form into a smooth paste. Add the remainder of the milk and heat in a stewpan, stirring constantly until thick. Add the cheese and stir until it is thoroughly melted. Put a layer of the boiled samp in a baking dish or casserole. Add a layer of sauce and so on alternately until the material is all used. Sprinkle bread crumbs over the top layer of sauce and cook in a medium oven until the crumbs brown.

CORN CHOWDER

¼ lb. fat salt pork	1 T flour
1 onion	2 T butter
2 C diced potatoes	1 C sliced tomatoes
1 pt. corn pulp	1 celery stalk
1 pt. hot milk	1 C broken crackers

Cut the pork in pieces, place in a kettle and fry until crisp. Take out the meat leaving the fat, add to it the sliced onion and let it cook until tender and lightly colored. Then add the raw diced potatoes, the corn pulp, sliced tomatoes, and the celery stalk cut into bits. Celery salt may be substituted for the celery. Meanwhile have the corncobs cooking in a pint of hot water. Cover the other vegetables with water and put on the fire. As soon as the potatoes are tender pour in the hot milk and the water strained off the cobs. Cook the flour and butter together as for white sauce and stir into the chowder. Simmer five min., put in the crackers and serve hot.

CORN CROQUETTES

6 ears corn	1 T flour
1 egg	1 T milk
¼ t pepper	½ t salt

Cut the kernals from the corn, mix and form in croquetts and fry in hot lard.

Mrs Cohn

CORN FRITTERS

4 ears corn	¼ t pepper
2 beaten eggs	1 C flour
½ t salt	1 C cold milk

Cut the kernals from the corn. Add the beaten eggs, salt, pepper, flour, and milk. Have ready a hot frying pan well greased and drop in the batter by spoonfuls. There should be enough for a dozen. Do not let the fritters touch Cook in relays, frying on one side 4 min., then turn and fry the other. These are delicious as an accompaniment for chicken or to serve for breakfast.

(NANTUCKET) CORN

1 doz. ears corn	1 t salt
1½ pt. rich milk	½ t pepper
4 eggs	2 T sugar

With a keen bladed knife score each row of kernels, then scrape out the pulp, leaving the hulls on the cob. To the pulp add the milk, the beaten eggs, salt, pepper and if the corn lacks sweetness, the sugar. Bake in a well buttered deep dish for 2 hrs., in a slow, steady oven.

CORN PUDDING

1 can corn	2 T butter
2 eggs	⅛ t salt
1 C milk	⅛ t pepper

Put in baking-dish, stand in a pan of water, bake in a slow oven 30 min. Cover at first for awhile, then uncover and let brown.

Mrs. J. H. Black.

CORN PUDDING

1 can corn	1 T butter
3 eggs	⅛ t salt

Beat egg separately, mix with corn, melt butter, add salt; beat thoroughly, place in covered bake dish and bake 20 min.

Mrs. Chester Long.

CORN PUDDING

1½ C canned corn	4 T flour
1 C milk	1 T sugar
2 eggs	1 T melted butter

Put the corn through the food chopper, add milk, then the beaten egg, flour, B. P., sugar, melted butter and salt and pepper to taste. Turn into a buttered baking dish, and bake in a moderate oven until brown. This may also be used for fresh grated corn.

Mrs. R. Millison.

CUCUMBERS

Slice the cucumbers and put in a quart jar within an inch of top of can. Cover with vinegar and on top of vinegar and cucumbers put olive oil to the top of can

Mrs. Oscar Barnes.

EGG PLANT, FRIED

1 egg plant	½ t salt
2 eggs	¼ t pepper
1 C cracker crumbs	1 T milk

Peel egg plant and slice 3-8 in. thick. Soak 1½ hrs. in salted water. Let drain, dip in beaten egg and milk, roll in cracker crumbs and fry to a golden brown. Salt and pepper. Serve hot.

EGG PLANT (Stuffed)

1 pretty shaped egg plant	1 C white cream sauce
1-6 t pepper	2 eggs
1-3 t salt	

Boil eggs 20 min. Make a cream sauce by melting 2 T butter, rub in 4 T flour as this sauce must be thick; Add 4 T milk, beat well, add 1 C milk which you have brought to a boiling point. Boil until nicely thicken and smooth

Cut off top of egg plant, scoop out the inside, leaving enough inside so that it will stand up well. Put what is scooped out in salt water, cook until tender, about 20 min. Drain off the water, stir into this the cream sauce, chopped eggs, salt and pepper. Scald out the shell, fill with the mixture, sprinkle cracker crumbs and butter over the top. Place in a pan with a little water and bake 20 min

Mrs. A. O Rorabaugh.

DICED EGG PLANT

Pare and dice an egg plant sprinkled with salt, cover with boiling water, let stand 10 minutes, drain, then add 2 onions cut in small pieces, 1 t chopped parsley, ½ C rice. Put in a sauce pan with 1 qt. water, cook until water is nearly absorbed. Take from stove and add 1 t of butter, ½ C strained tomatoes, add 1 t salt. Put in baking dish and bake 20 minutes.

Mrs Henry Lassen.

GREEN PEPPERS (Stuffed with Asparagus Tips)

6 green peppers	Bread crumbs
White sauce	1 large can asparagus

Cut asparagus in pieces, add a rich white sauce and put in boiled peppers, with butterer bread crumbs on top. Bake a few minutes.

Mrs. Cohn.

STUFFED GREEN PEPPERS

12 green peppers	2 eggs
¼ lb. cooked ham	1 t salt
½ lb. cooked veal	¼ t pepper
½ C bread crumbs	

Wash peppers in cold water, cut off ends and scoop out the seeds. Mince the meat fine and stir in bread, seasoning and beaten egg. Fill the peppers with the mixture, set upright in basin or pan, pour one inch of hot water in pan and bake till the peppers pierce easily with a straw

They may be eaten hot or make a nice salad if sliced when cold and served on a lettuce leaf with mayonnaise dressing.

Mrs L C. Jackson.

HALIBUT POTATO

Bake potatoes, remove center by cutting the side into a cross; fill the shell with halibut flakes mixed with cream sauce and cover top with grated cheese, paprika and butter. Bake until brown.

HOMINY AND CHEESE

1 C hominy	1 C finely cut cheese
2 t butter	1 t salt
2 T flour	¼ t mustard, pepper or paprika
1 C milk	

Melt the butter in a saucepan. Mix into it the flour and seasonings. Add the milk and heat, stirring constantly until the sauce becomes thick and smooth. Add the hominy, and when hot add the cheese and stir until melted.

HOMINY CROQUETTES

1 C hominy (boiled)	1 t butter (melted)
1 t salt	1 egg

Beat eggs, add to hominy, salt and butter; shape into balls, roll in flour and set in cold place over night. Fry in hot fat for breakfast.

ITALIAN VEGETABLES

1 C spinach	1 C potato
1 C celery	1 C asparagus
1 C cauliflower	1 t salt
¼ lb. butter	½ t pepper
½ lb. cheese	

Cook well, and bake in covered dish alternating the layers of vegetables with butter and grated cheese. Bake 30 minutes.

Mrs. Chester Long.

LETTUCE ROLL

½ C peas (cooked)	½ C mashed potatos
½ C beans (cooked)	½ C onion sliced
½ C celery (cooked)	1 egg
½ t salt	½ C tomato juice
6 lettuce leaves	

Split beans, cut celery in ½ in. slices, onions diced, egg beaten, all vegetables mixed together, salted and rolled in lettuce leaf. Put in buttered covered bake dish and pour over all tomato juice. Bake 20 min.

LIMA BEANS

To cook quickly by removing the skins, which require the long cooking, wash and throw the beans in boiling water for 10 min. Dry and rub off the skins. Then put to cook in 2½ C of boiling water for every C of beans. Cook slowly 45 min. or 1 hr. A little celery improves the flavor. Add salt 1 T carrots sliced thin also adds to the flavor.

MACARONI LOAF

1 C milk	¼ t curry powder
1 C bread crumbs (fresh)	1 small onion
¼ C butter	1 t parsley, chopped
3 eggs	

Scald the milk, pour over bread crumbs, add macaroni that has been cooked in salt water. Add other ingredients. Line a mold with oiled paper. Place loaf in steamer ½ hr. Serve with tomato sauce.

(SPANISH) MACARONI

1 C macaroni	1 T Worcestershire Sauce
2 onions	1 t chili powder
1 T olive oil	½ can tomatoes
3 T butter	½ C cheese (grated)

Boil macaroni until tender. Fry onions in olive oil and butter, add while frying, the sauce, chopped onion and chili powder. Put this mixture and the macaroni together, add tomatoes. Put in baking dish, grated cheese sprinkled over top Bake ½ hr. in moderate oven

Mrs. Erwin Taft

MUSHROOMS AND ASPARAGUS

1 lb. mushrooms	½ t celery salt
2 T butter	1 pt cream
6 pieces toast	¼ t pepper
½ t salt	1 lb. asparagus tips

Peel mushrooms and fry light brown in butter. Add cream and asparagus. Let it boil up just once and add pepper, celery, salt and serve on toast.

MUSHROOMS AND TOMATOES

1 large onion, cooked brown in 1 T flour. ⅛ t each of nutmeg, celery, salt, cloves and pepper. Pour juice of tomato over this and cook well. Make layer of tomato and layer of mushrooms. Pour above sauce over and cover with cracker crumbs Bake 20 min. slowly.

Mrs Warren Brown

MUSHROOM TEST

Put solid silver knife or fork in cooking mushrooms. If it discolors the silver the mushrooms are poison.

ONION JUICE

To get onion juice, peel the onion and grate on a large grater, using much pressure to extract the juice

ONIONS AND POTATOES (FRIED)

4 onions	1 T butter
4 potatoes	1 T lard
½ t salt	1 T bacon grease

Slice onions and potatoes, place fat in pan when hot, add onions and potatoes and salt Cover for the first 15 min., then watch carefully and stir occasionally for 10 or 15 min. longer. Sometimes water is added for 10 min

ONIONS (STUFFED)

6 onions
6 T bread crumbs
¼ t pepper

½ t sage
2 T butter
½ t salt

Scoop out center of onions, fill with bread crumbs, crumbled sage, pepper and salt, well mixed and moistened with the melted butter. Place the onions after stuffing on a bake dish, put a lump of butter on each, cover and bake 1 hr., in a very slow oven.

PARSNIP CROQUETTS

6 parsnips
⅛ t pepper
2 T sugar

1 T butter
2 eggs
½ t salt

Scrape parsnips, cook till tender, remove hard centers and mash. Add salt, pepper, butter, sugar, eggs and beat well. Mold in round balls and roll in cracker crumbs and fry in deep fat.

Mrs. English

PARSNIP FRITTERS

4 parsnips
3 eggs
½ t salt

2 T flour
1 C milk
2 T butter

Boil and mash parsnips. Beat eggs stiff, mix all well and fry on buttered griddle.

Mrs. G. M. Dickson

PEAS WASHINGTON

1 pt. peas (dried)
2 eggs
1 T butter
½ C cooked peas

1-3 t salt
⅛ t pepper
5 drops onion juice
½ C white sauce

Rub the one pint of dried peas after cooking, through a sieve, add the well beaten eggs, butter melted, salt, pepper and onion juice. Put in buttered molds and bake in a moderate oven Serve with ½ C white sauce to which has been added the ½ C cooked peas.

PECANS AND CELERY

1 C pecans
2 C celery, cooked
1 t salt

1½ C rich white sauce
½ t paprika

Drain celery, add to pecans in stew kettle, add cream sauce, salt and paprika. Cook 10 min.

Mrs. Chester Long

POTATO BALLS

2 C mashed potato	6 eggs
2 T melted butter	1 t cream
½ t salt	¼ t pepper

Beat potatoes and butter very light, add beaten eggs, beat again. Then add cream, salt and pepper. Beat again Bake in quick oven until brown Then beat 4 eggs separate and put on top of dish. Return to oven, brown again. Scoop out in shape of balls.

POTATO BALLS CURRIED

2 T butter	½ t salt
1 T onion	1 C milk
1 T flour	1 pt. potato balls
1 T curry powder	

Melt butter, cook in it the minced onion. Add flour, curry powder, salt and milk. Let boil 5 min., strain over 1 pt. hot boiled potato balls. Serve hot with cold meats.

POTATO BALLS IN PARSLEY

6 potatoes mashed	½ C minced parsley
½ can pimentos	3 T butter

Cut the pimentos into bits with the chopping knife, drain out all juice. Mix with the mashed potatoes which have been salted, peppered and beaten thoroughly adding 3 T butter. Make into balls and roll in parsley, and place on dish in oven for five min Serve with fried chicken or meats.

Mrs. Chester Long

POTATO EGGS

6 potatoes	4 eggs
½ t salt	2 T paprika

Mash potato, salt, mold with hands into shape of eggs. Press hard boiled yolks and whites separately through presser. Cover one half of each potato egg with egg whites and the other half with egg yolk. Dust with paprika and pile on plate.

POTATOES WITH CHEESE

Cut cold potatoes in slices. Put a layer of potatoes and a layer of grated cheese in bake pan. Alternate till filled. Salt and pepper. Fill pan with milk and bake.

Mrs. P. C. Lewis

POTATOES CREAMED WITH CHEESE

Cube cooked potatoes, cover with hot cream sauce, and add grated cheese. Heat till cheese melts.

POTATO CORN

1 C milk	1 C corn meal
1 C mashed potato	½ t salt
1 T sugar	2 t B. P.
1 egg	

Mix potatoes with milk. Beat egg well. Beat all together. Bake in muffin pans..

PINEAPPLE AND SWEET POTATOES

1 large can of pineapple cut in half. 6 large potatoes, sliced the same thickness, partly cooked. 1 C sugar and the juice of the pineapple boiled into a syrup. Put a layer of potato and then one of pineapple alternately in a bake pan. Pour the juice or syrup over this and bake about 20 min.

Mrs. F. G Smyth

DELMONICO POTATOES

Layer of diced potatoes, layer of cheese until dish is full, use drippings from ham of bacon to make thin cream sauce, pour over till it just comes to top. Bake till brown.

DUCHESS POTATOES

Bake potatoes, put through squeezer in circle or fancy shape, sprinkle on parsley.

ESCALLOPED POTATOES

Slice thin cold boiled potatoes. Put layer of potatoes, salt, pepper, then a layer of bread crumbs. Alternate the potatoes and bread crumbs until the dish is full, having bread crumbs on top. Put little butter on top, then pour over it a sauce. Bake ½ hr.

Sauce:

1 C milk	1 T butter
2 T flour	Cook till thick.

FRENCH FRIED POTATOES

Pare potatoes and put in cold water 1 hr. Cut in strips or slices and dry throughly on cloth. Drop into deep fat, boiling. They are done when they float. Drain on brown paper and salt and pepper. Do not add too many at once to fat, as it cools it.

KING'S POTATOES

6 small potatoes	2 T butter
6 small onions	1½ t salt
½ C celery	⅛ t pepper
½ C parsley	⅛ t paprika

Pare potatoes and cover bottom of dish, add onion, celery, parsley and seasoning mixed and cover with milk or cream. Dot with butter and cover. Cook until potatoes are soft, ½ hr. This is best with small new potatoes but can be used with old potatoes.

MARBLE POTATOES

3 C mashed potatoes	2 T butter
½ t salt	1 egg

Beat mashed potatoes light with salt and butter. Divide into 2 parts, into ½ stir the beaten egg-white, into the other stir the beaten egg-yolk. Mold into balls alternating yellow and white. Bake 10 min., in greased pan.

Mrs. Chester Long

POTATO NESTS

2 C peas	2 C potatoes
1 T butter	2 egg-yolks

Mash potatoes and mix with 1 well beaten yolk and melted butter. Beat thoroughly, make into small cake, roll in cracker crumbs and 1 egg-yolk, fry in butter, remove and scoop out inside of top making a large nest in which place the hot peas with a dot of butter on each cake. Serve hot.

NEW POTATOES

12 small new potatoes	4 T butter

Heat plenty of butter in closely covered pan. Scrape potatoes (not sliced) put them into hot butter, cover down air tight and cook till potatoes are done and well browned outside and white and mealy inside, about ½ hr.

PARSLEY NEW POTATOES

10 new potatoes	1 T butter
½ C parsley	2 C cream sauce
½ t salt	

Scrape potatoes and boil. Then drain, chop parsley very fine and add to cream sauce and salt. Cover potatoes with this and make dots of the butter over top.

POTATO PUFFS

1 C mashed potato	2 t B. P.
2 C flour (sifted)	3 eggs
½ C milk	½ t salt

Roll into balls and dip in bread crumbs. Fry in fat.

SOUFFLED POTATO

6 potatoes	1 C cheese
4 eggs	2 T butter
1 pt. milk	

Slice potatoes, grate cheese and put layers of each alternate in covered bake dish, dotting with butter and salt between. Bake 45 min., add milk to beaten egg and pour over all and bake 20 min. longer.

POPCORN BALLS

2 C sugar   ¼ C vinegar
1 C water   2 T butter
3 qts. popped corn

Use freshly popped corn. Make syrup by boiling sugar, water, vinegar and butter, pour over corn and mold while hot into balls. Wrap in oiled paper.

FRIED RADISHES

Cut large fresh radishes in half and fry in oil, 1 min. Serve with meat.

PLAIN BOILED SPAGHETTI

Fill a deep vessel with boiling water. Take a dozen spaghetti sticks full length, and push into the water without breaking as they soften. Boil just 22 min. Take out and drain. Cover with butter or grated cheese or stewed tomatoes while hot.

SPAGHETTI AND CHEESE

2 C cooked spaghetti   1 C cheese
1 C creamed sauce

Cut spaghetti into inch strips. Alternate layers of cheese and spaghetti in a bake pan. Pour over all cream sauce and bake 10 min.

SPAGHETTI AND TOMATO

2 T butter   2 C spaghetti
2 C tomato   1 t salt

Alternate spaghetti and tomato, salt and butter, in a bake dish. Cover and bake 30 min. 1 C cream sauce may be added.

SPINACH

2 lbs. spinach   ½ t salt
3 T butter   ¼ t pepper
2 eggs cooked

Wash the spinach carefully and let stand in cold water until ready to cook, drain it and place in covered kettle. Lift carefully over with spoon until it starts to cook, then it will have plenty of its own water. Cook 20 min., season with the melted butter, salt and pepper. Serve with sliced eggs over top. This will serve 8.

Mrs A. O. Rorabaugh

STUFFED SPINACH

6 large spinach leaves   4 T bread crumbs
6 eggs   1 t onion
1 T minced parsley   ¼ t salt

Soak bread crumbs in butter and water. Scald spinach leaves and drain. Hard boil eggs, remove yolks and mash with bread crumbs, minced onion, salt and parsley. Place on spinach leaf and roll. Place side by side in pan and cover with cream sauce and bake in covered dish 20 min. Press whites of eggs through ricer and sprinkle on top of dish when done.

SUMMER SQUASH

Mash and pare squash and cut in thick pieces 3 in. square. Bake, skin down and serve with butter while hot.

SUCCOTASH

1 qt. string beans	2 tomatoes
1 qt. corn	½ t salt
4 slices bacon	⅛ t pepper

Peel and chop tomatoes, add to cooked beans and corn Boil 20 min. with strips of bacon on top.

SUCCOTASH

1 C lima beans	1 t salt
2 T butter	1 C cream
1 can corn	½ t pepper

Drain beans and corn, mix with salt and pepper, when boiling add cream and butter.

SWEET CORN

Husk and silk the corn and cook in boiling salted water ½ hr., to which has been added 1 C milk.

6 ears corn on cob	1 T salt
2 qts. water	1 C milk

Steamed corn requires 45 min. to 1 hr to cook but it is much better

SWEET POTATO

Mash sweet potato, roll in corn flakes and bake in oven or fry in butter. Mrs. Millison

SWEET POTATO CROQUETTES

1 pt. riced potatoes	2 eggs
1 t butter	¼ t cinnamon
½ t salt	⅛ t nutmeg

Rice sweet potatoes, add butter, salt, eggs, cinnamon and nutmeg. Roll into croquettes, dip into egg, and then into bread crumbs, then fry.

GEORGIA SWEET POTATOES

Pare 4 large potatoes and cut in large slices lengthwise, let stand in cold water 20 min , take out and wipe dry and put in bake dish, cover with syrup made of

½ C butter	½ C water
½ C sugar	

Bake 1 hr., uncovered and turn top potatoes to bottom.
Mrs. Chester I. Long

SWEET POTATOES WITH MARSHMALLOWS

2 T butter
1 T cream
1 t salt

1 t sugar
1 doz. marshmallows

Cook potatoes until tender, remove the skins. Mash and add the seasoning. Place in serving dish, cover with marshmallows. Put in oven a min. before serving.

Mrs. O. D. Barnes

SWEET POTATOES AND NUT CROQUETTES

6 sweet potatoes
¾ t salt
1 T butter
⅛ t pepper
¼ lb. walnut meats

¼ C cream
1 C corn flakes
1 qt. lard
1 can peas

Boil and mash sweet potatoes, add salt, pepper, and butter, add walnut meats and moisten with cream. Form into croquettes, dip into beaten egg and corn flakes, drop into smoking fat and fry a golden brown. Serve hot with buttered peas.

Mrs. Ralph L. Millison

STUFFED SWEET POTATO

Bake sweet potato for 1 hr., in hot oven, then break in center. Scoop out center leaving shell whole. Put through ricer, add salt, butter, 1 egg-yolk, cream, brown sugar and beaten egg-whites. Stuff shells with this. Sprinkle top with sugar and butter. Put in oven until brown.

STUFFED TOMATOES BAKED

12 tomatoes
1 onion
1 C bread crumbs
1 t salt

¼ t pepper
1 T sugar
1 C cream

From blossom end of tomatoes cut a thin slice, scoop out pulp without breaking skin, chop onion finely and mix with bread crumbs and tomato pulp. Season with salt and pepper, add sugar and cream. Refill the tomato shells, place slice on top and place in buttered baking dish, the cut ends up, putting into the dish just enough water to keep from burning. Put small piece of butter on each tomato and bake 30 min., or until the tomatoes are done but not broken.

TOMATO MEXICAN

4 tomatoes green
½ green pepper
½ C olive oil

½ t salt
1 T meal
1 T flour

Slice tomatoes. Mix meal, flour and salt, dip tomatoes in the mixture, fry in hot olive oil adding the pepper chopped fine and seeded.

FRIED GREEN TOMATO

6 green tomatoes
½ t salt
4 T butter

½ C bread crumbs
⅛ t pepper

Cut tomatoes in ½ in. thick round slices without peeling. Mix salt and pepper with crumbs. Dip each slice in crumbs, fry in the butter and serve hot.

SCALLOPED TOMATOES

Butter baking dish, place in bottom a layer of tomatoes, add salt, pepper and butter, then a layer of toasted bread or cracker crumbs. Repeat until dish is full. Bake.

STUFFED TOMATOES

1 doz. tomatoes
2 eggs
1 C bread crumbs
1 C ham
4 T melted butter
Allspice
1 C tomato pulp

1 t minced onion
1-16 t pepper
½ t salt
1-16 t mustard
Mace
Cloves
1 C chicken

To bread crumbs, chicken and ham add butter, pepper, salt mustard, tomato pulp, hard boiled egg-yolks, minced onion, mace, allspice and cloves Stuff and bake.

VEGETABLE CUTLETS

1 C dried peas
2 slices onion
6 cloves
12 peppercorns
Bay leaf
8 T cream

2 t salt
¼ t soda
2-3 C peanuts
½ C dried bread crumbs
⅛ t pepper

Soak peas overnight in cold water to cover Drain, put in saucepan, cover with cold water and bring to boiling point. Again drain, cover with cold water and add onions, cloves, peppercorns, bay leaf, salt and soda. Cook until soft, drain and rub through seive Add finely chopped peanuts, dried bread crumbs, pepper and cream Shape in form of cutlets and saute in butter. Garnish with paper frills.

WAR TIME HASH

Use any kind of vegetables you may have on hand, peas, potatoes, celery, spinach, rice, asparagus, tomato or any kind of mixture, alternate each layer with grated cheese in a deep bake dish, with bread crumbs and butter on top Cover and bake ½ hr Small bits of meat or chicken may be added. This is a good way to use left overs.

PUDDINGS
━━ AND ━━
SAUCES

PUDDINGS AND SAUCES

Apple Pudding	Mrs. Geo. Whitney.
Apple Pudding	Mrs. Ralph Millison.
Apple Pudding and Sauce	Mrs. P. C. Lewis.
Beefsteak Pudding	Mrs. Governor Lewelling
Berry Pudding Steamed	Mrs. A. O. Rorabaugh.
Black Pudding	Mrs. A. O Rorabaugh.
Black or Ginger Pudding	Mrs. Harry Dockum.
Bread Pudding	Mrs. Chester Long.
Bread Pudding Caramel	
Bread Pudding with Fruit	
California Pudding	
Caramel Pudding	Mrs. E. Zartman.
Carrot Pudding	Mrs. Chester Long.
Carrot Plum Pudding	Mrs. H. W. Horn.
Cherry Pudding	Mrs. Howard Norton.
Chocolate Pudding	Mrs. W. E. Stanley.
Chocolate Pudding Hot	Mrs. Harry Dockum.
Coffee Tapioca and Sauce	Mrs. C. L Davidson
Cottage Pudding	Mrs. Geo Whitney.
Crumb Pudding	Mrs Geo. Steel.
Date Pudding	Mrs. A. O. Rorabaugh.
	Mrs. G. M. Dickson.
	Mrs C. W. Brown.
Date Pudding and Sauce	Mrs. Cleveland.
Date Pudding with Ice Cream	Mrs. W. E. Stanley.
Delicate Rice Pudding	Mrs. C. V. Ferguson.
Delicious Rice Pudding	Mrs. Henry Lassen
Easter Pudding	Mrs. C. F. Ferguson
Fig Pudding	Mrs. F. G Smyth.
Fig Pudding	Mrs. Geo. Whitney.
Fig Pudding Steamed	Mrs. Finley Ross.
Fig Pudding and Sauce	Mrs. C. V. Ferguson.
Foamy Sauce	Harriet Stanley
Frozen Pudding	Mrs. J. H. Black.
Frozen Pudding	Mrs C V. Ferguson.
Fruit Pudding	Mrs Warren Brown.
Fruit Pudding	Mrs. G. M. Dickson.
Graham Pudding	Mrs. Spangler.
Hard Sauce	Mrs. Finley Ross.
Hard Sauce	Mrs. G. M. Whitney.
Hasty Pudding and Hard Sauce	Mrs. J. H. Black.
Hingham Pudding and Sauce	
Indian Pudding Baked	Mrs. Howard Norton.
Kiss Pudding	Mrs. C. W. Brown.
Lemon Sauce	

Maple Pecan Pudding	Mrs. Harry Dockum
Macaroon Pudding	Mrs. F. G. Smyth.
Maple Pudding	Mrs Fred Robertson.
Maple Sauce	
Marchioness Pudding	Mrs. L C. Jackson
Marshmellow Pudding	Mrs. Murray Myers.
Marshmellow Cream Pudding	
Millionaire Plum Pudding	
Nation Pudding	
Nut Pudding	Mrs G. M Lowry.
Nut Pudding	Mrs Will Dixon.
Old Fashioned Rice Pudding	Mrs. Howard Norton.
Orange Pudding	Mrs O D. Barnes
Orange Sauce	C. C.
Pineapple Meringue	Mrs Frank Harryman
Pineapple Pudding	Mrs. C. V. Ferguson.
Plum Pudding Sauce	Mrs. H. W. Horn.
Plum Pudding Sauce	Mrs Geo. Steel.
Plum Pudding Cold	Mrs. F. G. Smyth.
Plum Pudding Steamed	Mrs. Baldwin.
Prune Pudding	Mrs J. H. Black.
Prune Whip	Mrs. A. O. Rorabaugh.
Prune Pudding	Mrs. Lewis.
Queen Pudding	Mrs. G. M. Dickson.
Snow Pudding	C C.
Souffle Pudding	Mrs W. E. Stanley.
Sponge Pudding	Mrs. Geo Steel.
Sweet Potato Pudding	
Tapioca Pudding	Mrs C. W. Brown.
Tapioca Fruit Pudding	Mrs. Spangler.
Tipsy Pudding	
White Pudding Sauce	Mrs. L. C. Jackson.
Woodford Jam Pudding	Mrs F. G. Smyth.

APPLE PUDDING

1 C bread crumbs
2 T butter
8 apples

1 C sugar
1 t nutmeg

Soak dry bread crusts in cold water, slice good cooking apples. Butter a baking dish, put a layer of soaked bread crusts in bottom of dish, then a layer of apples. Cover the top with bread crumbs. Bake half to three-quarters of 1 hr. till the crust is brown, serve hot with a good rich sauce, or sugar and cream flovored or a rich dip sauce.

Mrs. George Whitney.

APPLE PUDDING

½ C water
1 C sugar
¾ C flour

4 small apples
½ C butter

Peel apples and cut in 8 pieces, put in long shallow pan, then rub flour, sugar and butter together until it forms a soft dough, sprinkle over apples, bake in slow oven until the apples are tender; serve warm with whipped cream.

Mrs. Ralph Millison.

APPLE PUDDING AND SAUCE

½ C sugar
1 T butter
1 t nutmeg

½ C water
2 C apples

Line a round granite pan with raw sliced apples, sprinkle over the sugar, butter, nutmeg and water.

DOUGH

2 t B. P.
1 C flour
1 T sugar

1 T butter
1 C milk
⅛ t salt

Mix dough, spread over apples and bake slowly.

SAUCE

1 C sugar
3 T butter

1 t cream

Mix and cream well. Serve on Pudding.

Mrs. P. C. Lewis.

BEEFSTEAK PUDDING

1 lb. hamburg steak
1-3 C flour
1-3 C butter

2 eggs
1 pt. milk

Beat eggs, then add to meat, gradually add milk. Cream butter and flour first. Bake in pudding dish 1 hr.

Mrs. Governor Lewelling.

BERRY PUDDING (Steamed)

1 C sugar
1 egg
2 t B. P.

2 C flour
1 C milk
2 C berries

Stir as a simple cake, adding the well flavored berries last, strawberries or cherries are especially nice in this pudding. Steam 2 hrs.

SAUCE

1 C sugar
1 T butter
Nutmeg

1 pt water
1 T corn starch

Cream together sugar and butter, add boiling water to corn starch dissolved in cold water; boil thoroughly. Season with nutmeg or what you like.   Mrs. A. O. Rorabaugh.

BLACK PUDDING

1 C flour
1 C hot water
2 egg-yolks
1 t soda

1 C seeded raisins
2-3 C dark molasses
½ C Eng. walnuts
½ t salt

Separate the eggs placing the yolks in a crock—add molasses and salt—beat, sift in half of the flour, add ½ C hot water. Sift the soda thoroughly through the rest of the flour and add ½ C hot water, the floured raisins and nuts.

Place in buttered, floured cans; steam for 2 hrs

Mrs. A. O. Rorabaugh.

BLACK OR GINGER PUDDING

1 C molasses
1 egg into the molasses
1 t cinnamon
1 t ginger

2-3 C boiling water
1 t soda into the water
1½ C flour

Put together as they come. Bake 1 hr. and serve with hard sauce.   Mrs. Harry Dockum.

BREAD PUDDING

5 slices dry bread
1 C milk
2 eggs
1 t nutmeg

½ t salt
1 t vanilla
½ C sugar

Cover stale bread with milk and set over fire. When soft mash with spoon Add sugar and salt, add beaten egg-yolks and cook 2 min., adding vanilla Remove from fire and add stiffly beaten egg-whites. Pour into dish and add nutmeg sprinkled over top. Do not soak bread for Bread Pudding for that is what makes pudding heavy   Mrs. Chester I. Long.

BREAD PUDDING—CARAMEL

1 pt. bread crumbs	1 C milk
½ C seeded raisins	½ t salt
2 T sugar	2 T butter
2 eggs	

Soften bread crumbs with melted butter and milk. Add beaten eggs, raisins, salt and sugar. Bake. Make following sauce·

1½ C brown sugar	½ C milk
4 T grated chocolate	

Boil sugar, milk and grated chocolate and pour hot over pudding.

BREAD PUDDING WITH FRUIT

3 eggs	1 C sugar
1 C bread crumbs	1 pt. milk
2 C peaches	1 T butter

Butter hard bread, then crumble into bits. Butter pudding dish, put in layer of crumbs, then a layer of peaches, then bread. Beat eggs, add sugar and milk, pour over pudding and bake. Dot butter on top Any fruit, canned or fresh, or dried can be used. Do not use juice.

CALIFORNIA PUDDING

2 C bread crumbs	1 t cinnamon
2 t B. P.	½ t allspice
2 eggs	1 t nutmeg
1 C sugar	2 apples (chopped)
1 C raisins	3 T butter (melted and mixed
2-3 C milk	in bread crumbs)

Mix dry ingredients together, then add eggs and milk. Bake 30 or 40 min. in moderate oven.

SAUCE

1 C sugar	3 T butter
1 T flour	Juice and rind of.small lemon

Add boiling water a little at a time until of proper consistancy.

CARAMEL PUDDING

1 C tapioca	3 C B. Sugar
1 pt. water	1 can grated pineapple
1 qt. warm water	⅛ t salt
Whipped cream	

Pour cold water over tapioca, let soak 1 hr. then cook with the warm water, B. sugar and salt slowly for 20 min. Add pineapple. Serve with whipped cream.

Mrs. R. E. Zartman.

CARROT PUDDING

1 C ground carrots	1 t salt
1 C ground potato	1 C flour
½ C suet	1 t cloves
1 C sugar	1 t cinnamon

Chop suet fine, mix all together well. Steam 3 hrs

SAUCE

2 eggs	½ C hot water
2 C powdered sugar	½ C butter

Beat eggs separately. Add melted butter to boiling water and sugar and when boiling pour over eggs. Serve hot.

Mrs. Chester I. Long.

CARROT PLUM PUDDING

1 C grated or ground raw carrots	2½ C flour
	7 t B P
1 C grated or ground raw potatoes	1 C brown sugar
	1 t each cinnamon, cloves and
1 C chopped suet	nutmeg .
3 C seeded raisins	

Add nuts and currants, if desired. Steam 3 hrs

Mrs. H. W. Horn

CHERRY PUDDING

½ C sugar	2-3 C flour
½ C milk	2 t B. P.
2 T butter	1 pt can cherries

Cream the butter and sugar, add the flour and milk alternately, and B. P. Put the cherries into a baking dish and boil them adding more sugar if they are very sour. While boiling pour the batter over the fruit, but do not mix it in. Be sure that the fruit is entirely covered. Remove at once to hot oven and bake about 20 min. Serve with hot sauce or whipped cream.

SAUCE

1 T butter	1 C cold water
1 T flour	Juice of 1 lemon
1-3 C sugar	

Melt the butter, add the flour, then the sugar and lemon and last the water, stirring constantly while it thickens and boil several minutes.

Mrs Howard Norton.

CHOCOLATE PUDDING (Steamed)

¾ C sugar
¼ C butter
2-3 C milk
1 egg

1½ C flour
2 squares chocolate
1 t B. P.
1 t vanilla
3 T boiling water

Mix butter and sugar together, add the egg, milk, flour, etc. Melt chocolate, add water, stir in last. Steam 2½ hrs. Serve with whipped cream or hard sauce.

Mrs. W. E. Stanley.

HOT CHOCOLATE PUDDING

2 T butter
¼ C flour
¾ C milk
1½ sq. chocolate

½ C sugar
3 eggs
¼ vanilla

Melt butter, add flour, then milk and chocolate. When thick, remove from fire and add well beaten yolks and sugar. Let cool and add the egg-whites beaten very stiff and flavor. Bake about 35 min. and serve hot with frozen whipped cream that has been sweetened and flavored.

Mrs. Harry Dockum.

COFFEE TAPIOCA

2 C hot coffee
1 C milk
½ C tapioca

½ C sugar
¼ t salt
2 eggs (whites)

Stir into hot coffee and milk the tapioca, sugar, and salt; cook 15 min. Remove from fire and add the beaten whites of eggs. Pour into molds and serve cold, with custard dressing.

CUSTARD DRESSING

½ C sugar
1 C milk

2 eggs (yolks)

Boil in double boiler, stirring constantly until thick; add vanilla flavoring

Mrs C. L. Davidson.

COTTAGE PUDDING

2 C flour
2 t B. P.
1 t salt
3 T melted butter

1 egg
¾ C sugar
1 C milk

Mix salt and B. P. with flour, beat egg. Add sugar, butter and milk. Bake in shallow dish and serve with lemon, wine or foamy sauce. This may be steamed.

Mrs. Geo. Whitney.

CRUMB PUDDING

1½ C flour   1 T butter
2 t B. P.   ¼ t salt
¾ C sugar

Mix as for pie crust, moisten with milk the same as for cake batter. Bake in pie tin. Serve with lemon sauce.

Mrs. Geo. Steel.

DATE PUDDING

1 C dates   1 C Eng. walnuts
3 T flour   4 T milk
2 eggs   1 C sugar
1 t B. P.

Cut the dates with scissors, break up the nuts, separate the eggs, beat the egg-whites until stiff, beat the egg-yolks thoroughly. Put together again, add sugar, put the B. P. in half of flour, roll dates and nuts in other half, mix all together, place in a buttered pan, set in a pan of boiling water, bake 40 min. in slow oven. Serve with either ice cream or whipped cream.

Mrs. O. A. Rorabaugh.
Mrs. G. M. Dickson.
Mrs. C. W. Brown.

DATE PUDDING

5 eggs   ¼ lb. dates stoned and chopped
1-3 C powdered sugar

Beat eggs stiff, add powdered sugar and dates. Bake in pan set in pan of water.

HARD SAUCE

½ C butter   ½ C sweet cream
1 C powdered sugar

Cream, sugar and butter and work in gradually cream.

Mrs. Cleveland.

DATE PUDDING
(With Ice Cream)

1 C sugar   1 C dates
2 eggs   1 t B. P.
4 T cracker crumbs   1 saltspoon salt
1 C Eng. walnuts   1 t vanilla

Beat yolks of eggs with sugar. Then add cracker crumbs rolled but not pounded. Add nuts chopped. Add beaten whites the last thing. Bake slowly in a flat pan 25 min. This serves 9 people. To be served with ice cream.

Mrs. W. E. Stanley.

DELICATE RICE PUDDING

1 pt cream whipped
1 C cooked rice
1 package gelatine
½ C cold water

1 t vanilla
½ C nuts
½ C candied cherries

Dissolve gelatine thoroughly in the cold water. To the whipped cream add the rice, then sugar and vanilla; then add gelatine. Let stand 10 min. in ice chest; then add chopped nuts and candied cherries. Will serve 8 to 10 persons.

Mrs. C. V. Ferguson.

DELICIOUS RICE PUDDING

2 egg-yolks
¾ C sugar
1 T lemon extract

3 C milk
1 T corn starch
1 C well cooked rice

Mix egg-yolks, sugar, milk and corn starch together. Put on the stove and when warm add the rice, boil until thick and smooth. When done add the flavoring, pour into a pudding dish, cover with meringue made of whites of 2 eggs. Put in the oven to brown. Serve either hot or cold.

Mrs Henry Lassen.

EASTER PUDDING

4 eggs
4 lady fingers
½ C sugar
¼ C blanched almonds cut in
  small pieces

½ envelope of Knox Gelatin
¼ C candied pineapple cut in
  small pieces
½ pt whipping cream
1 t vanilla

Dissolve gelatine in ¼ C of cold water then place over hot water till thoroughly dissolved Beat yolks of eggs to stiff foam, add sugar and flavoring and the lady fingers broken in small pieces, 1 t vanilla. To the beaten whites, add the whipped cream and gelatin—blend well—then stir in the egg-yolk and lady finger mixture—Add the pineapple and nuts Pour into a mold Set in ice chest 4 hrs or more

Mrs. C. V. Ferguson

FIG PUDDING

1 lb. raisins
1 lb figs, ground
2 C bread crumbs
2 C suet
2 C B sugar
2 C nuts, chopped
2 C citron, cut fine

1 C flour
1 C fruit juice or coffee
½ nutmeg
1 lemon rind
1 t soda
⅛ t salt
4 eggs

Run figs through grinder, chop nuts and citron fine, grate rind of lemon. Mix well all together, put in B. P. cans ¾ full, add cover and steam 4 hrs. Must not let it stop steaming or pudding will be soggy.

Mrs. F. G. Smyth

FIG PUDDING

2 C flour	1 C minced beef suet
2 t B. P.	½ t cloves
2 t cinnamon	½ t nutmeg
2 t ginger	1 C chopped figs
½ t salt	1 C New Orleans molasses
3 eggs	½ t mace
1 C milk	

Mix together flour, B P , cinnamon, ginger, salt, cloves, mace and nutmeg, add suet, add chopped figs, rubbing them through the prepared flour (as above) then add milk, molasses and eggs, stir the mixture well, pour into a pudding mold and steam 3 hrs. If cooked in little cups, will steam in half hr

Mrs Geo. Whitney

FIG PUDDING (Steamed)

½ C suet	1 t cinnamon
½ C seeded raisins or figs chopped	1 t cloves
	½ grated nutmeg
½ C molasses	1 egg beaten lightly last
1½ C flour	1 t soda with sour milk
½ C milk, sour or sweet	1½ t B P. with sweet milk
2 t ginger	

Steam 25 or 30 min. in individual tins or 3 hrs in pudding dish Serve with sauce.

SAUCE

½ C butter	1 pt boiling water
1 C sugar	1 t lemon
2 T flour	1 T vanilla

Mrs. Finlay Ross.

FIG PUDDING AND SAUCE

½ lb. B . sugar	3 acid apples
½ lb. figs	¾ C sweet milk
½ lb. suet	3 eggs
½ lb. bread crumbs	¾ C nuts
5 T flour	

Grind figs, suet, bread crumbs and apples; to these add flour and sugar, mix thoroughly, add milk, then eggs beaten separately, then nuts. Put in buttered pudding molds. Steam 3 hrs.

SAUCE

2 egg-yolks	1-3 C butter
1 C sugar	1 C water
3 T flour	1 lemon

Mix flour and sugar; add water, then grated rind and juice of lemon, add butter, then well beaten yolks and cook over boiling water 15 min. Will serve 20 to 24.

Mrs. C. V. Ferguson.

FOAMY SAUCE

2 T butter
1 C powdered sugar
2 egg-yolks

⅛ t cinnamon
⅛ t nutmeg
½ pt. whipped cream

Cream together butter and sugar add the beaten yolks of eggs, add cinnamon and nutmeg. Then add whipped cream and beat well.

This sauce is very nice with any steamed or baked pudding.
Harriet Stanley.

FROZEN PUDDING

4 eggs
½ C granulated sugar
1 T flour
1 qt. milk

1 C strawberry preserves
1 C walnuts (chopped)
1 C raisins (chopped)
1 t vanilla

Beat the yolks of the eggs with the sugar until light. Dissolve the flour in a little cold milk, add to it the mixture and boil in double boiler until it thickens, stirring all the time. When cold add preserves, raisins and nuts. Flavor with vanilla. Freeze as ice cream, when half frozen add the whites of eggs well beaten, finish freezing. Whip a C of cream until stiff, add 2 T of powdered sugar. Flavor with vanilla and serve on top of pudding.
Mrs. J. H. Black.

FROZEN PUDDING

3 C cream
2½ C milk
1 C sugar

⅛ t salt
½ C macaroons
½ C candied cherries

Scald cream, milk, sugar and salt in double boiler, but do not boil. Let cool, freeze, when almost frozen add powdered macaroons and candied cherries cut in small pieces. Serve 10.
Mrs. C. V. Ferguson.

FRUIT PUDDING

1 can diced pineapple
2½ C water including juice
  Boil this 10 min.

1 C sugar
1 t butter

SAUCE

½ C sugar
1 egg
1 T melted butter

2 t B. P.
½ C flour

Drop in above and bake 25 min. Serve with whipped cream.
Mrs. W. E. Brown.

FRUIT PUDDING

2 T gelatine
1 C sugar
¼ C water
½ C milk

1 C peaches
2 egg-whites
1 C cream

Whip egg-whites and mix with whipped cream Into this fold other mixture. Set on ice.
Mrs. G. M. Dickson.

GRAHAM PUDDING (Steamed)

1½ C Graham flour
½ t salt
½ t each of cloves, cinnamon, and nutmeg
1 C milk
½ C molasses
1 C raisins
1 t soda

Steam 1½ hrs.

Mrs E. R. Spangler.

HARD SAUCE

1 C powdered sugar
½ C butter
1 t nutmeg

Cream butter and sugar, add nutmeg.

Mrs. Finlay Ross.

HARD SAUCE

1 T butter
4 T sugar
1 T cream whipped

Cream butter and sugar, add cream.

Mrs. Geo. Whitney.

HASTY PUDDING

2¼ C water
1 C sugar
1 T butter
3 t orange extract or juice of fresh orange

Boil a few minutes, then mix following and drop in the above boiling syrup. Bake 25 minutes.

HARD SAUCE

1 C flour
1 T butter
½ C milk
1 t B. P.
½ C sugar

Stir all together and drop off spoon into hot syrup Serve 6.

Mrs. J. H. Black.

HINGHAM PUDDING

¾ C New Orleans molasses
¾ C brown sugar
1 C cold water
3 C flour
¼ C butter
1 C raisins
1 t soda
2 t B. P.

Cream butter and sugar, then add molasses with soda in it. Be sure and stir soda in well until it foams before putting it into the sugar and butter. Then add alternately flour and water. Flour raisins out of the flour and put B. P. in the last of the flour added. Put in baking powder cans and steam 3 hrs.

Sauce for this pudding:
2 eggs
¼ C melted butter
1 C powdered sugar
1 t vanilla

Put eggs in bowl, beat with dover beater until very light then add melted butter. Add slowly the powdered sugar beating constantly, add vanilla. This sauce is good with any pudding.

INDIAN PUDDING (Baked)

1 pt. milk	½ t grated nutmeg
½ C corn meal	2 T butter
½ C molasses	1 pt. milk
1 t salt	1 pt apples, if desired
¼ t ginger	

Put milk in a double boiler. When it boils, pour it gradually over cornmeal. Return to boiler and cook half hr. stirring often. Then add molasses, salt, apples cut small Bake in a deep pudding dish, buttered, slowly for 3 hrs. or more. Add 1 pt. cold milk, just as you put it into the oven, without stirring Serve with cream or butter.

Mrs. Howard Norton.

KISS PUDDING

1 pt. milk	⅛ t salt
4 eggs	1 C powdered sugar
1 T cornstarch	½ C cocoanut
4 T sugar	

Dissolve cornstarch in little milk, beat yolks and strain mixture. Place in double boiler, (milk and sugar), beat well, then stir in eggs and cook well done. Put on platter, beat whites with cup of powdered sugar, add cocoanut and pour over pudding and put in oven for a few minutes.

Mrs. C W. Brown.

LEMON SAUCE

2 T butter	4 eggs
1 t flour	3 T sugar

Place in saucepan the butter and stir in flour, then stir in beaten eggs, sugar and juice of lemon strained and ½ rind grated. Do not cook too fast nor too long.

MAPLE PECAN PUDDING

2 C maple syrup
1½ T gelatine soaked in 2 T cold water
1 C heavy whipped cream
1 C pecans broken up

Bring syrup to a boil. Take from fire and add gelatine. When cold add cream and nuts and put into mold and dot the top with whole pecans.

Mrs. Harry Dockum.

MACAROON PUDDING

½ C water	1-3 box gelatine
1 C cream, whipped stiff	1 C macaroons
1 C sugar	½ t vanilla
Cherries	

Dissolve gelatine in cold water, roll enough macaroon to fill 1 cup. Put all together in a mold to cool. Add cherries on top when serving

Mrs. F. G. Smyth

MAPLE PUDDING

1 C maple sugar   4 egg-yolks

Cook 20 min. or until thick   Cool and add 1 pt whipped cream. Add nuts if wanted. Pack in ice 4 hrs.

Mrs Fred Robertson

MAPLE SAUCE

½ C maple syrup   ½ T cornstarch
½ C water   1 T butter

Dissolve corn starch in 2 T of the water. Boil the rest of the water, sugar and the syrup, stir in cornstarch and cook 8 min Serve on pudding or ice cream.

MARCHIONESS PUDDING

1 pt. cream   Flavoring
1 C sugar, pulverized   1 C hot water
1 T gelatine   ½ pt. grated pineapple
2 egg-whites

Dissolve gelatine in hot water. Cool, add to whipped cream, sugar, pineapple and the beaten egg-whites. Flavor to taste. This should be placed on ice to mold, and will serve 6 or 8. It is very nice to add chopped nuts or candied fruits.

Mrs. L. C. Jackson

MARSHMALLOW PUDDING

1 T Knox gelatine in   1 C hot water
4 T cold water   2-3 C sugar
Flavoring   3 egg-whites

Dissolve gelatine in cold water, add sugar and hot water, then pour over the stiffly beaten egg-whites and whip 20 min. Serve with whipped cream or make a custard of yolks and serve with it   This serves 10 persons and will keep for days in a cool place.

Mrs. Murray Myers

MARSHMALLOW CREAM PUDDING

1 T gelatine   2 t vanilla
½ C cold water   1 C chopped nuts
Whites of 4 eggs   Whipped cream
2 C granulated sugar   Brandied cherries

Dissolve gelatine in cold water   Put over fire and bring to boil stirring constantly. Then beat the egg-whites and add to them sugar, and the cooled gelatine. Beat steadily until it begins to thicken. Stir into it the vanilla and nuts. When very thick pour into molds and set upon ice. Serve with whipped cream and brandied cherries.

MILLIONAIRE PLUM PUDDING

1 qt. bread crums	1 nutmeg
1 pt. currants	2 T butter
1 pt. raisins	½ t citron
4 T suet	½ C milk
2 T cinnamon	1 C B. sugar
5 eggs	

Steam 4 hrs , and serve with the following sauce:

½ C butter	1 egg
1½ C pulverized sugar	

NATION PUDDING

½ sponge cake	1 C hot grape juice
2 T gelatine	1 C sugar
½ C cold grape juice	1 T lemon juice
2 egg-whites	1 C double cream
1 T orange juice	

Soak gelatine in cold grape juice and dissolve in hot grape juice, add sugar, lemon, orange. Cool. When cool add stiffly beaten egg-whites and set on ice 4 hrs. Serve on squares of thin sponge cake, topping all with whipped cream and candied grapes, or grape in candy fondant.

NUT PUDDING

1 C molasses	½ t soda
1 C sweet milk	½ t salt
1 C chopped suet	1 pound English Walnuts
2½ C flour	¼ pound chopped figs

Steam 2½ hrs. This to be served with sauce or whipped cream.

Mrs. G. M. Lowry

NUT PUDDING

6 eggs	1 T flour
1 C sugar	1 t B. P.
2 C English Walnuts	

Beat eggs separately. Add sugar to yolks and chopped nuts to whites, combine and add flour and B. P. Bake in individual molds. Serve with whipped cream.

Mrs. Will Dixon

OLD FASHIONED RICE PUDDING
(Sometimes called Poor Man's Pudding)

1 qt. milk	3 T sugar
3 T rice	⅛ t salt

Use new milk. Wash rice thoroughly. Put all in granite baking pan and cook 10 min. on top of stove. Then put into a slow oven and bake about 1 hour. It should be a delicate brown when done. Must not bake dry. Will serve 5 or 6 portions. This is an excellent dessert for the sick.

Mrs. Howard Norton

ORANGE PUDDING

3 eggs	3 t cornstarch
1 C sugar	2 oranges
2 C milk	½ t lemon flavoring

Beat the egg-yolks, add ¾ C sugar, cornstarch and milk. Cook in double boiler until thick. Add ¼ C sugar to the beaten whites, fold in the custard. When cool add flavoring and oranges cut in small pieces.

Mrs. O. D. Barnes

ORANGE SAUCE FOR PUDDINGS

1 C powdered sugar	1 orange
½ C butter	1 pt boiling water
1 T flour	

Cream powdered sugar with butter, add flour and juice and rind of orange, set over fire and pour in pint of boiling water, let cook up well and it is ready to serve.

C. C.

PINEAPPLE MERINGUE

1 qt. milk	½ C flour
4 eggs	1 can sliced pineapple
1 C sugar	1 small stale sponge cake

Have boiling one qt. of milk. Take the beaten yolks of four eggs, add one cup sugar. One half cup flour, add all this to boiling milk. Then cook until quite thick, take off stove, cool a little and add 1 t vanilla. Have ready sponge cake broken into one inch pieces—also pineapple cut into small pieces. Fill dish alternately, with cake, pineapple and custard, until dish is full. Beat whites of four eggs, add a little sugar to whites, spread over top of pudding and brown in oven, serve very cold.

Mrs. Frank Harryman.

PINEAPPLE PUDDING

1 pt. heavy cream	2 egg-whites
¼ box gelatine	1 t vanilla
1-3 C cold water	1 C grated pineapple
1 C sugar	1 doz. lady fingers

Add cold water to gelatine, when partly dissolved add 2 T hot pineapple juice. Beat cream, add sugar and egg-whites beaten stiff, then add vanilla, then pineapple. Let stand ½ hr. in ice box. Serve on lady fnigers

Mrs C. V. Ferguson

PLUM PUDDING SAUCE

¼ C butter	1 t extract lemon
1 C powdered sugar.	2 egg-yolks, well beaten

Cream butter and sugar. Add extract and beaten yolks. Add 1 C rich milk or cream. Cook in double boiler as a custard. Pour over 2 whites of eggs, well beaten. Serve.

Mrs. H. W. Horn

PLUM PUDDING SAUCE

1 egg
1 C sugar
1 t vanilla

¼ C melted butter
½ pt. cream, beaten stiff

Beat egg and sugar until light, then add butter. Beat, add cream and vanila last.

Mrs. Geo Steel

PLUM PUDDING (cold)

1 box gelatine
1 C water
1 pt. milk
1 C sugar
3 T chocolate
1 C raisins

½ C currants
¼ C citron
½ t vanilla
¾ C chopped nuts
⅛ t salt
Whipped cream

Soak gelatine in cold water, heat milk and sugar, grind chocolate and citron and chopped nuts. Dissolve gelatine, adding to milk and sugar, mix all together. Let stand, slice and serve with whipped cream or hard sauce.

Mrs. F. G. Smyth

PLUM PUDDING (Steamed)

½ C suet chopped fine
½ C black molasses
½ t soda

½ C chopped raisins
½ C flour
1 egg-yolk

Steam in individual molds.

Sauce for pudding·
1 C sugar
4 T hot water

Flavoring
½ C butter
1 egg-white

Mrs. Baldwin.

PRUNE PUDDING

5 eggs
½ t cream tartar
½ t salt

1 C pulverized sugar
¼ lb. prunes (cooked)

Beat together egg-whites, cream tartar and salt, add sugar and prunes (seeded and chopped). Mix all well together, pour in mold, set bake-dish in a pan of hot water. Bake 20 min. When cool turn out and serve with whipped cream.

Mrs. J. H. Black.

PRUNE WHIP

3 eggs
½ C sugar

7 prunes
1-16 t salt

Beat the three egg-whites until very stiff, add the seeded and cut prunes, lightly beat in sugar. Bake 20 min. Set bake-dish in pan of water.

Mrs. Rorabaugh.

PRUNE PUDDING

½ lb. prunes   1 C sugar
2 T gelatine   ½ lemon

Let prunes stand in water over night. Cook next morning till tender   Add 1 C sugar. Quarter prunes. It 2 C of liquor are not left add water   Dissolve gelatine in cold water then add juice. Put on stove to heat. Remove, add juice of lemon   Stir in prunes. Mold and serve with whipped cream. Mrs. Lewis.

QUEEN PUDDING

1 pt. milk   Walnut or butter
1 C bread crumbs   1 C sugar
2 eggs   Grated rind of 1 lemon

Mix the above, leaving out whites of eggs, add ½ lemon. Bake until done but not watery. Spread with jelly or jam   Beat whites of eggs, add sugar and juice of half lemon   Spread on top and brown lightly.

Meringue:
2 eggs   3 T sugar
½ lemon   Mrs. G M. Dickson.

SNOW PUDDING

½ box gelatine   1 C sugar
½ C cold water   1 lemon (juice)
1 pt. boiling water   4 egg-whites

Dissolve gelatine in cold water. When dissolved, pour in boiling water. When nearly cool add sugar and juice of lemon strain, add beaten whites of eggs; beat all well and chill

Custard:
4 egg-yolks   1 pt boiling water
½ t corn starch   ¼ t sugar

Beat egg-yolks, sugar, corn starch, add boiling water and cook.   C. C.

SOUFFLE PUDDING

2 T butter   1 C milk
2 T flour   4 eggs
2 T sugar

Let milk come to boil. Beat butter and flour together, then add slowly the boiling milk. Cook 8 min. stirring often. Beat sugar and egg-yolks together. Add to the cooked mixture and set away to cool. When cool, beat egg-whites to a stiff froth, add to the cooked mixture, and pour all into well greased pan, baking 20 or 30 min. Serve immediately

SAUCE

1 pt. milk   2 T sugar
2 eggs   ½ t vanilla

Let milk come to boil, then add eggs and sugar well beaten together. Flavor with vanilla. It should be about as thick as cream.   Mrs W. E. Stanley.

SPONGE PUDDING

1 pt. milk
½ C flour
½ C butter

½ C sugar
5 eggs

Dissolve flour in half pt. of milk, then stir in remainder of milk and cook in double boiler, add butter, let cool, beat yolks of eggs, with sugar and add to mixture; then add beaten whites, bake in pan set in hot water about 30 min. Serve with hard sauce.

Mrs. Geo. Steel.

SWEET POTATO PUDDING

1½ lb. potatoes
1 t nutmeg
½ lb. butter
1 C milk

¾ lb. sugar
4 eggs
1 lemon rind

Boil and mash potatoes with butter, add egg-yolks, sugar, milk, grated lemon rind and nutmeg. Add stiffly beaten whites last. Bake 1 hr.

TAPIOCA PUDDING

2 pt. water
1 C tapioca
3 C B. sugar

⅛ t salt
1 C walnuts
Whipped cream

Soak tapioca over night in 1 pt. of water. In morning add other pt. of water and B. sugar and salt. · Bake 3 hrs., when nearly done add nuts. Serve with whipped cream.

Mrs. C. W. Brown.

TAPIOCA FRUIT PUDDING

1 C pearl tapioca
1 pineapple
6 bananas
½ lb. nuts

1 C water
2 C sugar
3 oranges

Soak tapioca in water over night. Cook with sugar and pineapple until tender. Add oranges, slice the bananas, and nuts, and cover all with whipped cream, garnish with chocolate cream or marshmellows.

Mrs. Spangler.

TIPSY PUDDING

Use Loganberry juice instead of grape juice in Nation Pudding.

WHITE PUDDING SAUCE

½ C butter, creamed
1 C fine sugar
4 T boiling water

1 egg-white, beaten stiff
½ t vanilla

Mrs. L. C. Jackson.

WOODFORD JAM PUDDING

1 C blackberry jam   1 T buttermilk
½ t soda   Egg of butter
3 egg-yolks   Nutmeg
Snappy flavoring

Beat whites and add enough sugar for meringue, spread on top and brown, serve with a good butter sauce, with some snappy flavoring in it.

Meringue: 2 egg-whites, 1 T sugar.

Mrs F. G. Smyth.

DESSERTS

DESSERTS

Almond Cream
Almond Custard
Angel Charlotte Russe   Mrs. Harry Dockum.
Angel Food Loaf
Angel Snowballs
Apple Dumpling   Mrs G. M. Dickson
Apples, Fried   Mrs. Chester Long.
Apple Jinx
Apple Roley Poley
Apples stuffed with nuts   C. C.
Apricot Jelly a la Regiment
Bananas, Baked   Mrs. Chester Long.
Banana Sponge
Banana and Whipped Cream
Boston Cream Puffs   C C.
Blackberry Mush   Mrs. W. B. Buck.
Bridge Coffee
Candied Orange Peel   Mrs. Finlay Ross.
Caramel Tapioca   Mrs. Cohn.
Charlotte Russe   C. C.
Clotted Cream or Devonshire
  Cream
Cherry Pudding   C. C.
Charlotte Russe   Mrs. W. B. Buck.
Coffee Butter
Coffee Italian Cream   Mrs. Chester Long.
Coffee Souffle
Cocoanut Pudding   Agnes Long.
Chocolate Ice Box Desert   Mrs. W. B. Buck.
Chess Tarts   Mrs. Oak Throckmorton.
Chocolate Souffle   Pauline Brown Gillespie.
Chocolate Macaroon Pudding   Madeline Butts Lewis.
Cream Pudding   Mrs. L. C. Jackson.
Delicate Rice Pudding   Mrs. Coler Sim.

CUSTARDS

Custard   Mrs. Weiss
Custard, Baked
Caramel Custard   Mrs. Will Dixon.
Crystal Custard
Maple Syrup Custard   C. C.
Pineapple Custard
Tapioca Custard
Dates Stuffed
Easter Balls
Egg Sauce   Mrs. F. G. Smyth.
Floating Island   Mrs J. H Aley
Figs and Nuts   C. C.
Gelatine Loaf   Katherine Lewis Mechum.
Graham Fruit Mush
Grapes   Mrs. Geo. Whitney.
Grapefruit Frivol

Junket
Kingsleys Bivo   Mrs. Will Dixon.
Kisses
Lemon Filling   ,   Mrs. W. E. Stanley.
English Lemon Honey   Mrs. Chester Long.
Liberty Apples   Mrs. Ralph Millison
Loganberry Macedoine
Macaroon Souffle   Gaby Gouldner Powell.
Maple Sponge   ,   Mrs. F. G. Smyth.
Maple Whip   C. C.
Maraschino Rice Cup
Maraschino Russe
Marshmellows Toasted
Meringues and Whip Cream   Helen Brooks Hall.
Marshmellow Delight   Mrs. Oak Throckmorton.
Moonshine   Mrs. L. C. Jackson.
Mint Dry   Mrs. G. M. Whitney.
Mint Leaves   Mrs. Finlay Ross.
Moonshine   Helen Brooks Hall.
Niagara Foam
Nut Rings
Nut Sticks   Mrs. F. G. Smyth.
Oranges, Baked
Orange Desert   C. C.
Orange Float   Mrs. A. O. Rorabaugh.
Orange Hamburg
Peaches, Baked
Peach Balls   ,
Peach Puffs   Mrs. G. M. Whitney.
Paradise Pudding   Teresa L. Comley
Pineapple Desert   Mrs. Henry Lassen.
Peach Souffle
Pears in Cantaloupe
Peerless Desert   Mrs. C. W. Brown.
Pineapple Meringue   Mrs. J. H. Black.
Potato Crust for Dumplings
   and Sauce
Prunes
Prune Butter
Prunes, Stewed
Prune Whip   Mrs. Ralph Millison.
Raisin Puffs   Mrs. Geo. M. Whitney.
Refrigerator Cake   Mrs. F. G. Smyth.
Rhubarb   Mrs. W. E. Stanley.
Rhubarb Scalloped   Mrs. G. M. Dickson.
Rice and Apricots
Salted Nuts   Mrs. E. R. Spangler.
Short Cake Dough   C. C.
Sauce for Short Cake Dough   Mrs. F. G. Smyth.
Snowballs and Sauce   Mrs. Geo. Steel.
Snow Cream   C. C.
Snow Souffle
Snow Pudding   Mrs. Erwin Taft.
Stale Cake   Mrs. P. C. Lewis.

Strawberries, Escalloped
Strawberry Shortcake
Strawberry Sunshine
Strawberry Whip   Mrs. O. D. Barnes.
Tortion Tart
University Pudding   Mrs. J. H. Aley.
Washington Cream Pie
Wichita Special

ALMONDS AND NUTS BLANCHED

Put the nut meats over the fire in cold water, bring to a boil quickly, drain and rinse in cold water when the skins may be rubbed from the almonds.

ALMOND CREAM

1 pt. double cream	½ t vanilla
2 T powdered sugar	¼ lb. almond paste
6 mashed macaroons	⅛ box gelatine

Whip cream, add sugar and vanilla, mix almond paste and macaroons. Dissolve gelatine in hot water and beat all together. Put in dish and when cold cover with maraschino cherries quartered.

ALMOND CUSTARD

3 C milk	4 eggs
2 bay leaves	4 T sugar
⅛ t cinnamon	1 C cream
¼ lb. almonds	

Put milk, bay leaves and cinnamon in sauce pan, stir over slow fire until boiling, grind or grate almonds, mix egg-yolks. When milk is boiling, remove from fire, add cream and egg-whites, stir Put in double boiler and stir until thickened, then stir until cold

ANGEL CHARLOTTE RUSSE

1 T Knox sparkling gelatine soaked in ¼ C cold water. Dissolve this into ¼ C hot water. Whip 1 pt. cream very stiff. Add 1 C powdered sugar to gelatine. When cool, add whipped cream and half doz. macaroons rolled fine.

2 T candied cherries	1 C finely chopped blanched
½ doz. marshmellows cut very fine	almonds
	1 t vanilla or almond extract

Mrs. Harry Dockum

ANGEL FOOD LOAF

Bake Angel Food in square pan, when cold cut off top 1 in thick, remove center, leaving a square box, which fill with pistachio ice cream solidly, springle pistachio nuts over top, cover with lid which was cut from top of cake, cover all with stiffly whipped cream, flavor with vanilla, slice and serve.

Formula for above:

1 Angel cake square	1 pt. whipped cream
1 qt. ice cream	1 t vanilla
¼ C Pistachio nuts	

ANGEL SNOW BALLS

½ Angel Food cake	1 C grated cocoanut
1 C maple syrup	

Cut Angel Food in small round balls, dip in maple syrup and roll in cocoanut grated.

APPLE DUMPLINGS

Two C apples

Make rich biscuit dough and roll half in. thick. Spread over this tart apples cut fine. Roll together as for jelly roll and cut in pieces 2 in. thick. Drop in boiling syrup made of the following ingredients:

1 C sugar	¼ t nutmeg or
1½ pt. water	½ t cinnamon

Bake 20 or 30 minutes in hot oven. Serve with cream.

Mrs. G. M. Dickson.

APPLES, FRIED

2 C sliced unpeeled apples	¼ C butter
½ C sugar	¼ C water
1 T butter	

Put water in skillet, add apples, sugar and butter on top, cover 5 min. Let water cook out of apples. Stir, cook until brown.

Mrs. Chester Long.

APPLE JINX

8 apples cut in quarters	1 C flour
½ C water	1 C sugar
½ C butter	

Work sugar, butter and flour together until it crumbles and put on top of apples, bake ¾ hr. very slow oven. Grease pan.

APPLE ROLEY POLEY

½ C sugar added to biscuit dough	1 egg for 8 apples

Make a rich biscuit dough, adding sugar and egg. Roll out about one in. thick, have ready your apples pared and slice thin; lay them on top of the dough, then begin at the end and roll up like jelly-roll; put in cooker and steam one hour or more according to the size of the pudding. Serve hot with a suitable sauce.

APPLES STUFFED WITH NUTS

Core apples and fill in space with finely chopped nuts, sugar and cinnamon to taste. Bake and serve with whipped cream.

C. C.

APPRICOT JELLY A LA REGIMENT

2 lb. dried apricots	¾ C sugar
1 pkg. gelatine	1 C boiling water

Wash and soak dried apricots in cold water 2 hrs., simmer in same water to cover until soft. Then strain and mash through a seive. Stir briskly for a few minutes. Dissolve gelatine in boiling water and add the apricots, with sugar. Serve cold with heavy cream or whipped cream. This may be prepared in a chafing dish and set aside to cool.

BAKED BANANAS

½ doz. bananas   ¼ C butter
½ C sugar   ½ lemon

Cut bananas into halves lengthwise and pour over them the melted sugar and butter and lemon juice. Put in uncovered dish earthenware or glass, and bake 20 min. Small minced apples may be added.   Mrs Chester I. Long.

BANANA SPONGE

Make a custard and pour over sliced bananas, dotting over covering all with grated macaroons—any stale cake may be grated and used.

BANANA AND WHIPPED CREAM

Bananas may be mashed and beaten and served with whipped cream, flavored with Rose.

BOSTON CREAM PUFFS

1 pt milk   1½ C flour
2-3 C butter   5 eggs

Scald the milk and butter together, add the flour stirring constantly until mixture leaves the sides of the pan. Remove from the fire and beat well, adding the eggs which have been slightly beaten together. Bake in greased gem pans, 1 T in each, 30 min. in moderate oven. They will be hollow when done. When cold open at side and fill with mixture as follows:

1 pt. milk   1 T flour
2 eggs   2-3 C sugar

Cook together in a double boiler, stirring constantly until smooth and thick. Chocolate pie filling maye be used.

                                   C. C.

BLACKBERRY MUSH

1 qt. blackberries   1 C sugar
1½ C water   4 T flour

Wash and pick over berries, add water and boil until berries are tender. Moisten flour in water and stir until perfectly smooth Add to the cooked fruit and boil ten minutes, stirring all the time. Add sugar while still boiling, then take from fire and put in deep dish to cool. Serve very cold with heavy unwhipped cream.   Mrs. W B. Buck.

BRIDGE COFFEE

2 T gelatine   1 C water, boiling
½ C cold water   2 C black coffee, strong
1 pt double cream   ½ C sugar
3 drops vanilla

Soak gelatine in water half hr. Dissolve in boiling water, strain, add coffee and sugar, stirring well. Turn into mold when set, cover with sweetened whipped cream to which has been added 3 drops vanilla.

CANDIED ORANGE PEEL

2 C water   2 C gr. sugar
3 oranges

Boil sugar and water until blended. Cut orange peel on the round with scissors, cook in 3 changes of water, 15 min. each. Then put in syrup and cook until syrup boils down. While hot roll in granulated sugar. Two small C sugar, the same of water, is enough to cover the rind from three oranges.

Mrs. Finlay Ross.

CARAMEL TAPIOCA

1 C tapioca   1 C pecans
4 C water   Whipped cream
3 C B. sugar

Soak tapioca over night in the 4 C of water. Do not pour off water, but mix with other ingredients. Bake 1½ hrs., stirring occasionally when first put in oven. Serve cold with whipped cream.

Mrs. Cohn.

CHARLOTTE RUSSE

1 qt. cream, whipped   ½ box gelatine
1½ C powdered sugar   1½ t vanilla
3 egg-whites

Soak gelatine until dissolved, strain. Beat all together and serve. Either line a dish with lady-fingers or stale cake; or, serve in cups, without cake, with whipped cream.   C. C.

CLOTTED CREAM, OR DEVONSHIRE CREAM

Let milk stand 24 hrs. in cold weather, 12 in summer. Set on stove until nearly boiling, must come to the nearly boiling point, very slowly in order to be firm and must look thick when done. Set aside overnight in cool place and skim by rolling or folding over and over in rolls. Set on ice until used. Travelers in England know the Clotted Cream of Devon & Cheddar.

CHERRY PUDDING

1 C milk   ⅛ t salt
2 t B. P.   1 C cherries
2 eggs

Beaten eggs add milk, sifted flour enough to make a stiff batter, salt and cherries stirred in. Steam one hour. Serve with liquid sauce. Cranberries, peaches, currants, or any kind of tart fruit is nice used with this recipe. Serve with sweet sauce.

C. C.

CHARLOTTE RUSSE

1 qt. heavy cream   1 C sugar
2 egg-whites   1 C chopped almonds blanched
½ pkg. Knox gelatine   1 C candied cherries chopped
1 t almond extract   ½ doz. lady-fingers

Soak gelatine in one-half cup cold milk for 15 min. Beat cream stiff. Add stiffly beaten egg-whites. Fold in sugar, then the dissolved gelatine added carefully and extract. Line large mold with lady-fingers cut lengthwise. Add one-half of your mixture. Over this sprinkle the chopped fruit and nuts and last the remainder of the Russe. Now take a spatula and run it up and down through the Russe until well mixed. Set near ice, and turn on your dish from which it is to be served. Serve with whipped cream sweetened and flavored with a few drops of almond extract.

Mrs. W. B. Buck.

COFFEE BUTTER

½ C butter	1 egg-yolk
¼ C sugar	3 T coffee extract

Cream unsalted butter, sugar and add egg-yolk, well beaten, and coffee very strong may be used instead of extract.

COFFEE ITALIAN CREAM

1 C coffee	1 T gelatine
½ C milk	2 T water
½ C sugar	½ t vanilla
3 eggs	

Soak gelatine in 2 T cold water 5 min. Heat coffee until hot add milk and sugar and cook in double boiler. Add beaten egg-yolks and cook until thick, add gelatine and pour custard over them. Beat, add vanilla, mold and serve with whipped cream.

Mrs Chester I Long.

COFFEE SOUFFLE

2 T butter	1 C strong coffee
3 T flour	½ C cream
½ C sugar	3 egg-yolks

Melt butter, rub in flour, add coffee, remove from fire, add egg-yolks, sugar and cream. Add beaten egg-whites, last turn into bake dish and bake 30 min in slow oven. Serve with whipped cream or ice cream

Mrs L C. Jackson

COCOANUT PUDDING

½ C butter	1 t vanilla
1 C sugar	4 eggs
1 pkg. cocoanut	

Cream butter and sugar and then cream; into this the cocoanut. Add whites of eggs beaten very stiff. Flavor. Bake slowly until brown. Serve with following sauce.

Yolks of eggs	1 T butter
1 C sugar	½ t vanilla

Steam in double boiler until very thick syrup.

Agnes Long.

CHOCOLATE ICE BOX DESSERT

2 T boiling water
2½ T sugar
2 cakes sweet chocolate

4 egg-yolks and whites
1½ doz. lady-fingers

Melt chocolate in double boiler and add hot water, then egg-yolks one at a time, beat, let cool and add whites beaten dry. Line mold with lady-fingers cut in two lengthways. Pour over the mixture and let stand on ice 24 hrs. before using. Line mold with waxed paper before putting in pudding.

Mrs. W. B. Buck.

CHEESE TARTS

1 C brown sugar
1 egg
½ C raisins

1 T cream
1 t vanilla

Beat well and let stand for 30 min. Then bake in gem pans lined with rich pastry.

Mrs. Oak Throckmorton.

HOT CHOCOLATE SOUFFLE

2 T butter
2 T flour
⅞ C milk
½ C sugar

3 eggs
2 T hot water
2 squares chocolate

Melt butter in double boiler, add flour. Pour in milk gradually. Melt chocolate, add sugar and hot water, stir until smooth. Combine mixtures. Add egg-yolks well beaten, cool, fold in whites stiffly beaten, add ½ t vanilla. Bake in buttered pan. Set in pan of water, in moderate oven for 45 min. Serve with whipped cream.

Pauline Brown Gillespie.

CHOCOLATE MACAROON PUDDING

¼ lb. sweet chocolate
3 T hot water
3 T powdered sugar

2 eggs
1½ doz. macaroons

Melt chocolate in a double boiler. Add water and sugar and beat until smooth. Take off fire and add beaten yolks and let cool, add the stiffly beaten whites. Grind macaroons. Butter a shallow pan and line with alternate layers of macaroons and chocolate until you have 3 layers of macaroons and 2 layers of chocolate. Put in ice box for 24 hrs. Cut in squares and serve with whipped cream or ice cream.

Madeline Lewis.

CREAM PUDDING

1 qt. double cream, whipped
1 C sugar
1 C cherries
1 C nuts of any kind

1 small can grated pineapple
2 T heaping gelatine
½ C water

Cut the cherries and nuts in small pieces and dissolve gelatine in the water and add to the cream. Add sugar slowly, whipping all the time. Add pineapple last.

Mrs. L. C. Jackson.

DELICATE RICE PUDDING

3 C milk
½ t salt
1-3 box gelatine

½ C powdered sugar
1½ t vanilla
½ pt. cream, whipped

Cook rice, milk and salt in double boiler until milk is all absorbed. Then add dissolved gelatine. When cold and begins to thicken add powdered sugar, vanilla and whipped cream. Turn into wet molds.

Mrs. Coler Sims.

CUSTARDS

Custard are of two kinds, *Boiled Custards* and *Set Custards.* Boiled custards always cook in a double boiler and stir constantly while cooking and also until cold. Set custards are baked in oven and never stirred while cooking. Must be baked in a slow oven. When custard is watery the oven is too hot.

When boiled custard lumps it has been cooked too fast and too long *Tests for custards cooking:*

Soft custard is done when the froth disappears. Another test—when it covers the back of silver spoon.

Set custard is done when a silver knife can be run through the center and comes out clear.

Maple-Mousse unfrozen makes a fine custard.

Try Grape nuts instead of bread crumbs on top of custard.

Custards bake better in a shallow dish than a deep one. It must not stay in the oven too long or it becomes watery. Boiled custards are smoother if you use only the egg-yolks. Overbeating of eggs makes custards curdle. Beat just enough to have egg smooth and not stringy.

CUSTARD

1 egg
3 T flour

½ C sugar
1 C milk

Mix egg, flour and sugar, boil milk and pour over the sauce, put back on stove until thick, flavor and use.

Mrs. Weiss.

BAKED CUSTARD *

5 eggs
5 T sugar
1 t vanilla

1 qt. rich milk
¼ t salt

Beat yolks and whites separately; beat into the yolks the sugar, add whites beaten very stiffly, stir all together with the milk—previously boiled and cooled; flavor with vanilla, add salt, pour into a buttered pudding dish, set in a pan of hot water and bake in a moderate oven until a silver knife inserted will come out clean.

CARAMEL CUSTARD

4 T sugar
3 eggs
3 T sugar

1½ C cream
1 t vanilla

Melt sugar until a light brown, pour it into 6 custard cups, shake them quickly, so the caramel will line them, beat the eggs. Add sugar and cream. Mix thoroughly, add vanilla and pour mixture in cups, and stand them in a baking pan of hot water. Bake until set. Turn out while hot in individual dishes. Serve very hot.

Mrs. Will Dixon.

CRYSTAL CUSTARD

1 pt. cream
1½ C sugar, gr.

3 egg-whites
¼ t nutmeg

Pour cream on sugar and let stand until egg-whites are well beaten, add this to cream, beat lightly, grate in nutmeg, bake in cups in hot water closely covered. Can be tested with silver knife, if it comes out clean, custard is done.

MAPLE SYRUP CUSTARD

3 C milk
¼ C maple syrup

5 eggs

Beat yolks, add syrup and milk, add stiff whites the last thing. Bake in a pan of water in moderate oven or steam.

C. C.

PINEAPPLE CUSTARD

4 T sugar
2 T butter
2 T bread crumbs
2 T water

3 egg-yolks
1 egg-white
½ can grated pineapple

Cream sugar and butter. Add water to pineapple. Mix and place in a pan of water and bake 20 or 25 min., brown in oven. Serve with whipped cream if desired

TAPIOCA CUSTARD

4 T tapioca	⅛ t salt
4 eggs	½ t vanilla
1 qt. milk	½ C sugar

Soak tapioca over night in milk In the morning add salt, vanilla, sugar, beaten eggs and steam 30 min.

DATES—STUFFED

Stuffed dates or prunes. Dates or prunes may be stuffed by removing the seeds and filling with pecans and rolling in powdered sugar.

EASTER BALLS

Bake sunshine cake in deep iron round gem pans, dip in icing and roll in chopped pecans or macaroon crumbs toasted.

EGG SAUCE

2 eggs	1 t vanilla
1 C sugar	⅛ t salt

Beat the whites and yolks of two eggs separately, thoroughly to the yolks add sugar, flavoring, salt, beat and beat, then beat in your whipped whites and set in the ice box to get cold.

Mrs. F. G. Smyth.

FLOATING ISLAND

1 qt. milk	2 t flour
3 eggs	Vanilla
1 C sugar	

Beat the eggs separately. Scald milk and drop whites on the milk, dipping milk over the whites. Remove whites and mix the yolks, sugar and flour and add to milk. Cook until thick. Add a few drops of vanilla. Put into a dish to cool. Put whipped whites on top.

Mrs. J. H. Aley. ·

FIGS AND NUTS

1 C figs	1 C nuts
1 C cream, whipped	

Cut figs into bits, chop nuts, warm both in oven and pour whipped cream over all.   C. C.

GELATINE LOAF

½ C nut meats	1 C sugar
4 egg-whites	1 t vanilla
1 T Knox gelatine	1 t cocoa
2 T cold water	Fruit coloring
1 C boiling water	

Soak gelatine in cold water 15 min then dissolve in 1 C boiling water. Add 1 C sugar. Beat egg-whites stiff. Into them stir gelatine. Add vanilla. Beat well, divide in 3 parts. Use pink fruit coloring for one part. For another part use cocoa dissolved in 2 t warm water. When these 3 parts begin to thicken put them in a loaf pan in following order: white, brown, pink with nuts sprinkled between each layer. Let stand in cold place till firm. Serve in slices with whipped cream.

(Mrs. Kirk Mechem) Katherine Lewis Mechem.

GRAHAM FRUIT MUSH

1 pt. graham mush   1 C dates, figs or raisins
3 T cream

Make Graham mush. It must not be too thick. Steam 25 min. then stir in cream and dates, chopped. Cook 5 min. longer. Serve with hard sauce.

GRAPES

Add 1 T of water to 1 (not beaten) egg-white. Into this dip the grapes and then roll in granulated sugar, lay on oil paper, set aside in cool place to dry.

Mrs. Geo. Whitney.

GRAPEFRUIT FRIVOL

1 pkg. gelatine   1 T sugar
1 C warm water   3 C grape juice

Dissolve gelatine in water, add juice and sugar, let come to boiling point but do not boil, remove from fire, mold and serve with nut dressing.

JUNKET

1 pt. milk   ½ Junket tablet
2 T sugar   1 T water
½ t vanilla

Dissolve tablet in water, put milk in double boiler, when milk warm, remove from stove and pour over sugar. Add vanilla and dissolved tablet, stir until sugar dissolves. Put all in double boiler in boiling water, cover and remove from stove, let stand 15 min. and serve cold.

KINGSLEY'S BIVO

6 egg-whites   1 C hickory nuts
6 T sugar   ½ C shredded candied cher-
½ box geletine   ries

Beat stiff egg-whites, add sugar. Scatter nuts and cherries over the beaten eggs. Dissolve gelatine and pour it into the eggs, beat until it stiffins, put in paper lined mold by spoonfuls, let harden. Slice and serve with whipped cream.

Mrs. Will Dixon

KISSES

4 egg-whites   ¼ t vanilla
1 C sugar

- Beat eggs stiff, add sugar and vanilla, cook on oiled paper in pan in slow oven. Same recipe for meringue.

LEMON FILLING

1 C sugar   1 lemon-grated rind and juice
¾ C water   2 T cornstarch

Dissolve sugar in water then put in grated rind and juice of lemon and let come to a boil. Add to this the cornstarch which has been dissolved in a little cold water. Let boil until consistency of jelly. Remove from the fire and immediately spread between the layers and on top of the cake.

Mrs. W. E Stanley

ENGLISH LEMON HONEY

6 lemons   1 lb. strained honey
6 eggs   ½ lb. sugar

Put in double boiler, mix thoroughly, stir one way until boiling, add beaten eggs, stir and let simmer 5 min. Put in glass jar and seal when cool.

Mrs. Chester I. Long.

LIBERTY APPLES

6 apples   1 T butter
1 chopped lemon   ¾ C water
1 C sugar

Pare and quarter apples, place water in bake pan with apples, cover with lemon, sugar and butter. When half cooked, roll rich biscuit dough cut the size of a fifty-cent piece and lay these little biscuits over the apples. Cover and bake. When nearly done, remove cover and brown the biscuit. Serve with sauce or whipped cream.

Mrs. R Millison

LOGANBERRY MACEDOINE

6 peaches   ½ C sugar
1 C nuts   1 pt Loganberry juice
5 oranges

Slice peaches and oranges, add nuts, sweeten and chill. Pour over all 1 pt. ice cold Loganberry juice, chill.

MACAROON SOUFFLE

6 macaroons   2 T melted sugar or carmetez-
6 egg-whites   ed
·1 T sugar

To the stiffly beaten egg-whites add crumbled macaroons and 1 T sugar. Line a double boiler with the melted sugar, put in mixture and let it boil 20 to 30 min. Do not uncover any more than absolutely necessary.

CARAMEL SAUCE FOR SOUFFLE

3 egg-yolks   6 T sugar
1 C hot milk

    Caramelize sugar and add other ingredients.

                                  Gaby Gouldner Powell

MAPLE SPONGE

2 C cream   ¼ C water
1 t gelatine   1 C maple syrup
1 t vanilla ·   Oiled paper

    Whip cream very stiff, dissolve geletine in cold water, adding to this maple syrup and vanilla. Mix all together and pack in baking powder cans. Cover top with oiled paper before you add cover. Freeze 5 hrs. Serve 8 persons.

                                  Mrs. F. G. Smyth

MAPLE WHIP

½ C sugar   4 T cornstarch
1 C maple sugar   2 eggs
2 C water

    Beat yolks, add to water, sugar and cornstarch. Add whites when almost cool.

                                  C. C.

MARASCHINO RICE CUPS

½ lb. rice   ½ t salt
1 qt. milk   ⅛ C hot water
½ t vanilla   2 T gelatine
¼ C sugar   ½ pt. whipped cream
¼ C Maraschino cherries   1 T almonds ﹨

    Cook rice in milk, dissolve gelatine in hot water, add vanilla, sugar, salt and gelatine to rice, when cool fold in the cream, cherries cut in two and cut blanched almonds, press into ramekins and pour maraschino over each, serve with whipped cream.

MARASCHINO RUSSE

1 C Maraschino cherries   ½ C nuts

    Flavor Charlotte Russe with Maraschino and fill with Maraschino cherries, sprinkle nuts on top.

MARSHMALLOWS TOASTED

    Have long sharp pointed stick and run through marshmallows. Holding over coals or fire and turning stick continually. Do not burn and marshmallows will be brown and soft. Eat at once.

MERINGUES AND WHIPPED CREAM

3 egg-whites   1 t vanilla
1 C powdered sugar

Beat egg-whites, add sugar, gradually, then vanilla. Put oil-ed paper in a pan, drop meringue on paper, bake in a moderate oven one hour and a half Lift with cake turner, being very care-ful not to break. Put two together, whipped cream between and on top. You can serve just one person with whipped cream on top. This will serve four.

Helen Brooks Hall

MARSHMALLOW DELIGHT

Soak 1 pound of marshmallows in 1 pint of heavy cream over night. In morning whip until thick, then add ½ pound chopped almonds and 5 slices of Hawaiian pineapple cut fine. Serve in parfait glasses with whipped cream. Decorate each glass with bits of marshmellows, maraschino cherries and angel-ica.

Mrs. Oak Throckmorton

MOONSHINE

6 egg-whites   3 large peaches
12 T powdered sugar

Beat the egg-whites to a stiff froth and gradually add the sugar, beating not less than 20 min Then beat in the peaches, which have been cut in tiny pieces. Set on the ice till thorough-ly chilled and serve with whipped cream which has been sweet-ened and flavored with vanilla.

Mrs. L C. Jackson

MINT DRY

Pick before it blossoms and wash and lay out on paper and put in attic when dry, put in glass jar.

Mrs. J. M Whitney

MINT LEAVES

1 C leaves   1 C water
1 C sugar

Boil to a soft ball Add leaves, do not stir until thick. Then stir with fork carefully.

Mrs. Finley Ross

MOONSHINE

6 egg-whites   1 t vinegar
1 C sugar   1 t vanilla

Beat whites very stiff, add sugar, gradually then the vinegar and vanilla. After all the ingredients are in, stir as little as pos-sible. Paper the can, do not grease Have the oven hot when you put it in but bake slowly about 20 min. Serve with whipped cream. Put grated maple sugar on top of the whipped cream. Moonshine is hard to make and also expensive, but when made right it is delicious. Everything is in the baking.

Helen Brooks Hall

NIAGARA FOAM

6 egg-whites   15 T fine sugar
3 C apple pulp

Press cooked apples through sieve and chill. Beat eggs stiff, mix all together and chill, serve in sherbet glasses with whipped cream on top and green candied fruit.

NUT RINGS

1 C sugar   ½ t rose extract or lemon
2 T water   2 C pecans

Boil sugar and water 5 min   Stir into this pecans cut in half, remove and stir constantly until each nut is covered. Remove to buttered pans and cool. Do not stir until nuts are added.

NUT STICKS

1 C brown sugar   ¼ t B. P.
2 eggs well beaten   1 C nut meats cut small
⅛ t salt

Bake in a slow oven 20 min. Cut in sticks. Serves 8.

Mrs. F. G. Smyth

ORANGES BAKED

Use thin skinned oranges. Cut the tops off ¼ down, pull out the pith and fill the cavities with four T of sugar to each orange. Put the fruit in a casserole, fill a fourth full of water, cover and bake till they are tender. Remove from oven and make a sauce of the juices in the pan by stirring in 2 T of cornstarch, moistened with cold water. Put a half t of butter on the top of each orange. Pour the sauce over them and return to the oven uncovered to brown. Serve hot.

ORANGE DESSERT

1-3 box gelatine   1 lemon, juice
1-3 C cold water   1 C orange juice and pulp
1-3 C boiling water   3 egg-whites
1 C sugar

Soak gelatine in cold water until soft, then pour over it the boiling water. Add sugar, juice of lemon and juice and pulp of orange. Set on ice until it begins to harden, then add the egg-whites beaten. Beat all together until light and stiff. Put in cups to mold.

C. C.

ORANGE FLOAT

1 pt. milk	1½ T cornstarch
¾ C sugar	1-10 t salt
2 eggs	2 oranges

Place nearly the pint of milk on stove, when it reaches boiling point, stir in the two egg-yolks, cornstarch, sugar and salt, which have been well mixed with several T milk. Let this boil good stirring it   Remove from fire and while this cools a minute or two, grate just a little rind in dish then add the diced oranges. Now pour the custard over the oranges and place on top the nicely beaten whites, which have been sweetened with four T sugar and flavored with the grated rind or any extract.   Serve cold.

Mrs. Rorabaugh

ORANGE HAMBURG

1 large orange	3 eggs
1 C sugar	

Cook in double boiler, serve with cream.

. PEACHES BAKED

8 peaches	8 T sugar
32 cloves	2 t butter

Select fine peaches. Place in boiling water 3 min., then plunge into cold Remove skin. Leave whole and stick cloves into peaches. Place in deep bake dish, sprinkle with sugar and dots of butter Add boiling water and bake in moderate oven. Nuts may be added if desired. Apples and pears are good baked this way.

PEACH BALLS

6 peaches	½ C pecans
½ C Maraschino cherries	

Pear and roll in sugar, then in chopped nuts and chopped cherries. Set on ice when cold serve in a scooped out dish of almond ice cream or whipped cream.

PEACH PUFFS

Pare and halve fresh ripe peaches. Beat two egg-whites to a stiff froth, add 2 T powdered sugar, ⅛ t salt, 1 t vanilla. Heap the meringue in the peach cases, brown in a quick oven and serve cold with cream.

Mrs. G. M. Whitney

PARADISE PUDDING

¼ lb. blanched almonds chopped	1 doz. marshmallows cut fine
2 doz. candied cherries cut fine	½ doz. macaroons cut fine
	1 pkg. lemon jello
	1 pt. boiling water

When cold whip and add 1 C whipped cream, ¾ C sugar in cream. Pour over the above mixture, stir until firm

Teresa L. Comley.

PINEAPPLE DESSERT

1 can pineapple, diced   1 C juice and water
1 C sugar   1 T butter
      Boil 10 min.

FILLING

2-3 C sugar   2 t B. P.
½ C milk

     Flour to make a stiff batter, drop a spoonful at a time over top. Bake 20 min. Serve with whipped cream.

Mrs. Henry Lassen

PEACH SOUFFLE

6 peaches uncooked   6 egg-whites
1 C powdered sugar

     Peel and run peaches through ricer, stir in sugar, and whip eggs very light. Mix together and turn into dish. Bake 10 or 15 min.

PEARS IN CANTALOUPE

3 cantaloupe   12 pears
Juice 1 lemon   ½ C sugar

     Cut cantaloupe in halves, fill each case with sliced pears, and sprinkle with lemon juice and sugar.

PEERLESS DESSERT

1 box gelatine   1 lb. marshmallows
1 can sliced pineapple   1 lb. white grapes
½ lb. blanched almonds   ½ C Maraschino cherries

     Slice marshmallow, slice grapes, chop cherries, cut almonds. Put together with ½ pt. whipped cream and serve with whipped cream.

Mrs. C. W. Brown.

PINEAPPLE MERINGUE

1 doz. Lady Fingers or slices of   2 T flour
    sponge cake   1 C sugar
1 can grated pineapple   3 eggs
2½ C milk

     Line a baking dish with the cake, cover this with the pineapple. Make a cream as follows· milk, flour, sugar, egg-yolks, cook in a double boiler, stirring all the time to prevent lumps. Flavor if desired, pour over cake and pineapple. Beat whites into stiff meringue, put over top. Place in oven and brown.

Mrs J H. Black

POTATO CRUST FOR DUMPLINGS

1 C mashed potato
1 C milk
1 egg
½ t B. P.

2 T butter
¼ t salt
½ C flour

Mix well, roll, cut and drop around apple, peach or any kind of fruit. Steam or bake, use more flour if necessary to roll well

SAUCE FOR ABOVE

¼ C butter
½ C sugar

½ t vanilla
½ t cinnamon

Cream butter and sugar, add flavor and chill in ice box.

PRUNES

Prunes cooked and seeds removed and stuffed with pecans, served with whipped cream or ice cream.

PRUNE BUTTER

1 qt. prunes
1 t cinnamon
1 C sugar

1 t allspice
1 t cloves

Soak overnight, stew until tender, let cool, run through colander, add sugar and spices, boil all together ½ hr.

STEWED PRUNES

½ lb. prunes
1 qt water
½ C sugar

4 blades of mace
1 t lemon juice

Wash prunes, soak overnight in cold water and sugar, boil in same water with Mace and lemon juice until tender.

PRUNE WHIP

1 lb. prunes
1 C sugar

½ box gelatine
½ t vanilla

Wash the prunes thoroughly and soak over night. In the morning cook until tender; remove the stones; cut into small pieces. Add sugar, gelatine after it has been soaked in a ½ C water to the juice in which the prunes have been cooked, put on stove and let come to a boil, pour over prunes and mold, serve with whipped cream.   Mrs. Ralph Millison.

RAISIN PUFFS

1 C flour
2 t B. P.
¼ C sugar
4 T butter

1 C raisins
⅛ t salt
1 egg
½ C milk

Beat egg thoroughly. Divide into 6 jelly glasses. Place in steamer. Tie cloth over steamer, cover so water will not drip into puffs. Water under steamer must boil before placing glasses in and enough water so as to not add water, steam 1 hr. Serve with hard sauce   Mrs Geo Whitney.

REFRIGERATOR CAKE

1 lb. macaroons
½ lb. almonds blanched and
  broken not too fine
½ lb. butter

½ doz eggs
1 lb. powdered sugar
1 t vanilla

Cream butter and sugar thoroughly, add beaten yolks, then broken nuts, lastly beaten whites—very stiff—then vanilla—beat mixture well. Crumble macaroons and cover the bottom of square cake pan—line first with oiled paper—then a layer of the above mixture and repeat until ingredients are used. Put in the refrigerator and let stand 30 hrs. Then melt a couple of squares of Bakers unsweetened chocolate and pour over top—serve in squares with whip cream—this serves 16 good portions.

Mrs F. G. Smyth.

RHUBARB

2 lbs rhubarb   2 C sugar

Rhubarb and cut into small pieces—put into double boiler with 2 C of sugar and let boil until tender.

Mrs. W. E. Stanley.

RHUBARB—ESCALLOPED

2 C rhubarb   1 C sugar
3 C bread crumbs

Escallop with buttered bread crumbs, putting a layer of each. Last layer bread crumbs. Bake in slow oven 30 min. Serve with meats.   Mrs. G. M. Dickson.

RICE AND APRICOTS

3 C cooked rice
½ C sugar
1 C double cream

1 can apricots
½ pecans or any nuts pistachio

Cook rice until dry—pour in large dish and cover with apricots not using the juice. Then on top of this, pour stiff whipped cream, sugared, covering all with chopped nuts. Serve cold.

SALTED NUTS

1 lb. nuts
½ C salt

1 pt. water

Boil nuts and salt in water 8 min. drain, grease pan with either butter or olive oil and brown in slow oven.

Mrs. R. E. Spanger.

SHORT CAKE DOUGH

1½ C flour
1 T sugar
1 T butter
Berries

1 t B. P.
Milk
1 egg

Mix ingredients, add milk enough to make a drop batter, last add beaten egg. If your wish to serve individual cakes, bake in gem pans, cut in two, butter. Pour crushed berries over and sauce.   C. C.

SAUCE FOR SHORT CAKE

2 C sugar   ½ C water
Whipped cream   1 T whipped cream

Boil to a syrup, add cream—add this when serving the short cake.

Mrs. Smyth.

SNOW BALLS

½ C butter   2 t B. P.
½ C sugar   ½ C milk
2 C flour   2 egg-whites
⅛ t salt

Cream sugar and butter together. Add milk and flour and B. P. and salt. Lastly, the beaten egg-whites. Steam 25 min. in individual cups.

THE SAUCE

Make a hard sauce. Crush strawberries or red raspberries, mix with hard sauce or jam can be used.

Mrs. Geo. Steel.

SNOW CREAM

4 egg-whites   1 t vanilla
4 T powdered sugar   1 pt. whipped cream

Beat the whites of eggs until foamy, then add gradually powdered sugar, beating all the while, then beat until stiff enough to stand alone. Add vanilla and stir in carefully whipped cream. Serve in small glasses. Enough for 8 persons.

C. C.

SNOW SOUFFLE

4 eggs   ½ t vanilla
2 T sugar   1 C whipped cream

Beat the whites of eggs to a stiff dry froth and beat in gradually the sugar, add vanilla, add well beaten yolks then fold in carefully the cream. Turn into quart pudding dish lightly buttered and bake in hot oven 12 min. Serve at once—it will fall.

SNOW PUDDING

1 pt. boiling water   ½ C sugar

Three T corn starch wet in a little cold water, let cook a few min. until perfectly clear, stirring constantly. Take from stove, add juice of half lemon, then beat slowly into stiffly beaten whites of 3 eggs. Pour into individual molds.

SAUCE

3 egg-yolks   1 C milk
1 C sugar   1 t vanilla

Cook milk to boiling point in double boiler, add beaten eggs and sugar. Cook until a smooth custard. This will serve 8 people.

Mrs. Erwin Taft.

STALE CAKE

Cover stale cake with enough milk to moisten and bake. Make sauce of eggs beaten separately and sugar.

FORMULA FOR SAUCE

3 eggs   1 C sugar

Mrs. P. C. Lewis.

STRAWBERRIES—ESCALLOPED

1 pt. cream   1 pt. pineapple
1 pt strawberries   ½ C powdered sugar

Escallop Strawberries—whip the cream to a stiff froth. Arrange on the bottom of a glass dish a layer of pineapple, add a sprinkling of powdered sugar and cover with the whipped cream, make another layer with the strawberries, sugar and cream So continue the alternate layers until all are used and there is a pyramid of fruit with strawberries last. Heap the cream on top and keep on ice until ready to serve.

· STRAWBERRY SHORT CAKE

2 qts. berries to 1 C sugar

Wash and pick off stems—cut each berry in two, add ½ C of sugar and let stand on ice 2 hrs.

STRAWBERRY SUNSHINE

Prepare as for short cake and place between layers of sunshine cake. A bountiful supply of stiff whipped cream served on top and between each layer.

CRUST

1 C milk   ½ C lard and butter
2 T flour   1 T B. P.
¼ C flour   ⅛ t salt

Mix flour, salt and B. P. and shortening. Add sugar and milk. Stir, turn on floured board, bake in large biscuit pan, butter—cut in 4 parts and place berries between each layer.

STRAWBERRY WHIP

1 qt. strawberries   1 qt. cream
2 C sugar   1 C water
1 box gelatine

Dissolve gelatine in water and heat; when cool add whipped cream. When it begins to harden, add sugar and crushed berries. Fill individual glasses, cover with whipped cream and whole berries.

Mrs. O. D. Barnes.

TORTION TART

6 egg-whites	1 T vinegar
1 C sugar	1 t vanilla

Beat eggs stiff and add sugar and vanilla Have 2 pans greased with butter, very slow oven.

FILLING

1 pt. whipped cream	1 C maraschino cherries
1 C nuts	¼ C sugar

Cut nuts and cherries, mix with cream and sugar. Put between layers of tart.

UNIVERSITY PUDDING

Dissolve gelatin in cold water, beat egg-yolk and 3 T of sugar together, add 2 C of milk. Beat and cook till begins to thicken. Add gelatine, let cool—add the beaten egg-whites. When about to congeal, add the fruit and turn into molds.

FORMULA

1 T gelatine	3 T sugar
½ C water	2 C milk
3 eggs	1 C any kind of fruit

Mrs. J. H. Aley.

WASHINGTON CREAM PIE

Crust	1 C flour
6 eggs	1 C sugar
1 t vanilla	2 t lemon juice

Beat egg-yolks very stiff, add sugar, vanilla and lemon juice. Beat whites very stiff, fold half the whites into yolk mixture then half the flour, then remainder of whites and rest of flour Bake into 4 pie crusts

FILLING

1 T lemon juice	½ C flour
2 C milk	1 C butter
2 eggs	1½ t vanilla

Beat eggs very light, add sugar, flour and ½ C milk and beat until perfectly smooth. Put 1½ C milk in double boiler when scalding hot add above mixture. Beat till smooth. When cool add vanilla and lemon juice. Chopped nuts may be added

WICHITA SPECIAL

1½ pt. cream
6 eggs
2 T corn starch
1 t rose water
1 oz. citron

1 C powdered sugar
10 T grated chocolate
12 bitter almonds
¼ t vanilla
4 oz. sweet almonds

Fruit Charlotte over in double boiler, boil cream over slow fire stir in slowly the well beaten egg-yolks with corn starch, cook 10 min., stirring constantly, then divide mixture. To one-half add melted chocolate, simmer 3 min , take off fire and cool, then blanch bitter almonds and sweet almonds and pound in mortar with enough rose water to make a smooth paste. Add finely chopped citron and powdered sugar and stir these into the other one-half of cream mixture, simmer 3 min., set aside to cool and add ¼ T. vanilla. Cut a large Angel Food cake in slices crosswise half in. thick, spread 1 slice thickly with the chocolate cream. Put another slice on top of this and cover with the almond cream; dot this alternately, piling them evenly on a china dish until all ingredients are used, arrange in form of Angel cake before it was cut. Have ready 6 egg-whites stiffly whipped, add 6 T powdered sugar and with a spoon heap this all over top and sides of cake, then sift powdered sugar over and brown in oven, and use any preferred cake icing on top.

FROZEN
DESSERTS

FROZEN DESSERTS

Almond Ice
Angel Parfait
Apple Whip
Apricot Ice Cream   Mrs. G. M. Dickson.
Apricot Mousse
Baked Alaska
Baked Apple Ice Cream
Banana Sherbet   Mrs. Spangler.
Biscuit Glace   Mrs. Robert Campbell
Bisque Ice Cream
Blackberry Mold
Cafe Parfait   Mrs. Robert B. Campbell.
Cannon Balls
Cantelope Ice Cream
Cantelope Ice Cream
Caramel Ice Cream   Mrs. Gilbert Tucker.
Caramel Ice Cream   C. C.
Caramel Sauce, Plain
Caramel Syrup
Caramel Nut Sauce
Cherry Ice
Cherry Mousse
Cherry Parfait
Chilled Fruit   Mrs. J. H. Black.
Cranberry Sherbet   Mrs. Henry Lassen
Chocolate Sauce for Ice Cream
Chocolate Sauce Smooth
Custard Soft Boiled for Ice
  Cream   Mrs. Ralph Millison.
Chocolate Mousse
Coffee Mousse   C. C.
Cranberry Ice to serve with
  dinner course
Date Ice Cream
Delmonico Ice Cream
French Ice Cream
Frozen Roll
Fruit Milk Sherbet   Mrs. A. C. Jobes.
Ginger Ice Cream
Golden Rod Parfait
Lemon Ice   Mrs. Charles Smyth.
Lemon Ice   Mrs. W. E. Stanley.
Lemon Punch   Mrs. A. O. Rorabaugh.
Maple Mousse   Mrs. Oak Throckmorton
Maple Mousse   Margaret Long Stanley
Maple Ice Cream   Mrs. Howard Norton
Maple Parfait   Helen Brooks Hall
Maple Sugar Sherbet   Mrs. G. M. Dickson
Milk Sherbet   Mrs. Will Dixon
Meringue Glace
Nesselrode Pudding
Nut and Raisin Ice Cream

Orange Cream Sherbet
Orange Mousse
Orange Souffle
Peach Bombe
Peach Cream   Mrs. J. H. Black.
Peach Melba
Peach Parfait
Pineapple Frozen   ′ Mrs. Will Dixon.
Pineapple Ice
Pistachio Ice Cream   Mrs. A. O Rorabaugh.
Pudding Frozen   Mrs. C W. Brown.
Pyramids
St Patricks Ice Cream   Mrs. A. O. Rorabaugh.
Strawberries Frozen
Strawberry Mousse
Strawberry Mousse   Mrs B. H. Campbell.
Strawberry Parfait
Strawberry Sherbet
Strawberry Ice   Mrs. M Murdock
Soldier Boy Coupe
Sour Ice Cream
Thanksgiving Ice Cream
Three Sixes   Mrs. S. S. Noble
Yellow-Moose
Vanilla Ice Cream   Mrs. C. V. Ferguson.
Whipped Cream Sauce

FROZEN DESSERTS

Bombes are molds lined with water ice and filled with cream Parfait or Mousse and packed in freezer 4 hrs.

Biscuits are partly frozen yellow Parfait to which egg-whites are added, then packed in small boxes or molds in freezer for 2 or 3 hours.

Coupes are served in tall stemed glasses filled with a layer of ice cream, ice and whipped cream, with a bit of fruit on top or nuts may be added.

French Ice Cream is frozen custard.

Ice Cream is stirred while freezing. Mousses and parfait are frozen without stirring.

Ices are made from fruit juices, sweetened, and water added, sometimes egg-whites are added.

Mousse is frozen without stirring the freezer. It is simply whipped cream flavored and molded. It takes a long time to harden—4 hrs. It must not be stirred or the Mossy effect is lost.

Parfaits are composed of fruit juices sweetened, egg-yolks, or whites and whipped cream, packed, not stirred.

Sherbet or Sorbets. The same as water ice with egg-whites added.

Souffles, are composed of fruit or flavoring sweetened, whipped cream and gelatine, molded packed and not frozen as hard as other creams.

Frozen Fruits.

Fruits may be frozen whole or run thru sieve and sugar added. Packed in ice 1 hr. are delicious. Skins should be removed.

Berries should be hulled and sugared. Bananas should be sliced and peeled—add cinnamon and sugar.

Peaches and Pears should be peared. Stones or seeds removed and sugared; halved. Watermelon or Cantaloupe cut in squares or slices, or round balls, sprinkle with a little salt.

Iced Fruits may be dipped first in beaten egg-whites, then in sugar. Repeat the process then pack in freezer and surround with ice 3 hrs.

Fruit sauces for ice cream, Mash and sweeten to taste strawberries, raspberries, blueberries, cherries, peaches, pineapple or other fruits and serve over ice cream.

HOW TO PACK THE FREEZER

"The freezer must be packed carefully and accurately. Have ready a basket or a pan of ice finely and evenly crushed, a box of coarse rock salt and a dipper or a saucepan holding about a pint. Place three evenly measured dippers of crushed ice in the freezer tub, packing it down firmly. Over this put one evenly measured dipper of rock salt Repeat until the carefully measured layers of ice and salt reach to a place on the can higher than the mixture inside. This proportion of three parts of ice to one part of salt has proven to be the best for getting a fine-grained ice cream. Do not put in your ice and salt without measuring and then expect to get a perfectly frozen product.

"The freezer may be left for about five minutes after being packed while the ice begins to melt and the mixture becomes chilled. When the ice and salt have begun to work, it is time to turn the crank Begin by turning it very slowly. A slow song on the phonograph makes a good accompaniment, for the slower the freezer crank is turned for the first 10 min the finer grained will be the product."

FREEZING

Water ices should be frozen slowly. If milk is ice cold, fruit juice will not curdle it when added. Turn slowly at first then increase speed. Cream will be coarser grained if freezer is over ¾ full.

ALMOND ICE

6 T Almond Paste
½ C hot water
1½ C cold water

1 egg-white
3 drops vanilla

Dissolve Almond Paste in hot water until smooth. Add egg beaten until stiff, then cold water and flavor Freeze

ANGEL PARFAIT

¾ C sugar
½ C water
2 eggs

2 C whipping cream
1 T vanilla
3 T whipped cream

Boil sugar and water 3 min Pour boiling syrup over stiffly beaten egg-whites, beaten continually, whip cream stiff—add vanilla, beat all together and freeze. Serve in parfait glasses with a layer of parfait and then whipped cream alternate, topping with candied cherry and preferred flavor, or berries or fruit may be used.

APPLE WHIP

2 egg-whites
½ C apple sauce
½ C syrup

Beat egg-whites stiff.
Add apple sauce
Pack and freeze

APRICOT ICE CREAM

1 can apricots
1 C whipped cream

½ C sugar

Cook sugar and water 5 min Add strained apricots and add enough water to make 4 C in all. Then add whipped cream.

Mrs G M. Dixon.

APRICOT MOUSSE. Same as Cherry

BRICK BAKED ALASKA ICE CREAM

1 qt. ice cream   1 very hot oven
4 egg-whites

Place cream on very cold platter, have eggs beaten very stiff and cover ice cream entirely. Have oven at maximum temperature and let remain 5 min. Remove and serve at once. Is only a success if done quickly in a very hot oven. Macaroons may be ground and placed on top before serving.

BAKED APPLE ICE CREAM

Bake and run apples thru sieve and add sugar and cream, cinnamon and lemon juice.

Formula.
6 apples   ½ t cinnamon
1 qt. cream   2 T lemon juice
1 C sugar

BANANA SHERBET

3 oranges   1 C sugar
3 lemons   ½ C water
3 bananas   1 C cream

To the juice of the lemons and oranges, add the mashed bananas, sugar and water, when partly frozen, add the cream

Mrs. Spangler.

BISCUIT GLACE

2 C hot water   6 egg-yolks
2 C sugar   1 pt. cream

Boil the water and sugar together until it threads, add the beaten egg-yolks, cook 1 min. and beat until cold. Chill in freezer and add 1 pt. cream whipped dry, freeze and then pack in salt and ice. Flavor to taste.

Mrs. Robt. B. Campbell.

BISQUE ICE CREAM

Is made by the addition to any ice cream of dried and ground crumbs of any kind of cake. 1C to the qt. added last.

BLACKBERRY MOLD

1 qt. blackberries   6 T whipped cream
2 T water   ½ t salt
½ C sugar

Stem and mash berries in the water and sugar—mix with cream and freeze 4 hrs.

CAFE PARFAIT

½ C clear strong coffee   ¾ C sugar
1 pt. whipped cream

Add the coffee to the whipped cream, also the sugar, and whip until stiff enough to keep in shape Then pack in freezer or tin can with equal parts salt and finely crushed ice.

Mrs Robt. B Campbell

CANNON BALLS

Freeze cream very hard. Dip out in form of balls with a round scoop—roll in pulverized toasted macaroons.

CANTALOUPE ICE CREAM

Add to 1 qt French Ice Cream, 2 C mashed cantaloupes or muskmelon and ½ t vanilla

CANTALOUPE ICE CREAM

Ice cream served in ½ of a cantaloupe, ice cold.

CARAMEL ICE CREAM

½ C granulated sugar   3 pts. cream
1 pt. milk   1 C sugar

Melt the ½ C of sugar in an iron skillet and when boiling, and smoking hot, pour into it the boiling milk. Stir or it will crystallize. Set aside to cool, and then add 1 C sugar and 1 qt. cream, mix well and freeze. Remove the dasher, stir in the remaining pt. of cream whipped stiff, cover tightly and pack with ice and salt.

Mrs Gilbert Tucker.

CARAMEL ICE CREAM

1 pt milk   1½ t grated chocolate
1 pt. cream   1 C sugar
3 eggs   ½ C water

Dissolve sugar with water, then—not touching it— let boil to a golden brown, scald the milk and turn slowly on beaten eggs, add chocolate and cook in double boiler, stirring till custard coats the spoon, then add hot caramel, when cold add cream whipped Freeze.   C. C.

CARAMEL SAUCE—PLAIN

May be made without the nuts.

CARAMEL NUT SAUCE

1 C sugar .   1 C pecans
¼ C boiling water   3 T cream

Cook sugar until it browns; add boiling water, then broken pecans and cream.

CARAMEL SYRUP

1 C boiling water   1 C sugar

Put sugar in hot stew kettle and stir with wooden spoon until sugar is melted—add boiling water and simmer.

CHERRY ICE

1 can cherries   1 C sugar
2 C water   1 lemon

Boil water and sugar 10 min., then cool, add lemon juice and cherries chopped fine and juice. Freeze.

CHERRY MOUSSE

2 C cherry juice   1 t lemon juice
1 T boiling water   1 C sugar
2 C whipped cream

Mix same as chocolate mousse, adding sugar to fruit before cream is added.

CHERRY PARFAIT

Same as Strawberry Parfait.

CHILLED FRUIT

1 small bottle of red cherries   2 slices of pineapple
½ lb. white grapes—seeded   1 C pineapple juice
2 oranges—large   2 T sugar

Cut oranges and pineapple in small pieces, add sugar to pineapple juice and boil to a syrup. Pour over fruit. Put in freezer and pack with ice, not salt. Serve in sherbet glasses.

Mrs. J. H. Black.

CRANBERRY SHERBET

1 qt. stewed cranberries which have been put through a colander. Add the juice of 3 oranges and 1 lemon and 1 lb. sugar. Pack and freeze to a mush then stir in the stiffly beaten whites of 2 eggs Finish freezing

Mrs Henry Lassen.

CHOCOLATE SAUCE FOR ICE CREAM

2 squares of chocolate   ½ C sugar
1½ C milk   or ¼ T mint
½ t vanilla

Boil 5 min , can and set in ice box. This can also be used for an iced chocolate drink by adding cream.

CHOCOLATE SAUCE—SMOOTH

| 1-3 C cocoa | 2 C sugar |
| 1 C boiling water | ½ t vanilla |

Dissolve cocoa in boiling water, add sugar, boil 5 min. Cool and add vanilla. Seal in jar and keep cool. Makes 1 pt. and keeps indefinately. Is good to use for cold chocolate drink, by adding cream

All Mousse is made the same.

SOFT BOILED CUSTARD USED AS ICE CREAM

1 C milk	2 T sugar
1 egg	⅛ t salt
10 drops vanilla	

Heat milk scalding hot in double boiler. Add sugar and salt to egg and beat moderately. Pour hot milk slowly in to egg. Return to double boiler, cook, stirring constantly until spoon when lifted from mixture is coated. Add vanilla after custard is cooked When cold add 1 C double cream. For 6 pts. ice cream uses 6 times above recipt and 4 C maple syrup or caramelized sugar and 6 C of double cream

Mrs. Ralph L Millison.

CHOCOLATE MOUSSE

| 1 qt. cream | 1 T boiling water |
| 2 squares chocolate | 1 C sugar |

Whip cream, melt chocolate in water, add sugar, boil and stirring, pour over whipped cream cold, mix and freeze.

COFFEE MOUSSE

| 1 pt. cream | ¼ C sugar |
| ½ C coffee, strong | |

Stir together after whipping the cream, then turn into mold, cover with oiled paper and pack in ice and salt. 4 to 1, cover tightly with newspapers. Freeze 4 hrs. Serves 6 people.

C. C.

CRANBERRY ICE

To serve with dinner course.

| 3½ C water | 1½ C sugar |
| 1 qt. cranberries | |

Cook cranberries with water. Strain, add sugar. Set aside to cool, freeze. This will be a good half gallon when frozen, add the juice and rind of one lemon if liked.

DATE ICE CREAM

5 eggs	1 t vanilla
1 C sugar	2 C milk
1 qt. cream	½ C dates

Beat eggs, add sugar, milk, vanilla and rich cream. Chop dates very fine, mix well and freeze.

DELMONICO ICE CREAM

1 pt. milk	1 pt. cream
5 eggs	1 t flavor
1 C sugar	

Make milk, eggs and sugar into a cooked custard, add cream and flavor and freeze.

FRENCH ICE CREAM

1 C sugar	¼ t salt
1 C scalded milk	1 t butter
1½ C whipped cream	3 egg-yolks
1 T flavoring	

Pour milk over beaten egg-yolks, sugar and salt, cook 5 min. Add butter, if lumpy or coarse strain thru sieve and beat until cold. Add whipped cream and flavor.

FROZEN ROLL

1 qt. plain ice cream	½ C almonds
½ C pistachio nuts	½ C raisins, seeded

Make ice cream by any desired plain recipe, reserve 1-3 for the center of the roll, flavor the remainder with nuts pounded to a paste. Line mold with this mixture. To the other reserved plain cream add raisins, ground and sweetened and fill the center of the roll with this—cover the top with the lining mixture. Pack in salt and ice 4 hrs.

FRUIT MILK SHERBET

3 qts. milk	1 small can pineapple, grated
6 lemons	1 pt. canned cherries
2 pts. sugar	

Squeeze the juice of lemons in sugar, put on stove until dissolved, take off and cool, add pineapple and cherries. Put the milk in freezer and turn crank until cold or chilled then add the sugar, lemon juice, cherries, and pineapple.

Mrs. A. C. Jobes.

GINGER ICE CREAM

1 C milk	1 C sugar
3 C whipped cream	1½ preserved ginger
1 T lemon juice	1 t vanilla

Mix well together adding the ginger chopped very fine and freeze.

LEMON ICE

1 pt. sugar	4 lemons
1 pt water	1 orange
¼ box gelatine	

Boil sugar and water to thin syrup. Dissolve gelatine in water. Add juice of lemons and orange and add enough water to make 2 quarts.

Mrs Charles Smyth.

LEMON ICE

6 lemons	1 orange
4 C sugar	4 egg-whites
6 C water	

Prepare the juices, sugar and water as for lemonade. Set in the ice box to chill for an hour or more. Freeze until it seems to turn a little hard Now put in as quickly as possible the egg-whites which have been beaten to a stiff froth

Mrs. W. E. Stanley.

LEMON PUNCH

12 lemons	1 pt. grape juice
4 C sugar	1 qt. tea
4 qt. water	½ pt. mint leaves

Boil the sugar with 1 qt. of water, let it cool, add the grated rind of 2 and juice of all the lemons, add tea, grape juice, ice. Serve with a mint leaf in each sherbet cup. This will serve 60 cups. Mrs. A. O. Rorabaugh.

MAPLE MOUSSE

6 whole eggs or yolks of 8 eggs
1½ cups of maple syrup

Cook in double boiler until like custard. Let cool. Add 1½ pints of cream whipped. Pack in ice and salt for 4 hrs.

Mrs. Oak Throckmorton

MAPLE MOUSSE

4 eggs	1 C maple syrup
1 pt. whipping cream	

Boil syrup 5 minutes and then add to beaten yolks. Put on stove and just heat Cool Beat whites stiff and add to them the whipped cream. Beat. Add to this yolks and syrup mixture. Mix well. Pack in mold 5 hours in cracked ice and salt. This makes almost a quart. Margaret Long Stanley.

GOLDEN ROD PARFAIT

1 C sugar   ⅛ t salt
¼ C water   5 egg-yolks
1 T vanilla   2 C whipped cream

Boil sugar and water 5 min pour over beaten egg-yolks slowly, stirring—put in double boiler, add salt and cook until spoon is coated. Remove and beat until cold—add whipped cream and vanilla. Pack 4 hrs.

Mrs. Charles Smyth.

MAPLE ICE CREAM

1½ C maple syrup   2 C cream
4 eggs

Cook the syrup and the beaten egg-yolks together until thick, stirring constantly. When cold, add cream, and freeze, when nearly frozen, add the egg-whites. Will serve 6.

Mrs. H. G. Norton.

MAPLE SUGAR SHERBET

8 egg-yolks   1 C maple sugar
1 pt. whipped cream

Beat egg-yolks thoroughly and pour over them boiling maple sugar, beating all the time to make it smooth, let cool, then add 1 pt. of whipped cream and freeze.

Mrs. G. M. Dickson.

MILK SHERBET

4 lemons   1 C whipped cream
1 C sugar   1 qt. milk
4 egg-whites

Grate yellow rind of one lemon into milk and let it come to boil, and cook 2 min. Cool and put into freezer, turn 2 min. then add sugar and lemon juice mixed. Turn until nearly frozen, then open and add egg-whites well beaten and whipped cream. Repack and turn until done.

Mrs. Will Dixon.

MERINGUE GLACE

Divide egg-shaped Meringue into two parts, fill the centers with ice cream or mousse and put together to resemble egg.

NESSLRODE PUDDING

½ lb almond paste
1 pt. cream
1 pt. can pineapple
10 egg-yolks
30 small chestnuts or pecans
2 T grape juice

½ lb. candied fruit
1 T vanilla
2 C water
1 C sugar
¼ t salt

Boil sugar, water and pineapple juice 20 min. Blanch nuts and pound to a paste, rub almond paste smooth. Beet egg-yolks, stir into the syrup; cook in double boiler until it thickens. Beat over pan of cold water 10 min. Mix nuts and paste with the cream. Add the candied fruit. Pineapple cut fine. Mix with cooked mixture. Freeze as Ice Cream. Garnish with whip cream and preserved cherries.

NUT AND RAISIN ICE CREAM

1 pt. cream
1 pt. milk
3 C sugar

1 C raisins
1 C pecans
½ t vanilla

Grind raisins and nuts. Cover with milk and sugar and warm. Put cream in freezer. Freeze ½ and add mixture.

ORANGE CREAM SHERBET

2 egg-whites
2 C sugar
2½ boiling water
2½ C double cream

2 C orange juice
1 orange
½ C lemon juice
2-3 C powdered sugar

Cook sugar and water 5 min. Add the grated rind of 1 orange, 2 C of orange juice and lemon juice, turn into freezer and freeze to a mush. Whip cream until stiff, add the stiffly beaten eggs and add to frozen mixture and finish freezing

ORANGE MOUSSE

Juice 6 oranges
Juice 1 lemon
1½ C whipped cream

1 C minced pecans
1 C sugar
1 T boiling water

Add sugar to fruit before adding cream, mix, and freeze as for chocolate.

ORANGE SOUFFLE

6 oranges
1½ C sugar

4 eggs

Beat eggs separate and stiff. Cube oranges—add sugar, mix all together and serve as a breakfast dish

PEACH BOMBE

Line a mold with peach ice and fill with vanilla ice cream, sprinkle chopped pecans thru and grated macaroons on top when ready to serve

PEACH CREAM

12 large peaches   1 pt. water
2 C sugar   3 egg-whites, beaten

Beat egg-whites. Rub peaches through a colander and stir all ingredients together. Freeze like ice cream.

Mrs. J. H. Black.

PEACH MELBA—KANSAS

Place halves of canned peaches cold, on a mound of ice cream placed on a round cut of sponge cake. Whip cream on top of sponge cake. Topping all with minced peaches and a maraschino cherry.

PEACH PARFAIT

Same as Strawberry Parfait.

PINEAPPLE—FROZEN

1 can grated pineapple or   3 lemons
1 fresh pineapple grated   1 orange
1 qt. water   1 egg-white
2 C sugar   2 T powdered sugar

Add ½ C sugar to the pineapple, cook slowly 20 min. remove from the fire and cool. Boil water and remaining sugar with chipped rind of ½ lemon 10 min. Strain, when cold, add lemon and orange juice. Turn into freezer. When frozen, remove dasher and add pineapple, then stir in egg-whites beaten to stiff meringue with the powdered sugar. Repack freezer and let stand for 1 hr. before serving.

Mrs. Will Dixon.

PINEAPPLE ICE

1 can sliced pineapple   3 lemons
1 qt. water   4 egg-whites
3 C sugar   1 C cream

Chop pineapple rather fine. Boil sugar and water 5 min. Cool. When cool add lemon juice. Put in freezer and when partly frozen add stiffly beaten eggs and 1 C of sweet cream. Any kind of fruit juice may be used, or nuts may be added chopped fine. If sour fruit add more sugar.

PISTACHIO ICE CREAM

4 C light cream or   1 C sugar
3 C heavy   1 T flavoring—almond, vanilla
1 C milk   ¼ t salt
½ C Pistachio nuts   1 C almonds
coloring

Chop the nuts fine—mix all the ingredients—color a delicate green and freeze

You can with good result substitute ½ C pecans and 1 T pistachio for ½ C pistachio nuts.

Mrs. A. O. Rorabaugh.

PUDDING—FROZEN

1 pt. water

1 lb. sugar

6 egg-yolks

Nuts

1 qt. cream

Fruit

Orange juice

Boil water and sugar; add 6 egg-yolks beaten very lightly, beat over fire 1 min. Take from fire and beat until cold. Add cream and freeze. Add the fruit and nuts when it begins to freeze.

Mrs. C. W. Brown.

PYRAMIDS

Freeze ice cream very stiff, scoop out with lifter that forms a cone shape and roll in finely chopped pecans or almonds.

ST. PATRICK'S ICE CREAM

6 C milk

3 C sugar

½ C flour

2 C cream

1 t Pistachio Ex.

2 egg-whites

1 egg-yolk

¼ t salt

3 C nuts—1 pecan, 2 almonds

1 t almond ex.

GREEN FRUIT COLORING

Blend into a soft custard the sugar, flour, milk, eggs and salt by bringing 5½ C milk to the boiling point—add the remaining ½ C milk, sugar, flour, eggs and salt, which have been thoroughly mixed. Let all boil together for 3 min. Allow to cool, whip the cream and add flavor, color, add nuts, chopped fine and freeze. You have 3½ qts. ice cream.

Mrs. A. O. Rorabaugh.

STRAWBERRIES—FROZEN

1 qt. strawberries

Juice 2 lemons

1 lb. sugar

1 qt. water

Add sugar, water and lemon juice to berries, let stand 2 hrs. Mash berries, mix thoroughly and freeze slowly or do not mash berries but just chill by packing in freezer 1 hr.

STRAWBERRY MOUSSE

2 C whipping cream

1 C powdered sugar

2 C mashed strawberries

Whip cream stiff, add sugar and berries, turn into a mold and cover with oiled paper—cover tight, pack in 4 parts ice and 1 part salt, let stand 3 hrs. Any preferred berries may be used.

STRAWBERRY MOUSSE

1 qt. crushed strawberries

1 pt. whipped cream

1 C sugar

Mix and pack in freezer 3 hrs.

Mrs. B. H. Campbell.

STRAWBERRY PARFAIT

1 C sugar
1 C mashed fruit
½ C water
2 egg-whites

Juice of one orange
1 pt. heavy cream
5 drops almond extract—
  whipped

Boil sugar and water until it threads and pour slowly, beating over the stiffly beaten egg-whites. Mix orange juice and fruit together and beat in the egg-white mixture. Stir quickly until cold and then stir in the cream and almond Pour into a mold, cover with wax paper, and put on the lid. Pack in ice and salt for 4 hrs. If canned sweet fruit is used, use only ¾ C sugar.

STRAWBERRY ICE

1 box berries
1 C sugar

1 C water
Juice of one lemon

Crush the berries and run through sieve. Add sugar and water until dissolved. Cool, add to berries and juice of lemon and freeze.

Mrs. M. Murdock.

STRAWBERRY SHERBET

1 qt. milk
1 pt whipped cream
2½ boxes strawberries

1 2-3 pt. sugar
2 lemons, juice
¼ t salt

SOLDIER BOY COUPE

Fill tall glasses with alternate layers of vanilla cream, chopped cherries, whipped cream, topping all with a mound of cherries. A small flag stuck in the top makes a patriotic decoration

SOUR ICE CREAM

1 C sugar
1¼ C sour cream

Juice 2 lemons
3 bananas

Dissolve sugar in lemon juice, then mix with cream, whipped. Be careful not to whip enough to make butter. Beat in the bananas mashed. Freeze.

THANKSGIVING ICE CREAM

Scoop out the half of a pumpkin and fill with ice cream, colored with yellow vegetable coloring, stick in almonds to resemble seeds, and serve on large platter with pumpkin vines

THREE SIXES

3 lemons	3 C sugar
3 oranges	3 C water
3 bananas	3 egg-whites

To the juice of the lemons and oranges add the mashed bananas, sugar and water, when partly frozen add the egg-whites well beaten and freeze.

Mrs S. S. Noble

VANILLA ICE CREAM

1 qt cream	1 T vanilla
1 pt milk	Mix and freeze
1½ C sugar	

YELLOW MOOSE

7 egg-yolks	1 pt. heavy cream
1 C powdered sugar	2 T strong vanilla

Beat eggs well, then add powdered sugar and cook in a double boiler till thick—about 20 min. Stirring almost constantly Add flavoring and cream whipped Pack in salt and ice five hours. Will serve 8

Mrs. C V. Ferguson.

WHIPPED CREAM SAUCE

2 T butter	1 t lemon juice
¾ C powdered sugar	1 t vanilla
1 egg	1 t cinnamon

Cream butter and sugar, add egg beaten, vanilla and lemon. Then cream whipped, sprinkle cinnamon over top.

PIES

PIES

Apple Pie
Apple Cobbler
Apple Cream Pie
Apricot Pie
Banana Pie   Mrs Robert B. Campbell
Blackberry Pie
Boston Cream Pie
Butter Scotch Pie   Mrs. Ralph Millison
Caramel Pie   Mrs E. R. Spangler
Cheese Pie   Mrs Baldwin
Cherry Pie
Chess Pie   Mrs B. E. Zartman
Chiffon Pie filling   Mrs Harold McEwen
Chocolate Pie   Mrs. Robert B Campbell
Chocolate Pie   C C
Currant Pie   Mrs L C Jackson
    Mrs. Finley Ross
Custard Pie   Mrs G M. Dickson
Custard Apple Pie   Mrs. Chester Long
Cream Pie
Cream Pie   Mrs. O. D. Barnes
Cocoanut Pie
Delicious Pie   Mrs. Robert B. Campbell
Golden Sauce for Lemon Pie   Mrs C. V. Ferguson
Gooseberry Pie   Mrs. Chester Long
Huckleberry Pie
Lemon Pie   Mrs. Henry J. Allen
Lemon Pie with Milk   Mrs. L. C. Jackson
Lemon Pie   Mrs O. G. Hutchison
Lemon Custard Pie   Mrs. H. W. Horn
Lemon Sponge Pie   Mrs G C Purdue
Loganberry Pie   Mrs. J. H. Aley
Macaroon Pie
Meat Pie Crust   Mrs. F. G. Smyth
Mince Meat   Mrs G. M. Dickson
Mince Meat   Mrs. C. L. Davidson
Mock Cherry Pie   Mrs. G. M. Dickson
Mock Mince Meat   Mrs. Geo. Steel
Napoleons
Orange Pie
Orange Pie   C. C.
Peach Custard Pie   Mrs. H. W. Horn
Pearless Lemon Pie   Mrs G. C. Purdue
Patties
Peach Cobbler
Peach Mint Pie
Peach Pie
Philadelphia Butter Pie   Mrs. G M. Dickson
Pie Crust   Mrs. G. M. Dickson
    Mrs. O D. Barnes
Pineapple Pie   Mrs. Ralph Millison

Pineapple Pie	Mrs Geo. Steel
Preserve Pie	
Puff Paste	
Mrs. Farmer's Pumpkin Pie	Mrs. G M. Dickson
Pumpkin Pie	Mrs Henry J. Allen
Raisin Pie	
Raisin Pie	C. C.
Raisin Pie	Mrs Henry Lassen
Raisin Pie	Mrs. L. C. Jackson
Rhubarb Pie	Mrs F. G. Smyth
Rhubarb Pie	Mrs. W. E. Stanley
Rhubarb Pie	Mrs. Frank Harryman
Sweet Potato Pie	
Tarts and Tartlets	
Vinegar Pie	
White Pie	Mrs. O. D. Barnes

METHOD OF PIE MAKING

There are four distinct ways of mixing pie crust.

1—Cutting with one silver knife.

2—Cutting with two silver knives in opposite directions.

3—Mixing with finger tips.

4—Using both knife and fork.

The method with finger tips is objectionable on account of the fingers heating the ingredients. All things must be ice cold to insure good crust.

Mix all the dry ingredients. Then cut the fat into the mixture by any of the above methods, until the flour seems perfectly smooth. Then sprinkle ice water evenly over the mixture, use a fork to stir it in so that all the flour is taken up with the water. If it crumbles, cool the hands on ice, and quickly take up the dough and press together. Flour rolling-board lightly. Take ½ of dough for lower crust, roll quickly and in one direction about one-eighth inch thick, spread on pie tin, do not stretch, fit in closely and cut rim with knife. Put in desired filling and roll top crust, cutting a few gashes or prickling with a fork to let steam escape. Wet lower crust around the edge and put on top crust, pressing edges firmly together and trim. The edges may be crimped by pressing with tines of a fork, or with spoon handle.

PIE CRUST RECIPE I

2 T lard	1 C flour
¼ t salt	3 T ice water

PIE CRUST RECIPE II

1¼ C flour	½ C butter
¼ t salt	¼ C ice water

PIE CRUST RECIPE III

2 C flour	2-3 C equal parts lard and butter
½ t B. P.	
½ t salt	6 T ice water

All utensils should be cold.

Handle as little as possible.

One secret of crisp pie dough is in using as little water as possible.

OVEN TEMPERATURES

A slow oven—in five minutes glazed paper will brown.

A medium oven—in three minutes glazed paper will brown.

A hot oven—in two minutes glazed paper will brown.

Sprinkle flour over inside of oven If light brown in three minutes with the door shut, oven is right, if burned, oven is too hot.

The reason for having things ice cold in pie making, is that it will then raise to the maximum degree in the oven.

Pie crust must be rolled only one way, as rolling both to and from, breaks the air globbules and the rising quality is lessened.

To keep crust from puffing up when baking, turn one pan over the other.

In mixing, if material should be warm, use a little less water.

Cook pies in medium oven, that browns paper in three minutes.

To keep left over pie dough, wrap in oiled paper, and place in ice box.

Crisco makes a flaky crust. Butter makes a better crust, not likely to break and more tasty.

To bake under crust. Turn the pie tin upside down, put crust on outside of bottom, bake until just beginning to brown, take out and put in inside of pan for lower crust.

For liquid pie filling always partly bake under crust.

Pastry flour is made of winter wheat. Good pastry flour retains prints of fingers on flour when squeezed. Use 1½ T less of bread flour to the cup than of pastry flour.

Small tarts or pies may be made by baking dough on outside of tart pans, Gem pans, or muffin pans

For luncheons or picnics make individual pies.

If a cream pie or meringue just baked is set at once into a cold place it is apt to become watery. Keep it in the kitchen until cool.

When custard pies are cooked too fast, the custard will fall apart and become watery

To prevent fruit pies from boiling over while baking, add a T of corn starch to the fruit. Sweeten fruit to taste, add corn starch and heat before putting on crust.

Fruit Pies require three C fruit to each pie.

Puff Paste will rise to double its thickness

When making pies, cake or bread try a wire potato masher to mix the flour and shortening, or to mix the sugar and butter.

Corn starch must cook much longer than the flour in fillings.

Meringues become watery if cooked too fast.

Meringue:

1 T powdered sugar   1 egg-white

Beat egg-white well, add sugar. Flavor if desired.

When eggs will not whip add ¼ t salt to each egg This lowers the temperature of the eggs. Warm eggs will not beat well.

APPLE PIE

Fill lower half of pie crust (cooked) with pared and finely sliced juicy apples. Cover with ¾ C sugar, 3 T butter dotted in 1-8 nutmeg grated, 1 t flour and 3 T water. Cover with upper crust, pinch the edges closely together and bake.

APPLE COBBLER

Refer to Peach Cobbler

APPLE CREAM PIE

2 C mashed apple sauce	4 egg-whites
¾ C sugar	1 T cinnamon
⅛ t salt	1 T lemon juice
½ C cream	

Beat eggs stiff, add flavor, sugar, salt, cream and sauce. Place between layers in two crust pie and bake twenty minutes. By half baking the undercrust before putting in a liquid filling, it will not make it soggy.

APRICOT PIE

1 pt. apricots	½ C sugar
¼ C juice	

Run apricots through ricer and mix sugar and juice—if canned apricots. If fresh apricots are used, pare and cut in slices, make syrup of sugar and 2 T of water, cover apricots. Place between the two crusts of pie and bake thirty minutes.

BANANA PIE

1-3 C sugar	1 C milk
2 egg-yolks	⅛ t salt
½ T lemon juice	¼ C cream
3 T flour	1 large banana

Scald the milk, add the sugar and flour mixed together, and the beaten yolks, and salt. Cook fifteen minutes in a double boiler stirring while it thickens. Cool and add the cream, then lemon juice, and sliced banana, then turn into baked crust. Cover with meringue, and brown

Mrs. Robt. B. Campbell.

BLACKBERRY PIE

1 qt. ripe blackberries	2 T butter
¾ C sugar	

Cook undercrust one-half way done. Melt sugar and butter. Mix with berries and pour into undercrust. Cover with top crust and cook twenty to thirty minutes.

BOSTON CREAM PIE

Cake Part	Filling
3 eggs	1 C sugar
1 C sugar	2 C milk
1 C flour	3 eggs
3 T milk	2 T flour
1 T butter	½ C butter
1 t B. P.	1 pt. nuts

Cream butter and sugar, add milk and beaten eggs, add flour and B. P. Bake in layers. Put together with filling. Boil together the milk, sugar, butter and thicken with beaten yolks of three eggs and flour, add chopped nuts Put together when cold.

BUTTER SCOTCH PIE

1 C dark brown sugar	1 T butter
1 C milk	1 egg-yolk
1 rounding T flour	

Cook milk, sugar, flour and yolk of egg until thick, stirring all the time Drop in butter and pour into a baked crust with the beaten white of egg on top, put in oven and brown.

Mrs. Ralph Millison

CARAMEL PIE

1½ C B sugar	4 eggs
1½ C sugar	1 C milk
4 C water	1 C flour
2 T Powdered sugar	

Melt the sugar in skillet, on top of stove until it makes a syrup Beat the egg-yolks, add milk, water and flour, cook until thick in double boiler; add syrup Bake pie crust shell and fill. Cover with meringue of beaten white of eggs and 2 T sugar.

Mrs E. R. Spangler.

CHEESE PIE

2 C cheese	2 lemons
½ C sugar	½ t vanilla
6 eggs	4 T flour
1 C double cream	

Put cheese thru colander, add sugar, egg-yolks, rind of one lemon and juice of two, add vanilla, flour and egg-whites stiffly beaten. Bake crust about half done, then put in cheese filling and bake forty minutes. Serve with whipped cream.

Mrs. Baldwin.

CHERRY PIE

Take a deep earthen dish. Shallow pie pans will not do. Roll pie crust out thin and fit into the bottom of the dish and cut off at the edges. Cut a one inch strip of the pie crust and moistening the outer edge of the pie, place this strip around the edge, pressing it into place. Mix ½ C sugar with 1 T of flour and dust this evenly over the dough in the dish. Take an ice cold pat of butter and cut it into small bits, and dot the dish with these bits of butter.

In the meantime, the cherries should be stoned, drained and rolled in granulated sugar. Pour in the cherries and cover over them a thin top crust that has been cut through in the middle with three slashes of a knife. Press the edges of the upper crust well down on the lower crust and bake for about one-half hour in a quick oven.

The crust should not be crowded with cherries as this makes a tendency for the pie to boil over, and the burned juice causes an unpleasant smoke.

CHESS PIE

6 eggs
2 C sugar
½ C butter
½ C cream

1 C raisins
1 C pecans
Vanilla flavoring

Seed raisins and chop pecans. Put egg-whites in pie, either put the rest of whites on top as meringue or cover with whipped cream when ready to serve. Cream butter and sugar as for cake, then add eggs, and cream, and boil in double boiler until creamy like fudge and is a little dark. Stir continually. When off fire, add flavoring and seeded raisins and pecans Fill shells that have been baked. These pies will keep for several days. This recipe will make two large pies or twelve individual pieces.

Mrs. B. E. Zartman.

CHIFFON PIE FILLING

4 eggs
1 C sugar

1 lemon

Cook together in double boiler until thick, beaten egg-yolks, 1 C sugar, grated rine and juice of 1 lemon. When thick, pour over beaten whites of 2 eggs and beat in. Pour this in crust and put meringue made of 2 whites on top. Put in oven to bake until brown on top.

Mrs. Harold D. (Evelyn Rorabaugh) McEwen.

CHOCOLATE PIE

1 C milk
1 C sugar
3 T flour

2 egg-yolks
3 T grated chocolate
1 t vanilla

Mix the flour and sugar together, add the beaten yolks, and milk, cook stirring constantly until smooth and thick. Add the chocolate last, and after the mixture has been removed from the fire, stir in the vanilla. Put the whole into a baked pie crust, cover with a meringue made by beating two eggs very stiff, with 2 T sugar. Brown slightly.

Mrs. Robt B Campbell.

CHOCOLATE PIE

½ C sugar
1 C milk
1 T butter
1½ T grated chocolate

2 egg-yolks
1½ T corn starch
½ t vanilla
½ C sweet cream

Line a pie plate with a rich crust, bake. Make filling of sugar, milk, butter; when hot add grated chocolate, beaten yolks. Dissolve in cold milk corn starch, stirring over fire until thick and smooth, add vanilla. Fill shell with this mixture Whip cream to a froth, place on top of chocolate mixture and serve. (Very good).

C. C.

CURRANT PIE

1 C currants
1 C sugar
⅛ t salt

2 egg-yolks
3 T water
1 T flour

Mash currants, dissolve flour in water, mix all ingredients with egg-yolks, pour into a baked crust and when done, cover with frosting, browning in a slow oven

Frosting

2 egg-whites

2 T sugar

Mrs. Finley Ross.
Mrs. L. C. Jackson.

CUSTARD PIE

1 pt. milk

3 egg-yolks

Sugar to suit taste, flavor, and cook in double boiler, thicken with flour. Beat whites of egg to put on top and brown.

Mrs. G. M. Dickson.

CUSTARD APPLE PIE

3 ripe apples
1 C sugar
½ t cinnamon
¼ t nutmeg

2 eggs
1 C milk
1 T butter

Scrape apples, beat eggs, mix all together, dot butter on top and fill crust.

Mrs. Chester Long.

CREAM PIE

1 pt. cream
1½ C sugar
⅛ t rose flavoring

4 egg-whites
½ t nutmeg

Mix cream and sugar, nutmeg and rose. Beat eggs until they stand alone, mix all well together. Bake with the undercrust only Bake until set.

CREAM PIE

1 pt. milk	4 eggs (whites)
½ C sugar	Vanilla
1 t flour	Little pulverized sugar

Scald milk in double boiler, moisten sugar and flour and mix so it can be poured, cook until thick. Remove from fire and fold in beaten whites of two eggs. Flavor with vanilla. Put in baked crust and place in oven five minutes Make top of whites of two eggs, well beaten, and a little pulverized sugar. Whipped cream may be used and is delicious.

Mrs. O. D. Barnes.

COCOANUT PIE

Use custard pie recipe, add 1 T grated cocoanut to custard and 1 T grated cocoanut sifted over meringue on top.

DELICIOUS PIE

3 egg-yolks	½ C pulverized sugar
½ C butter	½ t vanilla

Cream the butter and sugar, add the well beaten egg-yolks and vanilla. Line a pan with pie crust or with puff-paste crust if a richer crust is desired, fill with the above mixture and bake until it sets. Remove from oven, and cover with a meringue made from three egg-whites, and ¾ C of pulverized sugar. Return to oven and brown slightly.

Mrs. Robt. B. Campbell.

GOLDEN SAUCE FOR LEMON PIE

1 C sugar	2 egg-yolks
½ C butter	1 lemon

Cream butter and 'sugar, add beaten yolks, cook in double boiler, add grated rind and juice of one lemon.

Mrs. C. V. Ferguson.

GOOSEBERRY PIE

1 can gooseberries	3 T butter
1 C sugar	1 t flour

Pour off juice and use for making jelly. Put gooseberries in partly baked under crust. Add sugar, dot in butter and sprinkle flour on top Cover with upper crust and pinch corners closely together Make a little richer crust 1 T butter extra for gooseberry pie crust.

Mrs. Chester Long.

HUCKLEBERRY PIE

Use blackberry pie receipe, and use ½ C of sugar, and 1 t lemon juice

LEMON PIE

¾ C sugar	1 C water
1½ T flour	1 lemon
3 eggs	⅛ t salt

To sugar, add flour and mix thoroughly, add yolks of eggs well beaten, add juice of lemon and one t grated rind. Beat smooth, adding the cold water. Cook in double boiler until thick Fill hot pie crust. Beat whites of eggs with three T sugar until stiff, spread over pie, return to over and bake until light brown.

Mrs. Henry J. Allen.

LEMON PIE WITH MILK

Three eggs	2 T butter
1 C milk	¼ t salt
1 C sugar	1 lemon
2 T flour	

Reserve the whites of two of the eggs for meringue

Mix the flour with the sugar and cream the butter into the sugar Stir in the beaten eggs and the juice and grated rind of the lemon, then add the milk very slowly

Cook and put into baked shell. Cover with meringue made with the whites of the eggs and four tablespoons of sugar, and bake till a delicate brown.

Mrs. L C Jackson.

LEMON PIE

Grated rind and juice of one lemon, add cup sugar, two level tea spoons of butter, ⅛ tea spoon of salt, two level table spoons of flour, add yolks of two eggs, one cup of milk Fold in well beaten egg-whites. Bake in raw crust in very slow oven.

Mrs. O. G. Hutchison

LEMON CUSTARD PIE

1 lemon grated	1 egg
3 t flour	⅛ t salt
1 C sugar	1 C sweet milk

Grate lemon, mix flour with sugar, add egg and salt, then add the grated lemon. Then mix in the sweet milk Bake with two crusts

Mrs. J. H Aley.

LEMON SPONGE PIE

3 T butter	1 C milk (later)
1½ C sugar	1 lemon
3 eggs	3 T flour
½ c milk	¼ t salt

Cream together the butter and sugar. When very light add the yolks of eggs beaten until lemon colored and the grated yellow rind of the lemon with the strained juice. Blend together the flour, the salt and the milk; then mix with the first ingredients, add the additional cup of milk and the stiffly whipped egg-whites. Turn quickly into a large pie plate that has been lined with pastry and bake as custard pie. Serve cold.

LOGANBERRY PIE

Use Blackberry Pie Recipe, use 1½ C of sugar to the pie and sprinkle berries with 1 T flour.

MACAROON PIE

1 T grated chocolate	¼ t nutmeg
8 macaroons	3 T sugar
2 C milk	½ t vanilla

Chop and roll and sife macaroons. Soak in chocolate and milk, ten minutes, then add beaten eggs, sugar and flavor. Mix well. Cook under crust half way done, add mixture and bake twenty or twenty-five minutes. May be served with molds of ice cream on top.

MEAT PIE CRUST

2 C flour	1 C milk
1 t B. P.	2 T butter
1 egg	⅛ t salt

Beat egg lightly, mix all together and it will be the consistency of a batter. Put chicken or meat in dish, pour batter over and quickly bake

Mrs. F. G. Smyth.

MINCE MEAT

6 lb. beef	1 T salt
3 lb suet	2 T cinnamon
4 lb. raisins	1 t pepper
4 lb. currants	1 T cloves
1 lb. citron	3 nutmegs
2 lb. sugar	1 qt. cider
4 qts. apples	1 qt. molasses

Cook beef slowly, let stand over night and chop fine. Mince beef suet. Seed and cut raisins, currants, citron, tart apples, put into large vessel together. Mix sugar, salt, molasses and let come to boiling point, then pour over ingredients in vessel, after having first mixed them well. Grape juice may be used instead of cider.

Mrs. G. M. Dickson.

MINCE MEAT

4 lbs beef
2 beef hearts (or
4 calves' hearts)
4 lbs. suet
5 lbs. currants
2 lbs raisins
5 lbs sultanos
½ lb. citron
1lb lemon
1 bu. apples

3 T cinnamon
2 T cloves
1 T allspice
1 T nutmeg
1 T ginger
6 oranges (juice)
6 lbs sugar
1 qt vinegar
1 orange rind
1 T mace

Boil meat until bones slip out, boil hearts until tender, chop and boil suet thirty minutes in salty water, leave hearts and meat in stock all night, well covered; leave suet to get cold in water in which it is boiled; mix raisins, currants, citron, and lemon It improves the mince meat to add a little of any preserved fruits you may have on hand. Peel and chop apples, weigh six pounds sugar, put in kettle with the vinegar and let come to a boil and stir with it all of the spices, first wetting them in vinegar; moisten fruits with this syrup, also the apples. Chop meat and hearts fine and break the suet up in it. Moisten all with the stock. Then measure one bowl of the meat and suet, one bowl mixed fruit and one bowl of the apples and mix all together, and continue this until all the mixed fruits are used and then put in juice of six oranges and grated rind of the one Put all on stove and cook until apples are well cooked, stirring constantly

Mrs C. L. Davidson.

MOCK CHERRY PIE

1 C cranberries
½ C raisins
1 t vanilla

1 C sugar
1 t flour
½ C water

Cut berries in half, wash in cold water to remove seeds and mix all together adding vanilla and boiling water last Bake with two crusts.

Mrs. G. M Dickson

MOCK MINCE MEAT

1 C chopped bread
1 C raisins
1 C molasses
1 C sugar
1 t cinnamon

2-3 C boiled cider or vinegar
½ C melted butter
2 C boiling water
⅛ t salt and pepper
½ t cloves and allspice

Stir all together, then warm. This will make three pies.

Mrs. Geo. Steel.

NAPOLEONS

Roll puff paste as thin as possible, set in ice box one hour. Bake in sheets a delicate brown. Cool and spread between the sheets a thick cream filling, making a Napoleon four layers high and each cream filling flavored differently. Cover top with icing and cut in blocks two by four inches Serve cold.

ORANGE PIE

3 egg-yolks	1 T flour
1 C sugar	3 T sweet milk
1 large orange (juice) (rind grated)	3 T butter

Combine. Bake in lower crust. Cover with meringue made of whites of three eggs, and 3 T of sugar.

ORANGE PIE

2 oranges	2 eggs
1 C sugar	1 T flour
1 C milk	1 T butter

Cream sugar and butter, mix milk with well-beaten yolks and add orange juice. Cook in double boiler. Have under-crust baked, and put in filling. Place in oven ten minutes, remove, putting on top of pie the whites of eggs stiffly beaten and 2 T sugar. Put in oven and brown.

C. C.

PEACH CUSTARD PIE

1½ C milk	1 T cornstarch
1 C sugar	1 baked pie crust
2 eggs separated	Fresh or canned sliced peaches

Dissolve cornstarch in some cold milk, then heat remainder of milk and pour over beaten yolks, sugar and cornstarch. Cook until a thick custard, by placing in double boiler and stirring continuously. Cover bottom of pie crust with peaches, pour over custard, turn pan over top and bake until peaches are cooked. Add meringue of two egg-whites, well beaten, two teaspoons sugar, two teaspoons baking powder mixed and added to beaten whites before putting on pie. Cover and bake until light brown.

Mrs. H. W. Horn.

PEERLESS LEMON PIE

¾ C sugar	1 lemon
1 T butter	½ C milk
1 T flour	3 eggs
⅛ t salt	

Cream sugar and butter, add flour and yellow part of grated rind of the lemon, salt, and well beaten yolks of eggs, the juice of

lemon and lastly milk. Be sure to beat mixture thoroughly with
each addition Bake in pastry lined pie pan. Beat whites of eggs
stiff, add two tablespoons sugar, and spread the meringue over
the pie and brown slightly in oven.

Mrs. G. C. Purdue.

PATTIES

Patties are made of puff paste baked in patty shells. The
filling gives the name to the patty. Meat, oysters, fish, or game
mixed with a cream sauce or brown sauce may fill patty shells.
Vegetable patties are filled with peas, beans, corn, asparagus or
cauliflower, mixed with a cream sauce.

PEACH COBBLER

3 sliced peaches	3 T. butter
1 C sugar	2 T water
¼ t vanilla	

Boil sugar, butter, vanilla and water three minutes. Pour
over peaches which have been placed in bottom of bake pan.
Cover with pie crust one inch thick and bake twenty to thirty
minutes.

A very rich biscuit dough made with butter is sometimes
made for cobbler

PEACH MINT PIE

Make crust and bake. When cold cover with peaches cut in
slices, arranged in overlapping rows. Add mint leaves to sugar,
sprinkle over peaches and cover all with stiff whipped cream
flavored with mint.

Recipe:	½ t mint flavoring
1 t sifted mint leaves	½ C whipping cream

PEACH PIE

8 peaches or 2 C sliced peaches   1 T butter
¾ C sugar

Pare and slice peaches. Warm with sugar and butter melted.
Bake undercrust and add filling. Cover with top crust and bake.

PHILADELPHIA BUTTER PIE

2-3 C sugar	1 T flour
1 C cream	Egg of butter

Stir butter, flour and sugar together. Stir in cream, pour in
pie crust and bake until brown.

Mrs. G. M. Dickson.

PIE CRUST

1 C flour	2 T lard
3 T water	¼ t salt

All ice cold. For one pie.

Mrs. O. D. Barnes
Mrs. G M Dickson.

PINEAPPLE PIE

Crust
2 C flour
1 C lard

Filling
2 eggs
2 T butter
1 C sugar

¼ C water, iced
1 t salt
1 egg-white
½ pt. can pineapple
1 C milk
1 T flour

Separate the whites and yolks of eggs using the yolks for the filling and then place in a double boiler the milk, yolks of eggs beaten, butter, sugar, flour and pineapple and cook like a custard until done.

Bake the crust first then pour the custard in, beat the whites of the two eggs stiff, and pour over top and brown.

Mrs. R. L. Millison.

PINEAPPLE PIE

1 can grated pineapple
3 eggs
½ C milk
½ C cream

2 T butter
1 T flour
½ C sugar or more

Beat yolks of eggs, add dissolved flour in milk, add cream, butter and sugar and pineapple. Cook all together in double boiler. Bake crust separately, do not put filling in crust until cold. This recipe 1½ will make two pies.

Put meringue on top.

Mrs. Geo. Steel.

PRESERVE PIE

Strawberry, peach, cherry, apricot or any kind of preserve is good placed on baked crust and served with whipped cream. Do not use the juice. This is especially good in warm weather.

MRS. FARMER'S PUMPKIN PIE

1½ C pumpkin
2-3 C B. sugar
1 t cinnamon
½ t salt

½ t ginger
1½ C milk
½ C cream
2 eggs

Mix all ingredients in order named and bake in one crust.

Mrs. G. M. Dickson.

PUMPKIN PIE

1¼ C pumpkin
2-3 C sugar
1C hot milk

2 eggs
1 t cinnamon
⅛ salt

Beat the eggs thoroughly, at least five minutes, add the pumpkin, sugar, hot milk, cinnamon and salt. Turn into a crust and bake.

Mrs. C. V. Ferguson.

PUMPKIN PIE

1 C pumpkin	½ t cinnamon
1 T flour	½ t ginger
½ C milk	½ t vanilla
2 eggs	⅛ t cloves
½ C light B. sugar	⅛ t salt
½ t nutmeg	

Stir the flour in the milk, add pumpkin, beaten eggs, melted butter, sugar and spices, vanilla and salt. Cook forty minutes in slow oven.

Mrs. Henry J. Allen.

RAISIN PIE

1 scant cup sugar   1 T butter

Cream together, add 1 T flour, 1 T vanilla, yolks of two eggs. While preparing this have 1 cup raisins simmering in 1 cup of water. Cook a few minutes then add other mixture to raisins and cook for a few minutes.

Put in your previously baked pie crust and cover with meringue made of the two egg-whites.

Mrs. Henry Lassen.

RAISIN PIE

1½ C raisins	½C water or fruit juice
2 C apples, chopped	2 t cinnamon
1 C walnuts, chopped	½ t cloves
1¾ C sugar	½ t salt
½ C vinegar	

Bake in crust with latticed top.
This makes two pies.

Mrs L. C. Jackson.

RAISIN PIE

1 C raisins (seedless)	1 lemon seeded and chopped
1 C sweet milk	1 egg
1 C sugar	2 T flour

Chop raisins. Bake between crusts.

C. C.

RAISIN PIE

1 C cooked raisins	1½ C sugar
2 eggs	2 T flour
1 lemon	

Beat eggs, add lemon juice, sugar and raisins floured. Cook until thick, then put in partly baked crust, and add top crust. Bake twenty minutes.

RHUBARB PIE

2 C rhubarb	1 egg
1 T flour	⅛ t salt
1½ C sugar	

Cut rhubarb in discs sufficient to make 2C. Mix well sugar and flour and salt, add beaten egg, make pie crust from pie crust recipe, and fill with the rhubarb mixture. Cover with strips of crust.

Mrs. F. G. Smyth.

RHUBARB PIE

1 C stewed rhubarb	1 T corn starch
1 C sugar	1 lemon
1 T butter	1 egg-yolk

Moisten the corn starch in a little cold water and cook until clear in ½C boiling water. Pour over the sugar and butter and allow to cool, then add lemon, eggs and rhubarb. Prepare crust first. Bake in one crust. When done spread with meringue made of the beaten white of the eggs and one small C of sugar. If pies are not desired very thick, this will be sufficient for two pies.

Mrs. W. E. Stanley.

RHUBARB PIE

Enough uncooked rhubarb to make pie.

2 egg-yolks	1 T butter
1½ C sugar	pinch of salt
2 T flour	

Make pie crust—fill with rhubarb and mixture, well mixed, bake in slow oven one hour, then put whites of 2 eggs on top and brown.

Mrs. Frank Harryman.

SWEET POTATO PIE

1½ C potato boiled and mashed	2 t cinnamon
5 C sugar	½ t nutmeg
5 eggs	¼ t salt
1 qt. milk	

Make and bake the same as Custard Pie.

TARTS AND TARTLETS

Tarts and tartlets can be made by cutting either plain or puff paste into small tarts, or baking in tart pans. Fill with the same filling used for pie, or fill with marmalade or jelly. Sometimes the plain pie crust is made richer.

VINEGAR PIE

2 egg-yolks	2½ T vinegar
2 C sugar	1 C water
2 T flour	1 T butter

Beat eggs well, add sugar and flour. Add vinegar and water. Cook in double boiler and then put in baked pie crust. Cover with meringue made of the two egg-whites and brown in oven.

WHITE PIE

1 C milk	1 t vanilla
½ C sugar	4 egg-whites
2 t flour	¼ t salt

Bake crust in deep tin Scald milk in double boiler. Add sugar and flour moistened with milk sufficient to pour, and cook until thick. Take from fire and stir in the beaten whites of two eggs, salt and vanilla. Fill the crust and put in oven five minutes or until set. Make meringue with two egg-whites and two t pulverized sugar. Cover pie and brown or use whipped cream.

Mrs. O. D. Barnes.

CAKES

CAKES

Apple Sauce Cake	Mrs. G. M. Dixon
Angle Food Cake	Mrs. Rorabaugh
Angle Food Cake, Small	Mrs J. H. Aley
Apple Cake, Dutch	Mrs. H. W. Lewis
Bread Cake	Mrs. G. M. Lowry
Brown Stone Front	Mrs. F. A. Amsden
Blitz Kugen	Mrs. Frank Harryman
Burnt Sugar	Mrs. R. B. Campbell
Chocolate Cake	Mrs. H. G. Norton
Chocolate Cake	Mrs. Gilbert Tucker
Chocolate Cream Roll	Mrs. Henry J. Allen
Cheese Cakes	Mrs. Ralph L. Millison
Coffee Cake	Mrs. Purdue
Custard Cake	Mrs. C. L. Davidson
Date Cake	Mrs. Erwin Taft
Delicious Cake, Allegretti Filling	Mrs. Frank Harryman
Fruit Cake	Mrs. G. M. Lowry
Favorite Sponge Cake	Mrs. C. W. Brown
Fairy Ginger Bread	Mrs. Frank Harryman
Ginger Bread	Mrs. J. H. Black
Grandmother's Ginger Bread	Mrs. G. M. Lowry
(Soft) Ginger Bread with Sour Milk	Mrs. C. L. Davidson
Hurry Cake	Mrs. Carrie Steel
Jam Cake	Mrs. B. H. Campbell
Kathryn's Chocolate Cake and Icing	Mrs. C. L. Davidson
Lady Baltimore and Filling	Mrs. Chester Long
Marble Cake	Mrs L. C. Jackson
One Egg Cake	Mrs. Warren Brown
Oregon Fruit Cake	Mrs. Erwin Taft
1-2-3-4 Cake	Mrs. R. B. Campbell
Potato Cake	Mrs. H. G. Norton
Sponge Cake	Mrs. M. Murdock
Sponge Cake	Mrs. Steel
Short Cake	Mrs H. W. Horn
Sour Cream Molasses Cake	Mrs. Steel
Sunshine Cake	Mrs. W. E. Stanley
Sunshine Cake	Mrs. Will Dixon
Surprise Cake	Mrs. C. V. Ferguson
Spice Cake	Mrs. C. V. Ferguson
Velvet Sponge Cake	Mrs. Henry J. Allen
Mrs. Woodrow Wilson's Wedding Cake	
White Layer Cake	Mrs. H. W. Lewis
White Fruit Cake	Mrs. Mary C. Todd
	Mrs. Steel
White Cake	Mrs. H. W. Horn
Yellow Sponge Tea Cake	Mrs. W E. Stanley
Cake Hints	

APPLE SAUCE CAKE

1 C Sugar	½ t Cloves
½ C Butter	¼ t Mace
2 C Flour	½ C Nuts
1 C Apple Sauce	1 t Soda
1 C Raisins	1 t B P
1 t Cinnamon	2 Eggs

Mix in usual manner and bake in loaf.

Mrs. G. M. Dickson.

ANGEL FOOD CAKE

11 egg-whites	1 1-3 C Granulated Sugar
⅛ t Salt	1 t Vanilla
1 t Cream of Tartar	1 t Orange Extract
1 C Flour "Swansdown"	

Break the eggs into a gallon crock, having crock and eggs cold. Add salt. Sift the flour five times, the sugar five times, measure the flour by t into measuring cup. Beat the eggs with wire whip two minutes, add Cream Tartar, beat seven or eight minutes, add the sugar gently but quickly, flavor, add the flour lightly. Place in an Angel Food Cake pan. Do not grease pan, bake in a moderately hot oven twenty-five minutes. When done turn upside down, leave for one hour, cut out and ice

Mrs. Rorabaugh.

SMALL ANGEL FOOD CAKE

1 C Milk	3 t B. P.
1 C Flour	2 Egg-Whites
1 C Sugar	⅛ t Salt

Scald milk in double boiler. Sift flour and sugar together four times Add to B P. and salt Pour the hot milk in mixture stirring constantly until smooth Fold in the beaten egg-whites by pushing the bowl of the spoon from you, then back, then from right to left and left to right until mixed. Do not grease the pan. Flavor the icing and not the cake. Bake in moderate oven

Mrs. J. H Aley.

DUTCH APPLE CAKE

1/3 C Butter	2 C Flour
1 C Sugar	2 t B. P.
2 Eggs	2 C Apples
½ C Milk	1 t Vanilla

Put mixture in shallow pan then 2 C sliced apples on top of batter. Sprinkle with sugar and cinnamon and bake. Serve with whipped cream.

Mrs. H. W. Lewis.

BREAD CAKE

1½ C Bread Sponge .
1 C Sugar
1 Egg
1 C Flour
¼ C Butter
1 C Raisins

1 C Chopped Nuts
1 t Soda
1 t B. P.
1 t Cinnamon
¼ t Nutmeg

Bake in a moderately hot oven.

Mrs. G. M. Lowry.

BROWN STONE FRONT

½ C Butter
1 C Sugar
½ C Sweet Milk
2 C Flour

2 Eggs well beaten
1 t Soda
1 t Vanilla
Mix in usual manner.

One C grated chocolate or 2 squares, ½ C sugar, ½ milk, 1 egg-yolk. Cook until smooth and add to above cake mixture while hot. Bake in layers and ice.

Mrs. F. A. Amsden.

BLITZ KUGEN

1 C powdered sugar
1 C butter
1 C pastry flour
4 eggs

1 t B. P.
1 t vanilla
1 small pinch salt

Separate eggs and beat yolks very light, add sugar and cream. Then add salt and vanilla, then add sifted flour, then fold in beaten whites of egg, then add B. P. last. Bake in greased flat pan. Cover top with shredded cut almonds, little powdered sugar and sprinkle little cinnamon on top. Bake in slow oven.

Mrs. Frank Harryman.

BURNT SUGAR CAKE

1½ C Sugar
½ C Butter
2 Eggs
1 C Water (cold)

2½ C Flour
2 t B. P.
1 t Vanilla
3 t Burnt Sugar Syrup

Cream butter and sugar, add yolks, beaten light, water, flour, B. P. and vanilla. Then add the burnt sugar and fold in the well beaten egg-whites Bake in layers and ice with caramel frosting. To burn sugar, put 1 cupful sugar in a skillet and stir constantly until it is melted and brown. Add one-half C hot water and boil to a thick syrup.

Mrs. R. B. Campbell.

CHOCOLATE CAKE

½ C Butter
1½ C Sugar
1¾ C Flour
1 t Vanilla
4 Eggs

5 T Boiling Water
½ C Milk
2 t B. P.
2 oz Chocolate

Dissolve chocolate in boiling water Cream butter and sugar, add the well beaten yolks, then chocolate, and the milk, and flour alternately, having sifted the B P. and flour together. Fold into this mixture the stiffly beaten egg-whites. Bake either in loaf or layers Use either white or chocolate boiled icing Use pastry flour.

. Mrs H G Norton.

CHOCOLATE CAKE

½ Cake Chocolate, melted
1 C B. Sugar
1 C Sweet Milk
1 Egg-Yolk
1 t Vanilla
Cook until smooth and let cool

1 C B. Sugar
½ C Butter
½ C Sweet Milk
2 Eggs and 1 Egg-White
2 C Flour
1 t Soda in 2 T Hot Water

Mix in usual manner, add the above mixture, and bake in layers in a moderate oven. This is very nice baked in gem pans, iced and served as tea cakes.

Mrs. Gilbert Tucker

CHOCOLATE CREAM ROLL

5 Eggs
1 C Sugar

2 T Flour
3 T Cocoa

To the well beaten yolks add the sugar and beat till creamy, add flour and cocoa, then fold in the stiffly beaten whites Spread over a pan twelve inches square Bake in a cool oven twenty or twenty-five minutes Turn on a damp towel; let cool Spread with one cup of heavy cream whipped and flavored. Roll. Then ice with the following

7 T Powdered Sugar
2 T Cocoa

3 T Cold Coffee

Mrs. Henry J. Allen.

CHEESE CAKES

2½ C B. Sugar
½ C Butter

2 Eggs
2 C Currants

Make a rich pie crust and put in gem pans. Wash currants until perfectly clean. Mix sugar and butter together then add currants and lastly the eggs beaten, pour this mixture into the gem pans and bake. Will serve fourteen people.

Mrs. Ralph L. Millison.

COFFEE CAKE

1 Cake Yeast
1 Pt. Sweet Milk
1/3 C Butter
1/3 C Sugar

¼ t Soda
2 Eggs
1 t Cinnamon

Mix yeast with ½ pint milk and flour at night mixing stiff. Add rest of the ingredients in the morning.

Mrs. Purdue.

CUSTARD CAKE

1 C Sugar
½ C Sweet Milk
1 Egg

3 t B. P.
2 C Flour (small)

Bake in jelly tins. Spread between layers of cake the following custard:

1 pt. Cream (thin)
1 Egg (beaten)
1 t Corn Starch

1 T Flour
½ C Sugar
Lemon (or any extract)

Boil cream, beaten egg, cornstarch, flour, sugar together, when cold flavor with lemon or any extract.

Mrs. C. L. Davidson.

DATE CAKE

1 C B sugar
2 Eggs
½ C Butter
½ C Sour Milk
1 t Soda

1½ C Flour
1 t Vanilla
1 t Lemon
1 lb. Dates (cut fine)
½ C Walnut Meats (broken)

Mrs. Erwin Taft.

DELICIOUS CAKE ALLEGRETTI FILLING

2 C sugar
1 C butter
3 eggs
3 C flour

1 C milk
2 t B. P.
1 t vanilla

Cream butter and sugar, add beaten yolks, milk, flour, vanilla. Lastly add beaten whites of eggs. Bake in two layers.

ALLEGRETTI FILLING

1 C water   1½ C sugar

Boil together until it will spin a thread, have ready the stiffly beaten whites of 2 eggs. Pour the hot syrup slowly over the whites, beating constantly. Beat until thick enough to spread, spread quickly on cakes when cold and firm. Melt about one-half cake of unsweetened chocolate and spread over icing, put layers together immediately.

Mrs. Frank Harryman.

FRUIT CAKE

Dark Part:
1½ C B. Sugar
1 C Butter
2 C Flour
6 Egg-Yolks
1½ lbs. Raisins
1 lb. Currants
½ lb Citron, cut fine

¼ lb English Walnuts
2/3 C Water, or Coffee
1 t Soda
½ t Cloves
½ t Cinnamon
½ t Allspice
½ t Nutmeg

Cream butter and sugar, add eggs and beat well, then add fruit and spices, and last soda.

White Part:
6 Egg-Whites
1 C Sugar
½ C Butter
½ C Sweet Cream
2 C Flour
2 Rounding t B. P.
1 lb. Almonds chopped fine

½ lb Citron cut fine
½ lb. Grated Cocoanut
1 t Rose Water
1 t Lemon Extract
1 Small Stick Sugared Orange
Cream, sugar and butter, add cream, nuts, flour, etc, and last whites of eggs

Line a pan with buttered paper, mixing the light and dark as desired, and bake slowly two hours.   Mrs. G. M. Lowry.

A FAVORITE SPONGE CAKE

1 C Sugar
½ C Water
6 Eggs

1 C Flour
1 t B P.

Boil sugar and water for five minutes. While hot, pour over the beaten egg-whites and beat until cold, add the well beaten yolks and flavor Add flour with B. P. sifted five times. Bake forty-five minutes.   Mrs C. W Brown.

FAIRY GINGERBREAD

½ C butter
1 C granulated sugar
¼ C molasses
½ C sweet milk
2 eggs

2 C flour
1 lb. ginger
½ t soda
½ t ground cinnamon
2 t B. P.

Cream, butter and sugar well together, add molasses, then milk, then add all dry ingredients which have been previously sifted three times together—then add eggs, well beaten, and pour into large buttered tin—Bake about 25 minutes Do not have oven extremely hot at first
                    Mrs Frank Harryman.

GINGER BREAD

⅛ C Lard   1½ t Soda
⅛ C Butter   ⅛ t Salt
½ C B. Sugar   1½ C Flour
2 Eggs   1½ t Ginger
½ C Molasses

Cream butter and lard, add sugar, beaten eggs and molasses, then add the mixed and sifted ingredients and half cup of boiling water. Pour into a greased pan and bake in a slow oven for thirty minutes.

Mrs. J. H. Black.

GRANDMOTHER'S GINGER BREAD

½ C Butter   2 Eggs
1 C Sugar   1 t Ginger
1 C Molasses   1 t Cloves
1 C Sour Milk   1 t Cinnamon
2 t Soda   1 C Raisins
4 C Flour   The grated rind of an orange

Cream the butter and sugar, add eggs beaten very light, spices and molasses. (Black New Orleans Molasses, not syrup.) Sift flour twice before measuring Add soda and sift again, mixing it in alternately with the sour milk. To be rather a soft mixture. Add the orange peel and raisins which have been rolled in flour. Bake one-half hour in a moderate oven.

Mrs. G. M. Lowry.

SOFT GINGER BREAD WITH SOUR MILK

1 C Sugar   4 Eggs
¾ C Butter   1 t Cinnamon
1 C Molasses   ¼ t Allspice
1 C Sour Milk   ¼ t Cloves
2½ C Flour   ½ t Vanilla
2 t Soda   ½ t Lemon

Cream butter and sugar. Add molasses, beaten egg-yolks, then sour milk alternately with the dry ingredients which have been sifted together; the flavoring and lastly the stiffly beaten egg whites. Bake in a slow oven forty-five minutes.

Mrs. C. L. Davidson.

HURRY CAKE

1 C Sugar   2 t B. P.
2 Eggs   Flavoring
1½ C Flour

Break eggs in cup, add enough sweet cream to fill the cup. Beat sugar, cream and eggs well. Add flour and B. P.

Mrs. Carrie Steel.

JAM CAKE

½ C Butter
1 C Sugar
3 Eggs, well beaten
3 T Sour Cream
1½ C Flour

1 t Soda
1 t Cinnamon
½ t Nutmeg
1 C Blackberry Jam

Add soda to cream. Mix in usual manner. Bake in layers, using white frosting. Other jams can be used.

Mrs. B. H. Campbell.

KATHRYN'S CHOCOLATE CAKE AND ICING

½ C Butter
1½ C Sugar
½ C Cold Water
¼ C Boiling Water

1¾ C Pastry Flour
3 Eggs
2 Squares Chocolate
½ t Vanilla

Cream sugar and butter. Add beaten egg-yolks, then chocolate which has been melted and mixed with the *boiling* water; add the cold water and beat well. Add 1 C of the flour which has been sifted three times; beat well and add the ¾ C of flour which has been sifted with B P three times. Add vanilla and lastly fold in the stiffly beaten egg-whites. Pour into an unbuttered tin which has a piece of oiled paper in the bottom and bake in a very slow fire at first. When cake has raised, increase the heat a little. Bake forty or fifty minutes

Icing—
1 C Sugar
1/3 C Water

2 Eggs
¼ t Vanilla

Boil sugar and water until a medium hard ball will form when dropped in cold water Let set until all the bubbles disappear; then pour over the stiffly beaten egg-whites and beat until the mixture is cold, add vanilla and spread upon cake.

Mrs. C. L. Davidson.

LADY BALTIMORE

1 C Butter
2 C Powdered Sugar
1 C Milk
6 egg-whites

4 C Flour
4 t B. P.
½ Lemon Juice

This is used at many Southern house parties.
Cream butter and sugar, add milk. When well mixed, stir in the juice of lemon and whip very light. Then stir in alternately the stiffened egg-whites and flour, which has been sifted twice with baking powder. Bake in three layers. When cold, put together with following filling:

LADY BALTIMORE (Filling)

3 C Granulated Sugar
1 C Water
3 Egg-Whites

1 C Seeded Raisins
½ C Halved Pecans
5 Figs

Boil sugar in water until it hairs, pour while boiling over the eggs, (which have been whipped to a standing froth). Whip quickly until you have a thick cream, then stir in raisins, pecans, and figs (that have been soaked soft in lukewarm water, dried and minced).

Mrs. Chester Long.

MARBLE CAKE

White Part
4 Egg-Whites
1½ C Sugar
2/3 C Butter

½ C Milk
1 t Cream of Tartar
½ t Soda
1 2/3 C Flour

Dark Part
4 Egg-Yolks
1 C B. Sugar
½ C Molasses
½ C Butter

½ C Sour Milk
1 t Soda
1 t All kinds of Spices
1 2/3 C. Flour

Bake in square tin. Place T of the light and dark cake batter in the tin, hit and miss. The light part makes a good layer cake.

Mrs. L. C. Jackson.

ONE EGG CAKE

1 C Sugar
2 C Flour
1 Egg
2/3 C Milk

1 T Butter
1 t Vanilla
2 t B. P.

Beat until light.

Mrs. Warren Brown.

OREGON FRUIT CAKE

2 C Sugar
2 C Butter
5 Eggs
2 pt Flour
1 t Soda (dissolved in a little
boiling water)
1 t Vanilla

1 t Lemon
1 lb. Dates (cut fine)
½ lb. Citron (cut fine)
1 lb. Currants
1 lb. Raisins
¼ C Candied Orange and
Lemon Peel (cut fine)

Bake in moderate oven.

Mrs. Erwin Taft.

1-2-3-4 CAKE

1 C Butter	1 C Milk or Cold Water
2 C Sugar	3 Level t B P.
3 C Flour	Flavoring
4 Eggs	

Mix in usual manner, bake in layers, and ice. This makes a good nut cake by adding one cup of nut meats and baking in a loaf.

Mrs. R. B. Campbell.

POTATO CAKE

1 C Butter	4 Eggs
2 C Sugar	1 t Cinnamon
2 C Flour	½ t Cloves
1 C Potato	½ t Nutmeg
½ C Milk	4 t B. P.
2 Squares Chocolate	2 t Vanilla
1 C English Walnuts or Pecans	

Mash potatoes as for table use; melt chocolate Cream butter and sugar, add yolks well beaten, potatoes and milk; then flour, B. P. spices, vanilla, chocolate and nuts. Beat well and last fold in whites stiffly beaten. Bake in layers Use either white or chocolate frosting.

Mrs. H. G Norton.

SPONGE CAKE

4 Eggs	2 t B. P.
1 C Sugar	4 T Boiling Water
1 C Flour	

Beat the yolks of the eggs until yellow and creamy, add sugar, beat well, and water, then add flour and baking powder. Add beaten whites last Bake in loaf or layers. Use any filling.

Mrs. M. Murdock.

SPONGE CAKE

1 C Sugar	1 t B. P.
2 Eggs	½ C Hot Milk
1 C Pastry Flour	⅛ t Salt

Put sugar in mixing bowl, break eggs into it, beat until very creamy with Dover egg beater, then add flour and B. P, last add hot milk. Bake in moderate oven twenty-five or thirty minutes.

Mrs. Steel.

SHORT CAKE

½ C Milk or Water	4 t B. P.
4 T Butter, Melted	½ t Salt
1 C Flour Sifted	2 T Sugar

Place in oven at once after mixing.

Mrs. H. W. Horn.

SOUR CREAM MOLASSES CAKE

1 C Molasses
1 C Sour Cream
2 Eggs well beaten
⅛ t Salt
1 t Cinnamon

½ t cloves
½ t Ginger
2 t Soda
2 C Flour

Dissolve the soda in sour cream. Beat mixture well and bake in moderate oven.

Mrs. Steel.

SUNSHINE CAKE

5 egg-yolks
7 Egg-Whites
1¼ C Sugar
1 C Swansdown Flour

1/3 t Cream Tartar
⅛ t Salt
Vanilla

Sift, measure and set aside flour and sugar. Whip whites to a foam, add cream of tartar and beat until very stiff, add sugar a little at a time. Beat yolks till thick, fold into whites, then gradually fold flour lightly through. Bake in Turks head pan in moderate oven from thirty to forty minutes.

Mrs. W. E. Stanley.

SUNSHINE CAKE

10 Egg-Whites
6 Egg-Yolks
1½ C Sugar
Juice ½ Lemon

1 C Flour
1 t Cream Tartar
⅛ t Salt

Beat whites until dry, add salt as you beat. Add cream of tartar when eggs are frothy and beat until stiff. Sift sugar three times, add to whites. Beat yolks, fold into whites, then add lemon juice. Sift flour three times, fold into batter. Pour into unbuttered pan. Bake fifty minutes to one hour in slow oven.

Mrs. Will Dixon.

SURPRISE CAKE

1 C Sugar
½ C Butter
2 Eggs
1 C Milk

2½ C Swansdown Cake Flour sifted before mixing
3½ t B. P.

Cream butter and sugar, add well beaten egg-yolks. Sift flour and baking powder together three times. Add alternately with milk. Fold in stiffly beaten whites and flavor. Bake in a layer or loaf, but is especially nice in loaf.

Mrs. C. V. Ferguson.

SPICE CAKE

2 C B. Sugar
½ C Butter
2 Eggs
1 C Sour Milk
1 t Soda
¼ Nutmeg, grated
⅓ t Salt

1 t B P
2½ C Flour, Sifted before
measuring
½ t Cloves
1 t Allspice
1½ t Cinnamon

Cream butter and sugar, add beaten yolks and salt. Then add the milk with soda, then 2/3 of flour. Beat thoroughly two minutes. Add remaining flour with B P Add spices and lastly fold in egg-whites. This makes two layers Spread with boiled icing.

Mrs. C. V. Ferguson.

VELVET SPONGE CAKE

4 Eggs
2 Scant C Sugar
2 C Flour

2 t B P.
2 t Vanilla
2/3 C Boiling Water

Beat eggs very light, add all sugar, beat, add flour sifted with B. P., add vanilla This makes a very stiff batter Then add slowly at first, boiling water. This makes a very thin batter Bake from thirty to forty minutes in very, very slow oven.

Mrs. Henry J Allen

MRS. WOODROW WILSON'S WEDDING CAKE

1½ C Sugar
¾ C Butter
6 Egg-Whites
1 C Milk

3½ C Swansdown Flour
3½ t B P
1 t Vanilla, Lemon or Rose
Flavoring

Beat whites of eggs very stiff—add spoonful at a time of the creamed butter and sugar to eggs, then add flavoring Pour in one C milk and before stirring add all at once flour previously sifted four times with B. P. Line bottom of pan with paper, if you use square pan, grease the corners slightly, otherwise, do not This makes a large loaf

WHITE LAYER CAKE

½ C Butter
3 t B. P.
2½ C Cake Flour
1 C Milk

1½ C Sugar
1 t Orange Extract
6 Egg-Whites

Cream well butter and sugar, add slowly milk, and flour with B. P., then add egg-whites, with extract

Mrs. H. W. Lewis

WHITE FRUIT CAKE

1 C Butter	1 lb. Figs
2 C Sugar	1 lb Almonds
1 C Milk	¼ lb. Citron
2½ C Flour	1 C Cocoanut
2 t B. P.	1 t Grated Lemon
7 egg-whites	1 t Vanilla

Cream butter and sugar, add sweet milk, flour in which B. P. has been sifted, egg-whites, well beaten, seeded raisins, figs and almonds chopped fine, citron, freshly grated cocoanut, vanilla and grated lemon. Bake slowly.

Mrs. Mary C. Todd.
Mrs. Steel.

WHITE CAKE

1½ C Sugar	3 t B. P.
2/3 C Butter	4 egg-whites, well beaten
1 C Milk or Water	1 t Vanilla
3 C Flour	

Mix in usual manner. Bake in layers.

Mrs. H. W. Horn.

YELLOW SPONGE TEA CAKES

4 Eggs	1 C Flour
1 C Sugar	1 t B. P.
¼ C Milk	1 t Vanilla

Beat yolks of eggs and sugar very light Add whites last thing and bake in little patty pans in a moderate oven.

Mrs W E. Stanley.

CAKE HINTS

Good cake is attained only by careful measuring, more careful mixing and most careful baking.

Pastry flour makes a finer and more delicate cake than ordinary flour.

Too much will cause a cake to bake with a hump in the center, to be tough and stiff and usually to crack open. Too much baking powder will make it coarse and cause it to dry quickly.

Give the batter a vigorous beating after you add the flour. The well-beaten egg-whites should be added last, folding them into the batter very gently.

Sweet milk makes cake that cuts like pound cake; sour milk makes spongy, light cake.

Always sift flour before measuring, then it may be sifted again with the baking powder to insure their being thoroughly blended.

In making fruit cakes, add the fruit before putting in the flour, as this will prevent it falling to the bottom of the cake. Flouring the fruit is unnecessary unless the fruit is damp.

In creaming butter and sugar, when butter is too hard to blend easily, warm the bowl and if necessary, warm the sugar, but never warm the butter, as this will change both texture and flavor of the cake

The smaller the cake, the hotter should be the oven. Large, rich cakes require very slow baking

FROSTINGS

FROSTINGS

Caramel Filling for Cake	Mrs. A. O. Rorabaugh
Chocolate Icing	Mrs. M. Murdock
Caramel Frosting	Mrs. L. C. Jackson
Custard for Filling	Mrs. Warren Brown
	Mrs. Ralph L. Millison
Caramel Fruit Icing	Mrs. R. B. Campbell
Chocolate Sauce	Mrs. J. H. Black
Coffee Filling for Cake	Mrs. Spangler
	Per Mrs. O. D. Barnes
Frosting for Cake	
Icing	Mrs. G. M. Dickson
Lemon Filling	Mrs. W. E. Stanley
Orange Filling	Mrs. F. G. Smyth
Reliable Frosting	Mrs. C. V. Ferguson
Uncooked Icing	Mrs. W. E. Stanley
White Frosting	Mrs. Warren Brown

CARAMEL FILLING FOR CAKE

2½ C light B. sugar   ½ C cream
½ C butter   1 t vanilla

Cook sugar and cream until a drop will go to the bottom of a glass of cold water and remain in a drop. Take off the fire, add butter and beat In about 10 min. add the flavoring, vanilla or other preferred. Continue to beat until of the right consistency to use.

Mrs. A O. Rorabaugh.

CHOCOLATE ICING

2 C powdered sugar
2 T cream heated to boiling point
Spuare and ½ of chocolate

Put sugar in bowl, add cream and melted chocolate. If too thick, thin with hot cream, if too thin, add more powdered sugar.

Mrs. M Murdock.

CARAMEL FROSTING

1 C of cream or rich milk   1 C chopped fruit
½ C of butter   1 C chopped nuts
3 C of light B. sugar

Cook sugar, cream and butter until it will form a soft ball in cold water. Beat until cool. Be careful about its granulating. Add fruit and nuts

Mrs. L. C. Jackson.

CUSTARD FOR FILLING

1 egg   3 T flour
½ C sugar   1 C boiling milk
1 t vanilla   lump butter

Mix egg, sugar and flour together, heat milk to boiling point, pour over mixture, add butter and cook until thick, add flavoring and serve with whipped cream. 2 C nuts can be added

Mrs. Ralph L. Millison.
Mrs. Warren Brown

CARAMEL FRUIT ICING

3 C B. sugar   ½ C chopped nuts
1 C rich milk   ½ C chopped raisins
½ C butter

Boil the sugar, milk and butter until it makes a soft ball when tested in cold water. Remove nuts and raisins. Put on cake when beginning to cool

Mrs. Robert B. Campbell.

CHOCOLATE SAUCE

1 C sugar
1 C water
½ C chocolate

1 t flour
½ t vanilla

Cook until thick, stir occassionally. Flavor with vanilla when cool. Makes ½ pint.

Mrs. J. H. Black.

COFFEE FILLING FOR CAKE

½ lb. unsalted butter
1 t vanilla

1 C pulverized sugar
½ C coffee

Cream butter and sugar, then drop by drop, add ½ cup strong Mocha coffee; beat all the time, add vanilla. Spread between layers of cake when cool.

Mrs. Spangler.
per Mrs. O. D. Barnes

FROSTING FOR CAKE

1 t gelatine
2 t cold water
6 T hot milk

2 T melted butter
2¾ C confectioners' sugar
1 t vanilla

Soak gelatine in cold water five minutes, and dissolve in hot milk then add butter Stir in sugar until mixture is of the right consistency to spread (the amount required being about 2¾ C, and add vanilla.

ICING

1 C sugar
½ C water

1 egg-white
2-3 C nuts

Cook sugar and water until threads, pour on beaten eggs, add chopped nuts

Mrs G. M. Dickson.

LEMON FILLING

1 C sugar
¼ C water

1 lemon
2 T cornstarch

Dissolve sugar in water then put in grated rind and juice of lemon and let come to a boil. Add to this the cornstarch which has been dissolved in a little cold water. Let boil until consistency as jelly. Remove from the fire and immediately spread between the layers and on top of the cake.

Mrs. W E. Stanley.

ORANGE FILLING

½ lb confection sugar
1 T melted butter

Juice of one small orange, beat together and spread on cake.
Mrs. F. G. Smyth.

—248—

RELIABLE FROSTING

Put in upper part of double boiler 1 unbeaten egg-white, 1 C granulated sugar and three table spoons of cold water. Place over boiling water and beat continuously with a dover egg beater for 7 minutes. Remove from the fire add 12 marshmallows then beat until smooth and cool enough to spread.

Mrs C. V. Ferguson

UNCOOKED ICING

1 C powdered sugar	1 t vanilla
2 T pulv. cocoa or chocolate	¼ C coffee
1 T butter	

Mix sugar and cocoa thoroughly. Put in butter and vanilla and last add the coffee Slowly stirring until right consistency for spreading on top of cake.

Mrs. W. E. Stanley.

WHITE FROSTING

1 C sugar	¼ t cream tartar
¼ C water	¼ t B. P.
Boil till it syrups—add when cool:	4 drops vanilla

Mrs. Warren Brown

COOKIES

COOKIES

Best Cookies in the World	Mrs. C. L. Davidson
Bread Doughnuts	Mrs. C. L. Davidson
Brownies	Mrs. O. G. Hutchison
Brambles	Mrs. B. H. Campbell
Butterscotch Cookies	Mrs. Oak Throckmorton
Berlinerkause—Danish Cookies	Mrs. W. B. Buck
Comfits	Mrs. George Whitney
Christmas Cookies	Mrs. R. B. Campbell
Cookies	Mrs. W. E. Stanley
Chocolate Brownies	Christina Ross Haun
Chocolate Doughnuts	Mrs. Norton
Chocolate Fruit Cookies	Mrs. P. C. Lewis
Chocolate Cream Puff Shells	Mrs. H. J. Allen
Cookies	Mrs. H. W. Horn
Date Bars	Mrs. G. M. Lowry
Date Cakes	Mrs. H. W. Lewis
Date Cookies	Mrs. O D. Barnes
Date Sticks	Mrs. G M. Lowry
Doughnuts	Mrs. G M. Dickson
Doughnuts	Mrs. Erwin Taft
Date Confections	Mrs Erwin Taft
Doughnuts	Mrs. B. H. Campbell (Given by Mrs. Norton)
Fruit Cookies	Mrs. C. V. Ferguson
Ginger Creams	Mrs. Henry Lassen
Ginger Wafers	Mrs. B. H. Campbell
Hermits	Mrs. W. E. Stanley
Hermits	Mrs. O. G. Hutchison
Japanese Hard Tack	Margaret Long Stanley
Kisses	Christina Ross Haun
Molasses Cookies	Mrs. P. C. Lewis
Molasses Cookies	Mrs. L. C. Jackson
Molasses Cookies and Snaps	Mrs. O. D. Barnes
Nut Cookies	Mrs. Carrie Steel
Oatmeal Cookies	Mrs. W. E. Stanley
Pecan Wafers	Mrs R. B. Campbell
Potatoe Doughnuts	Mrs. W. E. Stanley
Rocks	Mrs. G. M. Lowry
Sugar Cookies	Mrs. Ralph L. Millison
Sugar Cookies	Mrs. J. P. Allen
Vanities	Mrs. Barnes

BEST COOKIES IN THE WORLD

2 C flour	1 T soft butter
2 t B P.	1 T lard
2-3 C sugar	1 egg
¼ t salt	½ C milk (may not need all)

Sift flour, baking powder, sugar and salt together; rub in with a paddle, butter and lard. Beat egg to stiff froth, add milk and mix with other ingredients.

For soft cookies roll out and bake in quick oven. For crisp snaps knead in more flour and roll thin; any flavor may be added to the milk and eggs, or the three, vanilla, lemon and orange.

Mrs. C. L. Davidson.

BREAD DOUGHNUTS

1 cake Fleischman's Yeast	½ C sugar
1¼ C milk	3 T butter
1 T sugar	¼ t mace
4½ C sifted flour	1 egg
¼ t salt	

Dissolve yeast and T sugar in luke warm liquid. Add 1½ cup flour and beat well. Cover and set aside to rise in a warm place for about 1 hour. Then add to the mixture above the butter and ½ cup sugar well creamed, mace, egg well beaten, the remainder of flour to make a moderately soft dough, add the salt. Knead lightly. Place in well greased bowl, cover and allow to rise again in a warm place about one hour. Then roll out to ¼ inch in thickness and cut with a doughnut cutter. Place on greased tins; allow to rise one hour. Fry in deep fat until a golden brown. Drain on brown paper; roll in sugar.

Mrs. C. L. Davidson.

BROWNIES

3 well beaten eggs	2 squares chocolate—melted
1 C sugar	1 t vanilla
¼ C butter—melted	1 C chopped nuts
½ C flour	

Mix in the order given Spread thin on well greased pans. Bake slowly. When baked cut in squares while hot

Mrs. O. G. Hutchison.

BRAMBLES

1 C raisins	Crust
1 C sugar	2 C flour
1 egg	1 C lard
1 lemon	6 T ice water

Mix the flour and lard, moisten with the ice water and roll out as for pie crust. Beat the egg, add the sugar and raisins and the grated rind and juice of 1 lemon. Roll out the crust ½ inch thick and spread with a little butter cut into five inch squares. Spread one diagonal half of each square with the mixture, fold the other half over it, pinch the edges together, and bake. Will make little triangular cakes when done. Very good for luncheon.

Mrs. B. H. Campbell.

BUTTERSCOTCH COOKIES

1 C butter	1 t soda
4 C B. sugar	6½ C flour
4 eggs	

Make in loaf and let stand over night in ice box. In morning slice thin and bake.

Mrs. Oak Throckmorton.

BERLINERKRAUSE—DANISH COOKIES

1 lb. butter, fresh not too salty	7 egg-yolks
1 lb. flour	½ lb. sugar

Boil three eggs hard and pulverize the yolks. Mix butter well creamed with sugar and boiled yolks. Add flour. Make into sheet, cut in strips and roll with the hands forming circle four inches in diameter. Place one end over the other. Dip this into the white of eggs and sprinkle well with crushed loaf sugar. Bake in a moderate oven until a light brown.

Mrs. W. B. Buck.

COMFITS

4 eggs	5 C flour sifted
2 C sugar	5 t B. P. put in last with three
2 C milk	cups of flour

Cream the egg-yolks and sugar. Beat egg-whites, add butter, flour then little egg-whites and repeat the process—then add last three cups of flour with baking powder. 1 t salt and 1 t of vanilla or lemon, fry in deep fat. Dropping dough from spoon.

Mrs. Geo. Whitney.

CHRISTMAS COOKIES

1 C butter	2½ C flour
1½ C sugar	1 t cinnamon
3 eggs, beaten light	½ t cloves
1 lb. dates, cut small pieces	1 t soda in 3 T hot water
2 lb. English walnuts—broken up	1 T candied orange peel, chopped fine

Mix in order given—drop in small spoonfuls on greased pan, bake in moderate oven.

Mrs. R. B. Campbell.

COOKIES

1 C butter	1½ C sugar
½ C hot water	1 C currants
3 C flour	1 t soda
¼ t nutmeg	

Beat butter to a cream, add sugar, then eggs well beaten. Dissolve soda in hot water. Stir in flour and nutmeg, then currants. Drop batter by spoonsful in well buttered tins, allowing room for spreading. Bake in a moderate oven.

Mrs. W E. Stanley.

CHOCOLATE BROWNIES

½ C chocolate	1 C nuts
½ C butter	½ C flour
1 C sugar	1 t vanilla
2 eggs, well beaten	

Melt chocolate and butter together Add ingredients in their order. Bake slowly for 30 minutes Cut in squares while hot.

Christina Ross Haun

CHOCOLATE DOUGHNUTS

¼ C butter	1½ square chocolate
1¼ C sugar	1 t soda, dissolved
2 eggs	in milk
1 C sour milk	1 t cinnamon
4 C pastry flour	½ t vanilla

Mix in the order given, roll and fry in deep fat

Mrs Norton.

CHOCOLATE FRUIT COOKIES

¼ C butter	2 eggs
1 C sugar	1 C raisins
2 T grated chocolate	1 pt. flour (at first)
2 T water	2 t B. P.

Cream butter and sugar. Mix chocolate with one tablespoonful of sugar and the water and then add to the butter and sugar Add eggs, raisins, one pint of flour, baking powder. Then add more flour until stiff enough to roll out quite thin. Bake in moderate oven.

Mrs. P. C. Lewis.

CREAM PUFF SHELLS

4 eggs	1 C flour
1 C butter	1 C boiling water

Melt butter in boiling water and stir well, add flour while boiling, stir well and cook until a thick paste. Cool. When cool, add the eggs beaten well Drop on buttered tins, bake slowly 30 or 40 minutes Fill with cream custard when cold.

Mrs H. J. Allen.

COOKIES

2 C sugar
3 eggs
¼ C sour milk

1 t soda in sour milk
½ C butter
½ C lard

Cream shortening and sugar. Add well beaten eggs. Dissolve soda in the milk and add to the mixture. Add just enough flour to roll. Cut and bake in moderate oven.

Mrs. H. W. Horn.

DATE BARS

1 C sugar
3 eggs
⅛ t salt
1 C flour

1 t B. P.
1 t vanilla
1 lb. dates
1 C chopped nuts

Beat the eggs thoroughly, and add sugar, salt and flavoring. Mix dates, nuts, flour and baking powder, together, and add eggs and sugar. Bake in a slow oven. Cut while hot into bars of the size desired, roll in powdered sugar.

Mrs. G. M. Lowry.

DATE CAKES

1 C butter
1½ C sugar
¼ t cloves
3 T hot water
1½ lb English walnuts,
    unshelled

3 C flour
3 eggs
1 t cinnamon
1 t soda
1 lb. dates
1½ T vinegar

Cream, butter and sugar, add eggs, vinegar, soda, dissolve in hot water, flour sifted with cinnamon and cloves, then put in nuts and dates, drop by spoonsful on buttered tin or bake in small gem pans.

Mrs. H. W. Lewis.

DATE COOKIES

1 C butter
1½ C sugar
2½ C flour
3 eggs
1 lb. dates

1 lb. English walnuts
2 t soda
3 t hot water
1 t cinnamon
¼ t cloves

Dissolve soda in hot water; beat eggs; seed and chop dates; break nuts in small pieces; stir all together. Flour tins, drop with teaspoon far apart. Bake in moderate oven.

Mrs. O. D. Barnes.

DATE STICKS

2 eggs
1 C sugar
1 lb. dates
1 C nuts

3½ T flour
1 t B. P.
⅛ t salt

Mix in the order given. Bake in very slow oven in thin sheets, cut in sticks.

DOUGHNUTS

1 C sugar
1 C sour milk
2 eggs
5 T melted butter

1 t soda
¼ t salt
1 qt. flour

Mix sugar and milk first. Sift flour, soda and salt three times. Add 5 T melted butter.

Mrs. G. M Dickson.

DOUGHNUTS

2 C hot mashed potatoes
2 C sugar
1 C milk
3 eggs (beaten separately)
1 t salt

½ T nutmeg
3 T melted butter
5 C flour
5 t B. P.

Mix potatoes with sugar, add milk, eggs, salt, nutmeg, butter. Add flour into which baking powder has been sifted.

Mrs. Erwin Taft.

DATE CONFECTIONS

½ lb. almonds (unblanched)
½ lb. dates
4 egg-whites

2 C sugar
1½ t vanilla

Beat egg-whites. Add sugar, dates, almonds and vanilla. Drop on buttered tins, bake in moderate oven till light brown. Leave on buttered tins until cold.

Mrs. Erwin Taft

DOUGHNUTS

1 pt. sweet milk
2 eggs
1 1-3 C sugar
2 T butter, melted
¼ C melted lard

Juice and grated rind of 1 lemon
½ t soda
4 t B. P.
Salt and grated nutmeg

Flour enough to make a dough as soft as can be handled. Roll out on a floured board, cut into desired size, and fry in deep fat. When done roll in pulverized sugar. They should brown and cook quickly. To test break one open to see if it is cooked through.

Mrs. B H. Campbell.
(Given by Mrs. Norton)

FRUIT COOKIES

2 C sugar
1 C raisins
½ C lard
½ C butter
2 eggs

½ C nuts
½ C hot water
4½ C bread flour
1½ T vanilla
1 T soda

Cream butter, lard and sugar; then add the raisins chopped and mixed with a little of the flour; then the beaten eggs, nuts and soda dissolved in the hot water; then the flour and vanilla. Roll, cut, bake in moderate oven.

Mrs. C. V. Ferguson.

GINGER CREAMS

1 C sugar
¾ C molasses
½ C fat (butter or any of the substitutes)
1 egg
1 t ginger

½ t each cinnamon, cloves
    and nutmeg
2 t soda
1 C hot water
3½ C flour

Sift 3 cups of flour and spices together, the one half cup is set aside for further use. Mix sugar, fat and molasses together, then beat in egg until it is creamy. Dissolve soda in hot water and add to mixture then stir until smooth. Add flour and beat. This should be the consistence to drop easily from a spoon. If too thin add the half cup flour. Drop from spoon and bake. These cakes are glazed over with following icing.

2 T melted butter   2 C powdered sugar

1 to 3 T warm coffee, beat to cream and spread on cakes.

Mrs. Henry Lassen.

GINGER WAFERS

1 C butter
1 C water
Ginger to taste

2 C sugar, sifted
4 C flour, sifted

Beat thoroughly. Use if possible, baking sheets, or rimless cooking pans, or the bottom of baking pans turned upside down. Bake slowly, watch carefully to avoid scorching. Remove from oven to straight rolls or cornucopias. These wafers will be brittle as soon as they are cold, so must be handled quickly.

Mrs. B. H. Campbell.

HERMITS

3 C flour
1½ C sugar
1½ C raisins
1 t cloves
½ t ginger

3 eggs
1 C butter
1½ C nuts
1 t cinnamon
½ t soda

Cream butter and sugar and add eggs beaten light. Mix flour, spices, raisins, and nuts. Add soda, in ¼ C of boiling water to egg mixture, then combine the 2 mixtures.

Mrs. W. E. Stanley.

HERMITS

1 egg	½ t B. P
1 C sugar	½ t cloves
1-3 C butter	½ t cinnamon
2 C flour	½ t nutmeg
1-3 C sweet milk	½ t allspice
½ t soda	½ C chopped raisins

Cream butter and sugar. Add eggs well beaten   Mix soda and baking powder with the flour. Add alternately with milk to the mixture. Add raisins and spices   Drop from spoon into greased pan and bake.

Mrs. O. G. Hutchison

JAPANESE HARD TACK

12 dates	¾ C flour
12 walnuts	1 t B P.
1 lb orange marmalade	2 eggs
1 C sugar	

Stone dates and chop with walnuts. Sift sugar, flour and baking powder. Add beaten eggs then fruit and nuts. Mix well. Spread on greased roasting pan and bake 20 minutes in moderate oven. Cut in bars and roll in sugar.

To double recipe use 3 eggs, add a little water and double amount of other ingredients.

Margaret Long Stanley.

KISSES

2 egg-whites	½ C cocoanut (dry)
¼ C sugar	1 t vanilla
2 C Post Toasties	

Beat eggs stiff, add sugar gradually—then add Post Toasties, cocoanut and flavoring. Bake in a moderate oven. Makes 16.

Christina Ross Haun.

MOLASSES COOKIES

1 C sugar	1 t ginger
1 C molasses	2 t cinnamon
1 C butter (large cup)	1 t soda (in C water or C of
¼ t salt	coffee)

Mix in order given, knead the dough soft.

Mrs. P C Lewis.

MOLASSES COOKIES

1 C sugar	1 T ginger
1 C molasses	1 t cinnamon
½ C butter	½ t salt
½ C lard	2 eggs, well beaten
1 T soda	5 C flour

Reserve one C of the flour for rolling the cookies.

Mix in the order given. Roll one half inch thick and bake in a moderate oven.

Mrs. L. C. Jackson.

MOLASSES COOKIES AND SNAPS

1 C molasses	½ C raisins
1 C B sugar	2 t soda
2-3 C butter	½ t vanilla
1 t ginger	4½ C flour

Cream sugar and butter, add molasses and flavoring with 4 C flour and soda. Take one half of mixture and roll ½ inch thick; sift over with granulated sugar; place raisin in center, and bake in moderate oven Add ½ C flour to remainder roll, thin, and bake a golden brown.

Mrs. O. D. Barnes.

NUT COOKIES

1½ C sugar	1 lb. raisins
1 C butter	1 lb. nuts
3 eggs	1 t cinnamon
2½ C flour	¼ t cloves
1 t salt	1 t soda
8 T boiling water	

Cream butter and sugar, add eggs, salt and flour. Add soda dissolved in hot water. Then add raisins, nuts, cinnamon and cloves. Drop with spoon in baking sheets and bake in moderate oven.

Mrs. Carrie Steel.

OATMEAL COOKIES

1 C butter	2 C raisins
1 C sugar	8 t milk
2 C flour	1 t cinnamon
2 C oatmeal flakes	½ t soda
¼ t salt	

Beat butter and sugar to a cream, add other ingredients. Drop from a spoon on well buttered tins and bake in moderate oven.

Mrs. W. E. Stanley.

PECAN WAFERS

1 C B. sugar	¼ t salt
2 eggs	1 C pecans
3 T flour	1 t vanilla
¼ t B. P.	

Mix all ingredients together in the order given and spread out very thin on a baking sheet or buttered pan and bake 10 minutes in modern oven. Cut into squares while warm

Mrs. Robert B. Campbell.

POTATOE DOUGHNUTS

¾ C sugar	1 egg-white
2½ C flour	3 t B. P.
¼ C milk	1 T butter
1 C potatoes	1 t salt
3 eggs	1 t mace

Cream the butter and sugar and the well beaten eggs Stir in the potatoes and milk. Sift baking powder with the flour

and add salt, mace, and nutmeg, and add to first mixture work-
ing in additional flour as necessary to handle lightly. Roll and
cut all doughnuts before attending to frying. Have lard three
inches deep in kettle, and test temperature with a small cake
cut from the center of the doughnut.

Mrs. W. E. Stanley

ROCKS

1½ C B. sugar	1 C butter
3 eggs	A little salt
3 C flour	1 t soda
1 t cinnamon	1 C chopped nuts
1½ C raisins or dates	1 t B. P.

Cream butter and brown sugar, add well beaten eggs, cinnamon and salt. Add the flour, which has been sifted with the
baking powder and soda. Then add nuts, raisins and dates.
Mix well and drop on greased pan and bake.

Mrs. G. M. Lowry.

SUGAR COOKIES

2 C sugar	2 t B. P.
2-3 C butter	2 t vanilla
2 eggs	1 t salt
1 C sweet milk	

Cream butter and sugar together; add eggs well beaten then
the milk, B. P., vanilla and salt. Add sufficient flour to make a
soft dough; roll very thin; cut and bake in a hot oven.

Mrs. Ralph L. Millison

SUGAR COOKIES

1 C butter	3 eggs
2 C sugar	½ t nutmeg
1 C milk	3 t B. P.
2 C flour	

Cream sugar and butter. Add beaten eggs and milk. Sift
B. P. in flour. Roll out soft as you can, cut.

Mrs. J. P. Allen

VANITIES

2 eggs	1 C flour
1 T butter	¼ C powdered sugar
1 T sugar	

Cream butter and sugar, add beaten eggs and flour, roll
very thin, cut out with cookey cutter, drop in hot fat when
light-brown, turn over and lift out with large fork—sift over P.
sugar and a little cinnamon. Will make 25.

Mrs. Barnes.

PICKLES

PICKLES

Celery French Pickles	Mrs. G. M. Dickson
Cherry Olives for Pickles	Mrs. Smyth.
Chili Sauce	Mrs. Finlay Ross.
Chili Sauce	Mrs. W. E. Stanley
Chow Chow	Mrs. G. M. Lowry
Corn Relish	Mrs. C. V. Ferguson.
Corn Relish	Mrs. W E. Stanley.
Cucumber Pickles, French	Mrs. Steel.
Cucumber and Onion Pickle	Mrs. Oak Throckmorton.
Delicious Pickles	Mrs. R. L. Millison.
Favorite Pickle, My Mother's	Mrs G. M. Dickson.
Meat Relish	Mrs. Zartman.
Mexican Relish	Mrs J. H Black
Mixed Pickles	Cooking Club.
Mustard Pickles	Mrs. C. L. Davidson.
Pepper Hash Pickle	Mrs Gilbert Tucker.
Pickled Oysters	Mrs. Baldwin.
Sliced Tomato Pickles	Mrs. G. M. Lowry.
Spiced Pickled Eggs	Mrs R. L. Millison.
Sweet Pickled Peaches	Mrs C. L. Davidson.
Sweet Pickles	Mrs Cheser l Long.
Tiny Tim Pickles	Mrs. C. L. Davidson.
Tomato Pickle, Green	Cooking Club
Tomato Pickles, Sliced	Mrs. O D. Barnes.
Tomato Relish	Mrs H. W. Lewis.
Tomato Relish, Green	Cooking Club.
Tomato Sweet Pickles	Mrs. Strong.

CELERY FRENCH PICKLES

1 pk cucumbers, pared
2 heads cabbage
1 doz. green peppers
1 doz. large onions
1 gal. vinegar
¾ lb mustard seed
2 oz. celery
1 oz. tumerac
3 C sugar

Chop cucumber, cabbage, peppers and onions fine, salt down over night, squeeze out next morning. Then mix with celery, mustard, tumerac, sugar and vinegar. Let it come to a boil, seal in jars

Mrs G. M. Dickson

CHERRY OLIVES FOR PICKLES

Fill a jar with clean ripe cherries with stems. Mix 1 cup soft water, 1 cup vinegar, 1 T salt, 1 T sugar together and cover cherries. Seal. No cooking. Everything cold.

Mrs. Smyth.

CHILI SAUCE

½ bu ripe tomatoes
3 medium sized onions
5 t black pepper
5 T salt
5 C B. sugar (small)
1 doz. mango peppers
½ doz small red peppers
5 t ground cloves
5 C vinegar

Chop or run through grinder. Boil 1 hour. Will make 15 pts.

Mrs Finlay Ross

CHILI SAUCE

8 qt. tomatoes
1½ C green peppers, ground
½ C salt
2 t cinnamon
2 t nutmeg
¼ t red pepper
2 C onion, ground
3 C sugar
1 pt. vinegar
1 t ginger
1 t cloves

Add spices and vinegar and cook for about 2 hrs

Mrs. W. E. Stanley

CHOW CHOW

Chop fine one peck of green tomatoes, two heads of cabbage, six large onions, six green, and three red peppers. Sprinkle over the mixture one teacup of salt, let it sand for twelve hours, then drain. Heat two quarts of vinegar, two quarts of water, and lump of alum size of hickory nut dissolved in it. Put chow in and scald a few minutes, then drain. Heat one gallon of good vinegar with four cups of sugar, two tablespoons of cinnamon, two of allspice, one of cloves, one nutmeg grated. Put chow in and scald a few minutes, and it is ready for use.

Mrs. G. M Lowry.

CORN RELISH

12 ears corn
12 green peppers, chopped
1 qt. onions, after chopped
1 qt. cucumbers, after chopped
2 qts ripe tomatoes, after chopped

1 qt. C sugar
1½ qts. vingar
1 oz. celery seed
1 oz. white mustard seed
3 large red peppers

Cook 50 minutes or a little longer, if too thin. Can while hot.

Mrs. C. V. Ferguson

CORN RELISH OR DELICIOUS PICKLE

2 qt. tomatoes
1 qt. onion
1 qt. cucumbers
1 qt. sugar
2 qt. vinegar
½ oz. celery

1 doz ears corn or 2 cans
1 doz green mango peppers
3 red chile peppers
½ oz. tumeric
1 C salt

Cut corn off the cob, chop or put through the grinder tomatoes, onions, cucumbers and peppers. Put all the ingredients together and boil 40 minutes. Seal in glass jars while hot.

Mrs. W. E. Stanley

CUCUMBER PICKLES

1 gal vinegar
1 C mustard
1 C salt

1 C sugar
cucumbers (number depends on size of them)

To vinegar, add other ingredients and put in half gallon jars and seal.

Mrs. Carrie Steel.

CUCUMBER AND ONION PICKLE

12 large cucumbers, sliced
12 large onions, sliced
1 pound sugar

1 qt. vinegar
1 oz. mustard seed
1 t white pepper

Let cucumbers stand in salt water over night. Drain well and then add all other ingredients. Let boil up. Can and seal.

Mrs. Oak Throckmorton

DELICIOUS PICKLES

1 doz. ears corn
1 pt. onions after cut in small pieces
1 doz. green peppers
1 pt. ripe cucumbers
2½ pts. ripe tomatoes

½ C salt
2 pts. vinegar
1 pt. sugar
1 oz. mustard seed
½ oz. tumeric
3 large peppers

Cut corn from cob, add onions chopped fine then peppers, cucumbers, tomatoes, red peppers chopped fine. Add to this the salt, vinegar, sugar, mustard seed and last the tumeric. Boil 50 minutes and seal.

Mrs. Ralph L. Millison.

FAVORITE PICKLE, MY MOTHER'S

1 qt raw cabbage, chopped fine   1 C sugar
1 qt. boiled beets, chopped fine   1 t salt
1 t black pepper   ¼ t red pepper
1 t grated horseradish
     Cover with cold vinegar and keep from air

                                      Mrs G M Dickson.

MEAT RELISH

4 C beets   2 C cabbage
1 C sugar   ½ C horseradish, grated
⅛ t salt   vinegar to cover
     Mix diced beets finely chopped cabbage, sugar and grated horseradish (the bottled will do), salt, cover with vinegar It makes an unusually fine relish, can be made quickly and can be used at once.

                                 Mrs. Ed. Zartman.

MEXICAN RELISH

1 can pimento, cut fine   2 C chopped sweet cucumber
2 C chopped onion   pickle
¾ C sugar   1 C vinegar
2 C chopped cabbage   1 level t salt
     Mix well but do not cook.

                                  Mrs. J. H Black.

MIXED PICKLES

1 pk green tomatoes   3 C strong vinegar
1 good sized cauliflower   1 C water
3 cucumbers   2 C sugar
4 large onions, sliced   1 T salt
     Slice and let green tomatoes stand in salt over night, drain off in the morning. Cook thoroughly till done.

                                   Cooking Club.

MUSTARD PICKLES

1 qt tomatoes, green   1 qt vinegar
1 qt onions   2 C sugar
1 qt. cauliflower   1 C flour
1 qt cucumbers   6 T mustard
                             1 T tumeric
     Chop coarse and prepare for pickling
     Cook and then add chopped stuff   Seal

                                Mrs C. L. Davidson

PEPPER HASH PICKLE

12 red sweet peppers   3 onions
12 green sweet peppers
     Grind in meat grinder or cut in small pieces. Pour boiling water over mixture and let stand ten minutes Repeat second time; drain each time.
3 T salt   2 C sugar
2 pt vinegar
     Cook all 15 minutes. Can.

                                Mrs. Gilbert Tucker.

PICKLED OYSTERS

⅛ t salt
1 qt. large oysters
1 pt white vinegar
1 doz. blades mace

1 doz. whole cloves
1 doz whole black peppers
½ doz. red pepper, broken into bits.

Put oysters and liquor into a porcelain kettle, and heat slowly until very hot, not boiling. Take out the oysters and to the liquor add vinegar and spices. Let boil up fairly well, then pour this over the oysters Cover the jar and keep in a cool place. Next day put them into glass jars with tight tops. Keep in the dark where not liable to become heated. May be kept at least 3 weeks.

Mrs. Baldwin.

SLICED TOMATO PICKLES

1 peck green tomatoes
1 doz onions
6 red peppers
1 C sugar
1 T mustard

1 T cinnamon
1 T allspice
1 T cloves
Cayenne pepper to taste
3 pts vinegar

Put in preserving kettle, alternating tomatoes and onions. Mix spices and sugar with the vinegar; pour over all. Let boil slowly until very tender.

Mrs. G. M. Lowry.

SPICED PICKLED EGGS

Take as many hard boiled eggs as will fill a jar. Scald vinegar enough to cover, add pepper, allspice, cloves, and a stick of cinnamon. Pour boiling hot water over eggs and seal. Let stand a month before serving. Serve with cold meats

Mrs Ralph.L. Millison

SWEET PICKLED PEACHES

8 lbs. peaches
6 lbs. sugar
1 pt. vinegar

1 doz cloves
few sticks whole cinnamon

Boil all together until peaches are tender.

Mrs. C. L. Davidson.

SWEET PICKLE

2 T alum
7 lb. melon rind or fruit
½ C salt
2 gal. water
3 lb. sugar

2 oz. cinnamon
1 oz mace
½ oz. cloves
1 qt. vinegar

Lay fruit in brine over night made of the water and salt. In morning pour off brine and dissolve alum in 2 gal. of water. Pour over fruit and boil ½ hour. Pour off this water and add to the fruit the sugar, cinnamon, mace, cloves and vinegar, and boil 30 minutes. Or heat syrup daily and pour over fruit for 6 days, not boiling fruit.

Mrs. Chester I. Long.

TINY TIM PICKLES

\ Select tiny cucumbers of uniform size, pour on hot brine and boil 10 min., let stand 24 hrs. Take out and wash well, then cover them with vinegar and water (half and half) and let stand 5 days, put in glass jars and pour over them the following liquid:

1 gal. vinegar	2 oz white mustard seed
1 lb sugar	1 stick horseradish
1 T cloves	1 oz stick cinnamon
1 T black peppers, whole	1 oz ginger root
12 green peppers, cut up	½ oz whole mace
1 bunch garlic	½ oz. allspice

Put above ingredients on stove and boil together till peppers are perfectly soft It is better not strained. Recipe makes about 8 quarts

Mrs. C. L. Davidson.

TOMATO PICKLES, GREEN

1 pk green tomatoes	2 T cinnamon
½ pk onions	2 T ginger
½ lb. mustard seed	2 T black pepper
2 lb. B sugar	2 T Curry powder
½ t Cayenne pepper	2 T celery seed
2 t mace	2 T tumeric
2 t allspice	1 gal vinegar
2 t cloves	¼ C horseradish

Drain green tomatoes and onions over night Put in kettle and sprinkle with mustard seed. Mix brown sugar and spices together with a little cold vinegar, then add enough to make a gallon; sprinkle horseradish in, cook until tomatoes are a bright yellow. This is splendid

Cooking Club.

TOMATO PICKLES, SLICED

1 pk green tomatoes	6 large green peppers
12 good sized onions	½ C salt
3 large red peppers	1½ lb B. sugar
2 qts. vinegar	4 doz cloves
1 oz. celery	1½ T ground mustard
¼ lb. white mustard seed	2 T mixed spices

Slice onions, tomatoes, and peppers; salt; let stand over night, drain; cover with 1 pt vinegar, 1 pt. water, and cook 20 min. Let stand all day, and drain at night. Let vinegar, sugar and spices come to a boil, pour over pickles When cold add ½ C vinegar mixed with mustard. This will keep in stone jars where it is cool.

Mrs. O. D Barnes.

TOMATO RELISH

½ pk. tomatoes
6 large onions
4 bunches celery
1 oz. white mustard seed

1 C horseradish
1 C sugar
½ C salt
1 qt. cider vinegar

Chop tomatoes, tie in bag and let all water drop out over night, buy horseradish and grind in. Seal without cooking.

Mrs. H. W. Lewis.

TOMATO RELISH, GREEN

1 pk. green tomatoes
6 large onions
6 green sweet peppers
2 C celery, chopped
1 C salt

2 lb. B. sugar
2 T white mustard seed
1 T ground cinnamon
white vinegar

Chop tomatoes, onions, peppers, celery, fine, and mix salt with it. Then put in cloth and drain all night Then take brown sugar, mustard seed and cinnamon, cover with white vinegar, and it is ready for use.

Cooking Club.

TOMATO SWEET PICKLES

Slice green tomatoes and sprinkle with salt, let stand 24 hrs. and then soak fresh. Scald with weak vinegar and wash in fresh water. Let stand a while. To 5 lbs. of tomatoes, use 4 lbs sugar, and vinegar enough to make a syrup to cover them. After vinegar and sugar boil, put in tomatoes and scald until clear, add whole mace and cinnamon. Just before taking off range, add 1 lb. of raisins left on the stem. Let remain on fire until well plumped out.

Mrs. Strong.

Conserves

CONSERVE

Amber Preserves	Mrs. C. L. Jackson
Blue Plum Conserve	Mrs. R. B. Campbell
Cranberry Jelly	Mrs. Finley Ross
English Rhubarb	Mrs. J. H. Black
Four Fruit Jam	Mrs. F. G. Smyth
Fruit Conserve	Mrs. J. H. Black
Gooseberry Conserve	Mrs. Geo C. Strong
Green Grape Conserve	Mrs. G. N. Dickson
Grape Fruit or Orange Straws	Mrs. A. O. Rorabaugh
Ginger Pairs	Mrs. J. H. Black
Grape Conserve	Mrs. Harry Dockum
Peach and Orange Marmalade	Mrs. Black
Peach Pineapple	Mrs R. B. Campbell
Pear Conserve	Mrs. Ross
Quince Marmalade	Mrs. H. W. Horn
Red Tomato Preserves	Mrs. H. W. Horn
Rhubarb Raisin and Black-berry Conserve	Mrs. Newton Garst
Strawberry Preserves	Mrs. C. L. Davidson
Strawberry Preserves	Mrs. F. A. Amsden
Spiced Gooseberries	Mrs E. G. Robertson
Spiced Peaches or Pears	Mrs. W. E Stanley
Tomato Marmalade	Cooking Club
Tutti Frutti Jam	Mrs. F. G. Smyth

AMBER MARMALADE

Shave one orange, one lemon and one grapefruit very thin, rejecting seeds and cores. Measure fruit and add three times the quantity of water. Let it stand over night in earthen dish and in the morning let it boil for two minutes, only. Let stand another night, and the second morning, add pint for pint of sugar. Boil until it jellies, possibly two hours. Stir as little as possible, the strips of fruit should be well defined. This makes twelve glasses

Mrs L. C. Jackson.

BLUE PLUM CONSERVE

3 lbs. plum	1 lb English walnuts
3 lbs sugar	3 oranges
1 lb. raisins	

Cut raisins and nuts in small pieces and the rind of one orange cut small. Juice and pulp of three oranges. Mix all the ingredients except nuts, and cook one hour over slow fire. Add nuts just before taking from fire.

Mrs. R B Campbell.

CRANBERRY JELLY

1 qt. cranberries	1 pt. sugar
1 pt water	

Boil cranberries and water five minutes, then strain and boil five minutes, add sugar, boil five minutes more and turn in mold.

Mrs. Finley Ross.

ENGLISH RHUBARB JAM

3 lbs rhubarb	3 oranges
3 lbs. sugar	

Cut up rhubarb, put ¾ lb of sugar over it and let stand over night Chop, peel and pulp oranges separately and put 2¼ lb. of sugar over it and let it stand over night. In the morning boil rhubarb until tender, add oranges and cook thirty min. or until it jellies.

Mrs. J. H Black.

FOUR FRUIT JAM

2 qt. cherries	1 qt. currants
1 qt red raspberries	1 qt. gooseberries
12 cloves	¾ lb. sugar

Cook slowly for 3 hrs. or until the consistency required.

Mrs. F. G. Smyth.

FRUIT CONSERVE

1 qt. pie-plant
1 qt. cherries
1 qt currant juice
1 pt. raspberries
1 lb. seeded raisins

2 oranges
2 lemons
1 lb. English walnuts
1 lb. sugar to each lb. of fruit

Pare, rind and thick white of lemons and oranges Chop pulp fine. Stew like preserves, add lemons, oranges and nuts at the last

Mrs. J H. Black.

GOOSEBERRY CONSERVE

5 lb. gooseberries
4 lb. sugar

1½ lb. raisins
4 oranges

Chop raisins fine, add gooseberries and sugar, then oranges, juice and rind chopped fine. Cook 30 min.

Mrs Geo C. Strong.

GREEN GRAPE CONSERVE

1 glass grapes
4 T water

1 glass sugar

Cook sugar and water until it threads, then add grapes and cook until tender.

Mrs. G. N. Dickson.

GRAPE FRUIT OR ORANGE STRAWS

4 oranges

5 C granulated sugar

The rinds of four oranges or fruit, cut into fine strips. Put into a kettle, cover with cold water When it comes to the boiling point, pour off the water and again cover with cold water. Do this three times, then cook until tender— drain. Have ready a thick syrup jade of 4 cups sugar and 2 cups water boiled together 5 minutes. Drop straws into white paper over your bread-board, sprinkle with sugar and allow to dry over night.

Mrs. A O. Rorabaugh.

GINGER PEARS

8 lb. hard pears
6 lb granulated sugar
4 lemons

¼ lb. green ginger root
1 C water

Slice pears very thin, use juice and yellow part of lemons. Cut ginger in small pieces. Cook well for 3 hours, or until a rich golden color.

Mrs. J. H. Black.

GRAPE CONSERVE

5 lbs. New York grapes   1 lb. nut meats
3 lbs. sugar   2 lbs seedless raisins

Squeeze out pulp—cook—rub out seeds, add the skins to pulp and other ingredients—pour in glasses and cover with parafine.

Mrs. Harry Dockum.

PEACH-PINEAPPLE MARMALADE

6 lbs. peaches   4 lbs oranges
5 lbs. sugar   4 lbs. lemons

Use juice and grated rind of oranges and lemons. Cook until clear.

Mrs Black

PEACH-PINEAPPLE MARMALADE

2 qts. sliced peaches   sugar and water
1 pt. can grated pineapple

Peel, stone and slice enough peaches to make two quarts, then add a little water and stew until tender Mash the peaches, then add the grated pineapple Allow three fourths pound of sugar to each pound of pulp. Boil to a thick marmalade and seal.

Mrs R. B. Campbell

PEAR CONSERVE

6 lb. pears   3 oranges
5 lb. sugar   ½ lb raisins
1 lb English walnuts   Rind of 2 oranges, cut fine

Cut pears in cubes. Let stand in sugar all night, simmer slowly 20 min Then cook 2 hr. and add walnuts ½ hr. before done.

Mrs. Ross

QUINCE MARMALADE

7 quinces   5 pints sugar
2 sour apples   1 pint water

Put quince and apples through meat chopper, fine. Cook 15 or 20 minutes or until it jells

Mrs. H W. Horn.

RED TOMATO PRESERVES

Skin tomatoes, weigh, cook long enough to cook through. Skim out of water, and add, ¾ lbs sugar to 1 lb. tomatoes Let stand in sugar over night In A M. add slices of lemon to taste. Let cook until clear and preserved. Seal.

Mrs. H. W Horn.

RHUBARB, RAISIN AND BLACKBERRY CONSERVE

5 C Rhubarb 1 Box Blackberries
1 lb Raisins 8 C Sugar

Peel rhubarb, cut in small pieces, clean and seed raisins, pick over berries Arrange fruit in layers with sugar, let stand over night In morning cook over slow fire. Cook thirty minutes, counting the time when mixture begins to boil. Turn into glasses. Cover with paraffin when cool.

Mrs. Newton Garst.

STRAWBERRY PRESERVES

1 qt strawberries 1 C water
1 qt. sugar

Stem, wash and drain well the berries Cook sugar and water until ready to candy. Throw the berries into boiling water, let boil hard 2 minutes, pour immediately into a colander to drain, then cook 3 minutes in heavy syrup Can hot.

Mrs. C. L. Davidson.

STRAWEERRY PRESERVES

1 lb. strawberries 1 lb sugar
1 C water

Wash and stem berries. Add 1 cup water to sugar, cook to a good heavy syrup. Add berries and cook fast for 20 or 25 min. Take from fire When cold stir lightly as berries usually come to top. Can cold.

Mrs F. A. Amsden.

SPICED GOOSEBERRIES

5 lb. gooseberries 2 T cinnamon
½ pt. vinegar 1 t mace
4 lb. B. sugar 2 T cloves

Boil 2 hours Mrs E. G Robertson.

SPICED PEACHES OR PEARS

7 lbs fruit ½ oz. whole allspice
3½ lbs sugar ½ oz. whole cloves
1 pt. vinegar ½ oz stick cinnamon

Heat vinegar and sugar until the sugar is entirely dissolved. Tie the spices in cheese cloth bags. Boil these with the vinegar and sugar for 10 min. Then have peeled and cut in halve the peaches (quarter the pears unless very small.) Weigh the fruit and put the boiling syrup in Boil until tender, then fill sterilized jars with the fruit and pour over the boiling syrup and seal at once.

Mrs. W E. Stanley.

TOMATO MARMALADE

4 lb. yellow tomato   2 lemons
3 lb sugar

Chop lemons in tiny bits, boil tomato and lemon, heat sugar and add, boil until mixture thickens—20 minutes.

Cooking Club.

TUTTI FRUTTI JAM

15 lbs. grapes   3 lb. sugar
2 lb. seeded raisins   1 lb. walnut meats, broken

Remove skin from grapes. Put pulp on the fire and bring to a boil, put this through colander, to remove seeds, then put pulp, skins and sugar together and let this boil for 20 min Lastly add raisins and nuts, when thoroughly heated fill glasses, when cold, cover with paraffine.

Mrs F. G. Smyth

CEREALS

CEREALS

Bran and Dates
Bran Oatmeal
Bran and Prunes
Bran and Raisins
Breakfast Food

Cooking Mushes
Corn Meal Mush

Dates and Barley

Nut Croquettes

Nut Loaf

Oatmeal
Oatmeal, Baked

Rice au gratin
Rice, Boiled
Rice, Canned
Rice and Cheese
Rice and Chicken
Rice and Chipped Beef
Rice Croquettes
Rice Dressing
Rice and Fish
Rice with Fruit
Rice Griddle Cakes
Rice Hash, Baked
Rice Imperial   Mrs. F. G. Smyth.
Rice, Japanese, Boiled
Rice, Mexican   Mrs. A. O. Rorabaugh.
Rice Muffins
Rice Omelet
Rice with Pimentos   Mrs. Geo. Steel.
Rice and Salmon
Rice Sauce
Rice and Sausage
Rice, Spanish   Mrs. Ralph Millison.
Rice, Steamed
Rice Steamed   Mrs. W. B. Buck.

Soldiers Rice

BRAN AND DATES

1 C bran   1 C dates
3 C water   ¼ C oats
1 t salt
    Cook in double boiler 30 min. Add more water if too thick.

BRAN OATMEAL

    Half as much bran as oatmeal, add to the oatmeal when half done, makes a delicious brose. Serve with rich cream This requires 1-3 more water than plain oatmeal boiling.

BRAN AND PRUNES

1 C bran   ½ C fine breakfast food
3 C water   1 t salt
½ C cooked prunes, chopped
    Place in double boiler. Cook 20 min.

BRAN AND RAISINS

1 C bran   1 C raisins
4 C water   ½ t salt
1 C wheat meal   ½ C nut meats
    Cut nuts. Use seeded raisins. Mix all, stir well and cook 25 min.

BREAKFAST FOOD

1 C corn meal   1 C bran
1 C oat meal   4 C water
    Cook in double boiler. Stir in meal last. Serve hot

COOKING MUSHES

Oatmeal, 1 C; boiling water, 4 C; time, 3 hrs
Barley, 1 C; boiling water, 2 C, time, 3½ hrs.
Hominy, 1 C; boiling water, 3½ C; time, 4 hrs.
Meal, 1½ qts.; boiling water, 4 qts.; time, 4 hrs.
Graham, 1 pt., boiling water, 3 pts ; time, 1 hr.
Rye, 1 pt.; boiling water, 1 qt.; time, 10 min.

CORN MEAL MUSH FRIED

1 qt. water   1½ C corn meal
1 t salt
    Sprinkle the corn meal slowly into the boiling water season-ed with salt. Stir briskly to avoid lumping. When corn meal is all in, cook slowly 2 hrs., if for mush and milk. If to fry cook 15 min The secret of success in making this is to keep the water at the boiling point until after all the corn meal is added.
    To be crisp this mush should be fried at once. Dip out a spoonful at a time and place in a skillet containing 2 T butter and 6 T lard When brown on one side, turn; then brown. Have very hot lard, fry crisp and do not burn

DATES AND BARLEY

1 C barley	1 t salt
5 C water	1 C seeded dates

Cook washed barley 2½ hrs., in salted water in double boiler. Wash dates, seed and then measure, cut in small cubes and add to barley 15 min., before serving.

NUT CROQUETTES

½ pt. nut meats	1 t onion juice
1 pt. mashed potato	1 T chopped parsley
2 egg-yolks	¼ t pepper
1 t salt	¼ t nutmeg

Chop nuts, mix ingredients, mold into pyramids, dip in beaten egg-yolks then bread crumbs; fry in deep fat.

NUT LOAF

2 eggs	1 t salt
2 C milk	¾ C nuts
1½ C bread crumbs	

Stir the crumbs into the milk. Beat eggs and add chopped nuts and salt. Mix well. Bake. Serve with Nut Gravy:

1 C milk	½ t salt
1 C water	3 T flour
½ C walnuts	

Stir the flour into part of the milk, stir thickening into the rest of the milk and the water. Boil and stir 5 min. Add finely chopped nuts and salt

OATMEAL

2 T oatmeal	1 C milk
1 t sugar	1 t salt
1 C boiling water	

Cook and mold. When cool serve with hot cream. Oatmeal may be cooked in fireless cooker overnight and improve flavor. 1 t butter added to the oatmeal in boiling, always improves the flavor.

OATMEAL BAKED

1 C oatmeal	1 T butter
½ t salt	3 C water

Mix in sauce pan, bake in hot oven in covered dish 20 min Serve with cream and sugar.

RICE AU GRATIN

2 C rice cooked	1 C cheese
1 C white sauce	

Cover in bake dish with white sauce, bake 10 min. Add cheese and place in oven, covered for 1 min.

RICE BOILED

1 C rice   3 qts. boiling water
1 t salt

Wash rice thoroughly through 3 waters, drain and sprinkle slowly into boiling water. Cover and boil rapidly 20 min. Do not stir   When done drain and rinse with a qt of cold water. Drain again and set in oven 5 min , or until it steams itself dry. This leaves each grain whole and flaky.

RICE CANNED

A very convenient article to have ready to serve at once without long cooking necessary.

1 C rice   1 t salt

Wash and clean rice   Place in jar and fill with boiling water, add salt and process 1½ hrs   When ready to serve loosen lid and re-heat in jar   A quantity of rice may be canned at once. Oat meal may be canned the same way.

To re-heat rice, place in a colander over a pot of boiling water. Steam 5 min

RICE AND CHEESE

2 C rice boiled   2 C cheese

Boil rice according to directions   Serve hot on platter and pile grated cheese on top of hot rice   2 C hot white sauce may be poured over all.

RICE AND CHICKEN

2 C cooked rice   1 C chicken broth or cream
2 C cooked chicken   1 t salt

Escallop alternate layers of chicken and rice. Pour over all either broth or cream. Salt and bake 20 min.

RICE AND CHIPPED BEEF

½ lb chipped beef   ½ C boiled rice
1 T butter   2 C milk

Parboil beef if salty. Pour off water, shread into bits, fry in butter 3 min. Add milk and rice. Boil 5 min. May be thickened if desired.

RICE CROQUETTES

1 pt. boiled rice   1 T butter
1 t sugar   1 egg
½ t salt

Mix all together in desired form for croquettes. Roll in beaten egg, then in cracker crumbs, and fry in deep fat.

RICE DRESSING

1 onion	4 C boiled rice
1 T butter	1 C sausage
1 C milk	¼ t pepper
1 t salt	1 t celery
1 T parsley	1 C bread crumbs

Moisten bread crumbs with milk. Brown chopped onion in butter. Chop parsley and celery. Mix all together. Stir while cooking. Serve over toast or with fowl as a dressing.

RICE AND FISH

2 C cooked fish	1 C boiled rice
4 hard boiled eggs	1 t salt
1 C cream sauce	

Mash egg-yolks, add to rice and place alternate layers in bake dish. When baked 10 min., cover with hot cream sauce, and garnish with egg-whites.

RICE WITH FRUIT

1 C cooked rice	2 C canned fruit

Pour fruit over rice and serve cold. Whipped cream may be served on this.

RICE GRIDDLE CAKES

2 C flour	2 C milk
2 eggs	½ t salt
1½ C cooked rice	1 t sugar
2 t B. P.	

Beat eggs, mix ingredients and bake on hot griddle.

RICE HASH BAKED

1 C chopped beef	1 C milk
1 C cooked rice	2 T butter
1 t salt	1 egg
¼ t pepper	

Put beef, rice, milk, butter, salt and pepper in stew pan. Cook 5 min., add well beaten egg Put in bake pan and bake 20 min.

RICE IMPERIAL

1 pt. whipped cream	1 pkg gelatine
1 C cooked rice	1 t vanilla
½ C sugar	½ C water

Soak gelatine in cold water and vanilla; melt gelatine dissolved in the cold water by placing in a pan of hot water. Mix other ingredients. Mold. Serve cold.

Mrs. F. G. Smyth

RICE JAPANESE BOILED

1 C rice   1½ t salt
5 C boiling water

Pour boiling water over rice in colander to wash it and rinse through 3 waters. To the bubbling boiling water add the salt and rice, cover and set on back of stove, boiling slowly 15 min. Drain, then place in oven still covered, 15 min. The rice should then be tender and soft and each grain whole and separate.

RICE MEXICAN

1 C rice   4 slices bacon
1 onion (large)   3 green peppers
3 tomatoes   1 t salt
1-6 t pepper

Cook rice until tender. Fry and grind bacon, onion and peppers Cook and strain tomatoes. Stir these 2 mixtures together adding bacon fryings and bake 4 min, in a medium oven.

Mrs. A. O. Rorabaugh

RICE MUFFINS

1 C cooked rice   1 C milk
1 T melted butter   2 eggs
1½ C flour   1 T sugar
2 t B. P.

Combine rice, butter, milk, beaten egg-yolks and sugar; add flour and B. P Fold in egg-whites, stiffly beaten, last Put in hot buttered gem pans and bake in hot oven. Do not let stand.

RICE OMELET

1 egg   ½ t salt
½ C rice   ½ C cream sauce

Cook as omelette and pour over all ½ C cream sauce.

RICE WITH PIMENTOS

2½ C cold boiled rice   1 minced onion
1 can tomatoes   2 t salt
1 small can pimentos   ¼ t pepper
1 t sugar   2 T butter
½ C bread crumbs

Add salt, pepper, sugar and onion to tomatoes. Butter a baking dish. Spread over a layer of tomatoes. Then add rice and sprinkle with some of the pimentos, which should be chopped. Dot with bits of butter, repeat until dish is full. Sprinkle top with bread crumbs mixed with butter and bake about 40 min. in moderate oven

Mrs Geo Steel

RICE AND SALMON

2 C rice cooked   2 C cream sauce
1 can salmon

     Place rice in bottom of bake pan, mix salmon in cream sauce. Pour over rice, bake 10 min.

RICE SAUCE

1 C rice cooked   1 C cream sauce
½ C cheese   1 pt. tomato soup

     Brown rice, add cream sauce, cheese and tomato soup.

RICE AND SAUSAGE

1 qt cooked rice   1 lb. sausage

     Put layer of rice in casserole and alternate with layers of sausage, putting sausage on top and bake 30 min.

RICE SPANISH

1 C rice   1 onion
1 can tomatoes   1 C peanuts
1 good sized green pepper   ½ grated cheese
1 T butter

     Cook rice, season with butter and salt while cooking, put in a baking dish in layers, covering each with a sauce made with the tomatoes, chopped pepper, onion and peanuts. Spread the grated cheese over all and bake in a moderate oven.

                              Mrs Ralph Millison

RICE STEAMED

1 pt. rice   1 pt. water
1 t salt

     Put all in covered steamer and steam 1 hr. Do not stir.

STEAMED RICE

     Wash and drain rice, place in a double boiler and cook for ½ hr., with water to cover well. Remove from fire, toss into a colander and pour cold water through it. Then place colander with rice in a shallow pan of hot water in oven for 1 hr Keep well covered and steam.

                              Mrs. W. B. Buck

SOLDIERS' RICE

1 C cooked rice   1 t butter
1 t salt

     Warm all together, pack in square dish. When cold cut in ½ in. slices and fry brown in meat drippings.

Eggs---Omelets

EGGS

Asparagus tips with eggs   Mrs. James Buck
Baked with Bacon
Baked in Cream
Beaureguard   Mrs. Chester Long
Beets and Eggs
Boiled Hard
Boiled Soft
Breaded Eggs
Cheese and Eggs, baked
Coddled Eggs
Deviled
Egg Nog
Escalloped
Fried
Good Friday Eggs
Ham and Eggs
Stuffed Eggs with Ham
Japanese Eggs
Keeping Eggs for Winter   Mrs. C. V. Ferguson
Muffin Eggs
Mumbled Eggs
Nest Eggs
Omelet   Mrs. Newton Garst
Ox Eyes
Poached Eggs
Poached Eggs and Rarebit
Poached Eggs in Milk   Mrs. Murray Myers
Egg Rarebit
Scrambled Eggs
Eggs Scrambled with Rice   Mrs. F. G Smyth
Shirred in Cream
Shirred Plain
Souffle
Stuffed
Timballs
Tomato and Egg
Toast (egg)

FACTS ABOUT EGGS

On Cooking Eggs

The manner of cooking eggs is most important as the digestibility depends upon the cooking. A high temperature hardens and toughens the white, so the egg-white should never be boiled. The egg-white should be cooked below the boiling point. The yolk may be boiled, as the high temperature really makes it more mealy and digestible. The egg unbroken should be placed in a pan of boiling water, covered, and immediately set on the back of stove and let stand five min; the results will be a lovely soft-boiled egg. If a hard boiled egg is desired let stand thirty minutes in the same manner. Hard boiled eggs run through the colander are more easily digested

Olive oil, bacon or ham fat is best for frying eggs Butter burns before the cooking is done, and lard tastes badly. Eggs plunged into cold water as soon as taken from stove will not stick to the shell, but they will not slice smoothly.

Eggs may be separated, yolks and whites frozen, separately, and kept frozen until time to use them for cooking.

Never buy dirty looking eggs. It shows that the hens were not kept in a clean place and are likely to be diseased.

Some cooks scrape with the finger every particle of egg white sticking to the shell, claiming that this thick part of the egg contains most of the beating quality of the egg In six eggs 1 t of egg white is thus saved.

TESTING EGGS

One T salt to 1 qt. of water. Drop in the egg and if it is newly laid it will sink, if six days old it will float; if bad it will ride upon the top of the surface. An egg loses its density daily and the longer it is kept the lighter it becomes.

Sometimes eggs fail to beat when they are too fresh.

The whites of eggs will whip more readily if a pinch of salt is added to them If the eggs are placed in cold water for a time before being broken they will whip easily.

Be sure the vessel in which the egg is beaten is dry, as a drop of water may dilute the albumen sufficiently to prevent its beating.

COMPOSITION OF EGGS

The white has 86% water and the yolk 50%. The 33% fat in the yolk is the most concentrated food we have. The white cooks at a lower temperature than does the yolk. Eggs are mostly proteins; the egg-yolk contains fat, the egg-white is almost pure albumen, diluted with water.

Eggs are valuable for mineral salts, iron, phosphorus, and lime. The digestibility of eggs depends upon the cooking

The yolk contains 1700 calories per pound and the white 250. The white is a wonderful leavening agent, because so much air can be beaten into it. The colder and purer the air, the lighter will be the products cooked. The white is also used for clarifying.

EGGS WITH ASPARAGUS TIPS

6 eggs
2 T butter
1 T milk

Salt and pepper
Butter toast

Boil the asparagus tips. Put the butter, milk, pepper and salt in a pan, add the eggs and asparagus tips and scramble. Serve on toast.

Mrs. James Buck.

EGGS BAKED WITH BACON

6 eggs   14 slices bacon

Fry, bake or broil bacon crisp. Place in baking pan, cover with eggs. Bake in hot oven and serve for breakfast. This may be served on toast.

BAKED EGGS

Eggs in Cream.
6 eggs

6 T cream
1 t salt

Grease baking dish with butter, break the eggs into it, sprinkle with salt and pour cream over them If not sufficient cream, add enough to cover eggs. Set dish in water and cook in moderate oven, about ten minutes. Very digestible and nourishing.

BEAUREGUARD EGGS

5 eggs
6 slices of toast
2 C milk
Cream sauce

4 T butter
2 T flour
1/8 t milk

Make cream sauce of milk, butter and flour
Hard boil the eggs, press the yolks through the ricer, chop the whites, mix the whites and 1/2 the yolks with the sauce. Pour over freshly made and richly buttered toast, and sprinkle the remaining yolks over the sauce and toast, serve at once and hot.

Mrs. Chester I. Long.

EGGS AND BEETS

1/2 lemon
6 eggs

2 C beets
1/4 t salt

Hard boil the eggs. Run yolks and whites separately through ricer, slice beets in round pieces and cover with yolks and whites of eggs alternately, add salt and squeeze juice of lemon on top. This is a good luncheon dish.

EGGS HARD BOILED

Eggs hard boiled, 1 C boiling water to each egg. Have water boiling and put eggs in with shell on, set on back of stove covered, thirty minutes Be sure the water and eggs are boiling when set back. This cooks yolk and white evenly.

EGG BOILED SOFT

Have water boiling in deep pan, drop in egg in shell, and set on back of the stove covered. The egg will be soft boiled evenly in three minutes. Be sure the water and eggs are boiling when set off the fire.

EGGS BOILED

Put the egg in a sauce pan of cold water and when the water boils the egg is done. Remove from shell at once.

BREADED EGG

3 eggs   ¼ t salt
1 C bread

Cut bread in ½ inch cubes, beat eggs, salt, and pour over bread. Stir well and pour in greased buttered frying pan. Stir and fry brown.

EGGS AND CHEESE BAKED

1 C crumbs   6 eggs
1 C cheese   ½ C cream

Line baking dish with bread crumbs Cover with cheese, make pockets for eggs. Break one egg into each pocket, cover with bread crumbs Pour cream over all, dot on butter and bake in hot oven until eggs are set.

CODDLED EGGS

Have water boiling hard, set off fire, cover eggs, cook seven minutes. Whites should be soft and jelly like.

DEVILED EGGS

6 eggs   ¼ t celery salt
¼ t salt   ¼ t mustard
¼ t pepper   1 t vinegar

Hard boil eggs, cut in half, remove yolks and mix with above ingredients, making a paste. Fill the whites with this paste and serve cold

EGG NOG

6 eggs   4 t sugar
5 oranges

Beat yolk and white very stiff separately. Pare and cut oranges in small dices. Mix all together and sweeten. Serve at once. A little cinnamon may be sprinkled on top. Lemon juice, grape juice or any sour fruit may be used. A good breakfast dish.

ESCALLOPED EGGS

6 eggs
1 C ham cooked
½ C bread crumbs
¼ t salt

1 T melted butter
1 T cream
½ t paprika

Chop ham and mix eggs and bread crumbs. Place on bottom of bake dish, cook ten minutes. Break eggs into plate and slip off plate on top of ham mixture. Cover and cook 10 minutes. Serve with Maitre De Hotel Sauce if any sauce is desired.

FRIED EGGS

There are many ways of frying eggs. The best of which is to break all the eggs into a dish, have the frying pan oiled or greased with 3 T of liquid. When hot, pour in the eggs carefully, cover, and do not life the cover until done, which should be five minutes. The eggs will puff with the heat and be evenly cooked. Salt and pepper.

GOOD FRIDAY EGGS

6 slices bread
6 eggs
6 T butter

1½ C milk
¼ t salt
6 T cheese

Cut bread into thick slices and fry each slice in 1 T butter. Beat eggs separately, add milk and salt. Pour over fried bread in large shallow bake pan, and bake fifteen minutes. Grate cheese and sprinkle over mixture when taken from oven.

HAM AND EGGS

2 C cream sauce
5 hard boiled eggs
5 slices hard bread, toasted

1 C minced ham
½ t salt

Mix ham and minced eggs, place on top of bread in bake dish. Pour over all cream sauce. Bake 10 min. Serve hot.

STUFFED EGGS WITH HAM

Boil half a dozen eggs hard. Remove the shells and cut the eggs crosswise in two. Slice off a piece from each end to make them stand firmly. Remove the yolks and mix them with a little chopped ham. Fill the whites with this mixture, heaping it up in cone shape. Put the stuffed halves on a flat dish and pour over them this dressing.

Beat two egg-yolks with t of salt and 12 T salad oil added slowly as it is necessary with oil.

JAPANESE EGGS

1 C cooked rice
3 T cream

1 t salt
6 eggs

Mix rice and cream, spread on hot platter, break eggs on rice, bake until eggs begin to set. Salt and serve at once.

KEEPING EGGS FOR WINTER

1 Qt. liquid glass   18 doz. eggs
12 Qts water.

Mix together liquid glass and water, put in large jar Handle eggs carefully, having sufficient amount of liquid to cover them Will keep indefinitely. Purchase liquid glass at drug store.

Mrs. C. V. Ferguson.

MUFFIN EGGS

6 Eggs   6 Muffins

Heat Griddle, butter and place small rings on gridle, break an egg into each muffin ring, cook until as done as desired. Serve on bacon or on toast or on ham.

MUMBLED EGGS

6 eggs $\frac{1}{4}$ t salt
1 C milk   4 pieces toast

Put milk on fire in stew kettle. When boiling, add eggs unbeaten Stir quickly with fork until thick, salt eggs. This way is not as well cooked as scrambled eggs. Serve on buttered toast

NEST EGGS

6 eggs

Beat whites very stiff, lay spoonful on a greased platter that will stand the oven heat, hollow out a hole with the back of a spoon and lay the yolk in Heat in oven until meringue begins to color. Then add salt and pepper and a bit of butter on each egg. Serve in same platter

OMELET

Beat the whites and yolks of three eggs separately. Salt and pepper to taste One quarter of a cupful of bread crumbs with enough milk to make them soft. Mix with beaten yolks, and fold in the well beaten whites. Pour mixture into a hot omelet pan which is well-buttered. Cook until the egg is set Fold as usual.

Mrs Newton Garst

OX EYES

Make an attractive breakfast or luncheon dish. Cut rounds of bread and make an opening in the center of each which is large enough to take in a broken egg Dip the rounds of bread in melted butter and brown in the oven. Then put in each an egg, moisten the toast with cream, sprinkle with salt and paprika and heat in the oven.

POACHED EGGS

Only fresh eggs poach well. Have water boiling in shallow kettle, drop in broken egg, cover and set back on stove. The egg will poach soft in two minutes, medium three minutes, hard five minutes.

A spoonful of vinegar in the water will keep the egg from spreading in poaching. Do not let the water boil too hard in poaching or the egg will stick to the bottom of the pan.

POACHED EGG AND RAREBIT

Poach 6 eggs and put on top of 6 square of toast—pour over all a tomato rarebit.

POACHED EGGS IN MILK

A luncheon dish. Poach eggs in milk and place them on slices of buttered toast. Melt some cheese in the milk and pour it over the eggs and toast.—Mrs. Murray Myers.

EGG RAREBIT

2 C cheese   2 C cream sauce
2 eggs

Beat eggs, add to hot cream sauce, stirring when boiling remove from fire and add cheese.

SCRAMBLED EGGS

4 eggs   ½ C cream
¼ t salt

Beat eggs lightly, add salt or milk and cream or milk, have ready a hot greased pan, turn the eggs in quickly stirring constantly, until firm but soft.

Eggs may be scrambled with chopped ham, dried beef, salmon, spaghetti, cooked, or rice cooked   Eggs are always good served hard boiled chopped on spinnach.

SCRAMBLED EGGS AND RICE

Add 1 t of cooked rice to each egg and then scramble very good.   Mrs. F. G. Smyth.

SHIRRED EGGS IN CREAM

6 T milk   6 eggs
1 T butter   ¼ t salt

Divide 1 T butter into 6 shirred egg dishes and 1 T of milk, break 1 egg in each dish, set in oven until egg is cooked as soft or hard as desired.

SHIRRED EGGS—PLAIN

Oil or grease shirred egg dishes and break 1 egg in each dish, sprinkle with finely minced parsley, salt and a bit of butter set in oven and bake as soft or hard as desired. Serve at once as the egg hardens standing in the hot dish

EGG SOUFFLE

⅛ t paprika	1 C milk
2 T butter	4 eggs
2 T flour	1 t salt
1 C cream	

Cream butter, add flour and stir, pour on milk and cream which have been scalded, cook 7 min. in double boiler. Then add well beaten yolks, salt and paprika. Remove from boiler and add whites stiffly beaten, put in buttered ramekins and bake.

STUFFED EGGS

Hard boiled egg-whites may be stuffed with spinach mixed with lemon juice, and the yolked riced.

EGG TIMBALLS

5 eggs	1 t minced parsley
1 2-3 C milk	1 t salt
1 t onion juice	

Heat milk, add onion juice and parsley, add to well beaten eggs, then add salt and turn into timball cups. Place in pan of hot water in oven, bake in slow oven until firm. Serve with cream sauce on top in timball cups

TOMATO AND EGG

1 C tomato	½ t salt
6 eggs	

Beat eggs and salt and mix with tomato   Scramble in oiled pan on top of stove, stirring constantly.

EGG TOAST

4 rounds of toast	2 eggs
1 pt of milk	1 t salt
2 T butter	

Make toast and butter, heat milk and add eggs. When boiling salt and pour over toast. A little thickening may be added if preferred, or cheese may be grated on top while hot.

OMELET

Omelet   C. C.
Omelet   Mrs. Will Dixon
Apple Omelet
Asparagus Omelet
Baked Omelet
Baked Omelet   C. C.
Cheese Omelet
Chicken Omelet
Cream Omelet   Helen Brooks Hall
Economy Omelet
Ham Omelet
Jelly Omelet
Mushroom Omelet
Parsley Omelet
Plain Omelet   Helen Brooks Hall
Puffy Omelet   Helen Brooks Hall
Puffy Orange Omelet
Ripe Olive and Pine Nut
  Omelet
Spanish Omelet   Mrs. Chester Long
William Penn Omelet

OMELETS

Fresh eggs are most important for the success of an omelet.

Be sure the vessel is dry in which the egg is beaten; as a drop of water may dilute the albumen sufficiently to prevent its beating.

Omelets fall from being cooked too fast.

OMELET

1 t cornstarch	1-16 t salt
2 t cream	1-32 t pepper
2 eggs	1 t parsley

Beat cornstarch with cream, add egg-yolks, beat whites stiff, add salt and pepper, sprinkle parsley on buttered griddle, pour in the Omelet and fry. Use 2 pans, turn omelet upside down into 2nd pan which is hot and greased, then set in oven 5 min.

C. C.

OMELET

5 eggs	Salt
2-3 C milk	Pepper
1 T butter	

Beat eggs separately. Add milk to yolks, season, fold in egg-whites gently. Have skillet hot, put in butter. Pour in mixture, cover and cook slowly 15 min When done, fold over and turn on hot platter.

Mrs. Will Dixon.

APPLE OMELET

9 apples	1 T butter
4 eggs	1 t cinnamon.
1 C sugar	

Stew apples until soft, mash, add sugar and butter while hot, let cool. Add to beaten eggs Bake until brown. Good with any pork dish.

ASPARAGUS OMELET

Make creamy omelet, add ½ C asparagus tips to 1 C cream sauce and pour over omelet

BAKED OMELET

6 eggs	½ pt. milk.

Beat egg-yolks stiff, add milk, stir well. Beat egg-whites until they stand alone and gradually stir into mixture. Quick oven.

BAKED OMELET

4 eggs   1 C hot milk
3 t flour   1-16 t salt
1 T melted butter   1-32 t pepper

Beat eggs separately, add salt and pepper; dissolve flour in a little milk; add other ingredients, the whites last, just before placing in oven. Bake 20 min.

C. C.

CHEESE OMELET

Sprinkle 3 T cheese over omelet when it begins to thicken.

CHICKEN OMELET

1 C cooked chicken chopped fine to a plain omelet.

CREAM OMELET

An omelet cooked in a skillet on top the stove may be improved by covering. Do not lift the lid until done and then fold quickly.

CREAM OMELET

1 egg   ⅛ t salt
½ C white sauce   ⅛ t pepper

Combine ¼ C sauce, well beaten egg and seasoning. Cook as plain omelet. Serve with other ¼ C cream, same poured around omelet.

Helen Brooks Hall.

ECONOMY OMELET

1 egg   1 T flour
1 C cooked rice   ¼ t salt
1 C sweet milk   ⅛ t pepper

Stale bread or crackers soaked in hot water can be used in place of rice. Will serve 3 people

HAM OMELET

Add 3 T chopped ham to a plain omelet recipe.

JELLY OMELET

Make omelet and spread with jelly before rolling.

MUSHROOM OMELET

Make creamy omelet and add ½ C mushrooms to cream sauce poured over omelet.

PARSLEY OMELET

Make plain omelet and sprinkle with ½ C parsley before rolling.

PLAIN OMELETS

1 egg   ⅛ t salt
1 T milk   ⅛ t pepper

Beat eggs lightly, add milk and seasoning, pour into hot greased omelet pan. Shake quickly to keep loose from pan. When set and browned fold or roll, turn on hot platter.

Helen Brooks Hall.

PUFFY OMELETS

1 egg   ⅛ t salt
1 T milk   ⅛ t pepper

Separate egg—beating yolk thick and whites stiff, add milk and seasonings to yolk, cut well beaten whites into yolks. Cook and serve, folded, as for plain omelet

Helen Brooks Hall.

PUFFY ORANGE OMELET

3 eggs   ¼ t salt
2 T orange juice   3 T sugar

Beat eggs separately, add salt and juice to yolks and beat. Cut whites into egg-yolks. Heat pan, grease bottom and sides with 1 T butter. Spread omelet over bottom of pan, cook evenly, cover to finish top. Fold and turn from pan. Garnish with slices of orange. Cover with powdered sugar and score with hot iron.

Helen Brooks Hall

RIPE OLIVE AND PINE NUTS OMELET

4 eggs   ¼ C pine nuts
½ C ripe olives

Chop olives and nuts fine, add to plain omelet, using 4 eggs.

SPANISH OMELET

6 eggs   1 onion
1 t salt   1 t celery seed
8 slices bacon   6 mushrooms
¼ t pepper

Fry bacon, cut in small pieces and add the vegetables chopped fine. Cook 10 min. Beat eggs and turn in buttered pan, bake and when done mix tomato sauce with bacon and vegetables and salt, pepper and celery seed. Pour over omelet and cook 2 min.

Mrs. Chester I. Long.

WM. PENN OMELET

3 eggs	1 t butter
½ C milk	1 t paprika
1 ½ T cornstarch	2 t ham fat
1 t salt	

Put butter and ham fat in very hot omelet pan, beat egg-yolks well, add salt and cornstarch, then milk, adding stiffly beaten whites last, pour into pan, cover, cook 6 to 8 min. Fold, turn out on hot dish and pour a cream sauce over it. Be careful not to burn, serve immediately with ham.

CHEESE

CHEESE DISHES

Baked Cheese.   Mrs. C. V. Ferguson.

Cheese Balls.
Cheese and Jelly.
Cheese Fingers   Mrs. G. M. Dickson
Cheese Hail Stones
Cheese Harlequins.
Cheese Paste.   Mrs. G. M. Dickson.
Cheese Marbles.
Cheese Muffins.
Cheese Patties.
Cheese and Pineapple Salad.
Cheese Rarebit.   Mrs. O. D Barnes.
Cheese Souffle.   Mrs. Todd.
Cheese Souffle.   Mrs. R. B. Campbell.
Cheese Souffle Chafing Dish   Mrs. W. E. Stanley
     Mrs. Will Dixon

Cheese Sticks.
Cheese Straws.   Mrs. A. O. Rorabough.
Cheese Straws.   Mrs. W. E. Stanley.
Cheese Wafers.
Cottage Cheese
Cottage Cheese

Dreams.

Grated Cheese.

Jerusalem Krepza.
Macaroni and Cheese   C. C.

Spanish Rabbit

Under Cheese Relish.   Mrs. Brown.

War Bride Cheese.
Welsh Rarebit.
Welsh Rarebit.   Mrs. C. L. Davidson.

·BAKED CHEESE

1 C cheese
1 C bread crumbs
1 t salt

2 eggs
1½ C milk

To the milk add the grated cheese, bread crumbs and salt; then add eggs beaten separately   Bake 20 min. in moderate oven.

Mrs C V. Ferguson.

CHEESE BALLS

2 C cottage cheese
4 T cream

½ t salt

Mix cream and salt with cheese. Make into small balls. Cinnamon or nutmeg may be added.

CHEESE BALLS AND JELLY

Place a mound of tart jelly in center of round dish and surround with cheese balls. Serve cold.

CHEESE FINGERS

2 C cheese
½ t salt and 1-16 t pepper

2 eggs
Bread crumbs

Beat egg-whites and mix with cheese, salt, and pepper. Mold into finger shape. Dip in egg and bread crumbs and fry in lard

Mrs. G. M Dickson.

CHEESE HAIL STONES

1 lb. cottage cheese
1 t salt

1 egg-yolk
2 T cream

Mash the hard boiled egg yolk, add to the cheese, salt and cream. Roll into round balls and serve with powdered cinnamon on top, as an accompaniment to salad

CHEESE HARLEQUINS

Roll pastry thin, sprinkle cheese between the two layers, cut in strips and bake.

CHEESE PASTE

1 C cheese
½ C milk
2 eggs
½ small can pimentos

1 t salt
1 t dry mustard
Egg of butter

Put butter in double boiler, when melted, add milk, when heated, add salt and mustard. Mix well and smooth, then grate cheese into mixture and stir constantly until cheese melts and gets creamy. Beat eggs well and add, stirring until it pours like thick custard. Stir constantly. When cool add pimentos cut fine.

Mrs. G. M. Dickson.

CHEESE MARBLES

Add minced pimento to cheese balls.
Add minced pecans to cheese balls.
Add currant jelly to cheese balls.
Add minced parsley to cheese balls.

Serve all the different colored balls heaped on a round plate.

CHEESE MUFFINS

Melt cheese on toasted English muffins.

CHEESE PATTIES

¼ lb. cheese	1 C cream
3 eggs	½ t salt
¼ t paprika	1 t pimento

Line 16 patty pans with puff paste. Grate cheese and mix with beaten eggs, pimento chopped, cream, paprika and salt. Bake 30 min.

CHEESE AND PINEAPPLE SALAD

1 C neufchatel cheese   ½ C pineapple

Cut pineapple in cubes, cover with cheese and pour French dressing over all.

CHEESE RAREBIT

1 loaf bread	¼ t salt
½ lb. cream cheese	3 C milk

Trim the crust from a loaf of bread. Cut in slices half in. thick. Make a sandwich with thin slices of yellow cream cheese, sprinkled with salt.

Place in long pie tin. Grate cheese over the top and fill the tin 1-3 full of milk. Cover, and bake 20 min.

Mrs. O. D. Barnes.

CHEESE SOUFFLE

2 T butter	3 eggs (yolks and whites sep-
1 T flour	arated)
½ C sweet milk	1 C grated cheese

Cream butter and flour, add milk. Set it on the stove and stir until it comes to a boil. While hot add yolk three eggs, grated cheese. After it cools add whites of eggs, pour in buttered pan and bake 15 min.

Mrs. Todd.

CHEESE SOUFFLE

1 C chopped cheese	4 eggs
3 T flour	½ t salt
1½ C milk	½ t paprika

Mix the flour with half C cold milk, and add to 1 C hot milk, cook until thick, add cheese and stir until melted Add yolks well beaten Remove from fire, add salt and paprika, stir in carefully the well beaten whites Turn all into buttered baking dish and bake twenty min in moderate oven. Serve at once.   Mrs. R. B. Campbell

CHEESE SOUFFLE—CHAFING DISH

1 T butter	1 T flour
½ t paprika	1 C sweet milk
½ t mustard	1 C grated cheese
1 t salt	3 eggs

Put in chafing dish or double boiler the butter, paprika, mustard, salt, melt all together, then add flour, stir until thickened; add cheese, remove from fire and set in hot water. Beat eggs separately, add yolks and last stir in whites, cover and cook 30 min.   Mrs. W. E. Stanley
                                                 Mrs. Will Dixon.

CHEESE STICKS

Cover buttered crackers with grated cheese, set in oven until cheese is warm Serve.

CHEESE STRAWS

1 C flour	1-6 C ice water
3 T butter	¼ t salt
¼ lb. N. York full cream cheese	1-16 t cheyenne pepper

Mix thoroughly the flour, butter, cheese, salt and pepper, add just enough ice water to make a nice dough, roll out, cut into strips 4 in. long and ½ in. wide, also cut rings. Bake in a quick oven. When serving place three straws in a ring which will add an attractive appearance to the salad plate.
                                                 Mrs A. O. Rorabaugh

CHEESE STRAWS

½ lb. cheese	⅛ lb. butter
2 eggs	¼ t salt

Cut pie crust dough into strips 3 in long and 2 in wide. Mix grated cheese, well beaten egg and butter and dip straws into this. Fry in deep fat
                                                 Mrs. W. E. Stanley

CHEESE WAFERS

Cut pie dough into 3 inch squares. Cook and spread with creamed cheese. Place in oven, heat 3 min.

COTTAGE CHEESE

1 qt. clabber milk	1 T butter or 2 T cream
1 qt warm water	⅛ t salt

Heat milk until almost boiling, add water and turn into strainer lined with cheese cloth. Let drain until free from whey, and when cool add salt, butter or cream.

COTTAGE CHEESE

Place 2 qts. of sour milk in a gallon jar, pour enough hot water (boiling) into the milk to make the whole mixture luke warm. Let stand 3 hrs Pour through fine strainer and drain 2 hrs. Wash when cold and add salt and sweet cream to make rather soft.

DREAMS

12 slices bread   ½ lb. cheese
6 t butter

Toast bread on one side, butter toasted side, and pile cheese between buttered toasted sides of bread, place in oven and toast.

GRATED CHEESE

Grated Cheese is a fine accompaniment to soup. Place a dish heaped full of grated cheese on the table, and try some of it in the soup or on the salad. A tablespoonful of it is good after dessert on water biscuit or crackers.

JERUSALEM KREPZA

2 lbs. flour   ½ t sugar
3 eggs   1 t salt

Make a pyramid of flour on the dough board, make a depression in the center and break in the eggs, salt and sugar. Work flour into the eggs until there is a firm ball of dough. Form the remainder of the flour into a mold and follow the proceeding above until all flour is used up. Do not use any water. Roll out ⅛ in. thick and cut into 3 cornered pieces and spread with the following:

1 lb. cheese   ¼ t salt
2 eggs

Grate cheese, beat eggs and mix, fill Krepza with this mixture and fold over the corners tight pinching them together. Drop into pan of boiling water When they rise to the top take out and drain and fry until a light brown.

MACARONI AND CHEESE

1 can tomatoes   ¼ t pepper
½ box macaroni   1 C cheese (grated)
1 t salt

Boil macaroni 'til tender in salted water, drain. Grate cheese and arrange in layers in baking dish—macaroni, tomatoes and cheese. Season to taste and bake ¾ of an hour.

C. C.

SPANISH RABBIT

1 lb. cream cheese	½ can pimentos
1 can corn	1 egg
1 can Campbell's tomato soup	1 t flour

Melt cheese in double boiler, add corn, tomato soup, pimentos chopped fine, seasoning or paprika and salt. Let come to boil, then add one egg which has been mixed with 1 lb. flour. Serve on toast.

UNDER CHEESE RELISH

1 C grated cheese	1 C chopped nuts
1 C bread crumbs	1 egg
1 T melted butter	2 t chopped onions
½ C cold water	Juice 1 lemon
⅛ t salt	⅛ t pepper

Bake half hour, serve hot with tomato sauce.

Mrs Brown.

⸎ WAR BRIDES CHEESE

4 slices bread	1 egg
1½ C grated cheese	½ t salt
1½ C milk	Paprika

Cut the bread into slices 1 in. thick, remove crusts and save, toasted for soups. Grease baking dish, put in a layer of bread, then a layer of cheese and proceed until cheese and bread are all used. Mix beaten egg, salt, paprika and milk together and pour over bread and cheese. Bake in a moderately quick oven until nicely brown.

WELSH RAREBIT

1 T butter	¼ t salt
1 T flour or 1 t corn starch	1-18 t pepper
½ C milk	¼ t mustard
½ lb. cheese	

Make cream sauce of butter and flour, rubbing flour in the hot butter. When melted add milk, salt, pepper and mustard. When done add cheese grated but do not cook after cheese is added. Serve hot on toast Rice, macaroni or tomato may be added.

WELSH RAREBIT

2 C cheese	2 egg-yolks
½ C milk	½ t mustard
1-32 t pepper (red)	

Let milk come to boil, add cheese, when melted add egg-yolks, pepper, and mustard. Serve on toast

Mrs. C. L. Davidson.

Sandwiches

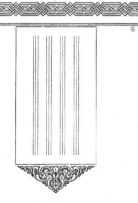

SANDWICHES

A Man's Sandwich

Bacon Sandwich
Bacon and Sardine Sandwich
Bridge Tea Sandwich
Brown's Sandwich   Mrs. Warren Brown

Caviar Sandwich
Checker Sandwich
Cheese Sandwich   C C.
Cheese Sandwich Hot   Mrs J. H.. Black
Cheese Sandwich, Hot   Mrs. C. L. Davidson
Cheese and Pineapple
  Sandwich
Cheese and Strawberry
  Sandwich
Cherry and Pecan Sandwich
Chicken Sandwich
Club Sandwich   Mrs. Chester Long
Cottage Chees and Jelly
  Sandwich
Cracker Sandwich
Chicken and Nut Sandwich   Mrs. L. C. Jackson
Cucumber Sandwich

Dream Cakes   Mrs. C. L. Davidson

Fig Paste
Filling for Sandwich
Finger Sandwich
Fresh Crisp Lettuce Sandwich
Fried Egg Sandwich

Ginger and Nuts Sandwich
Grape Marmalade and Nut
  Sandwich

Ham and Egg Sandwich
Ham (Potted) Sandwich

Lettuce Sandwich
Luncheon Sandwich   Mrs. C. L. Davidson
Macedoine Sandwich
Meat Sandwiches   Mrs. C. L. Davidson
New Sandwich

Nut Butter Sandwich

Olive Squares

Patriot Sandwich   Mrs. Robt. B. Campbell
Picnic Appetizers

Pimento Cheese and Nut
  Sandwich

Ribbon Sandwich
Rolled Sandwich

Sardine Sandwich   Mrs. Chester Long
Sorrento Sandwich
Spanish Filling
Sugar and Cinnamon   Mrs J. H. Black
Tartar Sandwich

Toasted Sandwich   Mrs. J. H. Black
Tongue Sandwich

Welch Rarebit Sandwich   C. C.

SANDWICHES

All meat sandwiches are made after the same recipe. The meat should be chopped fine, nicely seasoned and flavorings added to blend with meat. For instance, season mutton with a little mint or capers, salt and pepper. To chopped beef add tomato catsup in proportions of 2 T each ½ pt of chopped meat, add also salt, pepper and just a suspicion of onion. To chicken add salt, pepper, thick sweet cream and a little finely chopped celery. Spread these mixtures between thin slices of bread and butter. Cut into fancy shapes and serve.

Mrs. C. L. Davidson.

A MAN'S SANDWICH

6 pieces toast	12 sices tomato
6 crisp lettuce leaves	12 slices Bermuda onions
3 T chopped parsley	

Place between hot buttered toast, one lettuce leaf, on top of this 2 slices of tomato, 2 of onion and ½ t of parsley. Cover with mayonnaise. A little extra salt may be needed as tomatoes always absorb more salt than any other vegetable.

BACON SANDWICH

Bacon is always good between bread, and especially so between layers of cold buttered biscuit. Bacon must be hot.

BACON AND SARDINE SANDWICH

Bacon and Sardine make a good sandwich; equal parts with mayonnaise.

BRIDGE TEA SANDWICH

1 layer white bread	1 layer white bread
1 layer pink bread	1 layer pink bread

Put vegetable coloring in bread when baking. Fill with any favorite sandwich filling. Cut down and serve in oblong sandwiches.

BROWN'S SANDWICH

3 egg-yolks	1 package neufchatel cheese
½ can pimento	½ C mayonnaise

Crumble hard boiled egg-yolks Chop pimentos, add cheese and mayonnaise, mix well and spread between graham or whole wheat bread.

Mrs. Warren Brown

CAVIAR SANDWICH

Mix caviar with lemon juice and spread on thin slices of buttered white bread.

CHECKER SANDWICH

4 slices white bread   8 olives
4 slices graham bread   ½ t paprika
3 T creamed butter

Cut bread ¼ in. thick. Chop olives very fine and form a paste with paprika and butter. Spread bread and place alternate layers of graham and white, cutting in inch square sandwiches.

CHEESE SANDWICH

½ C cream cheese, grated or   1 chopped pimento
  mashed   ⅛ t salt
3 chopped olives   1 t melted butter

Mix and spread on thinly sliced bread.   C. C.

CHEESE SANDWICH HOT

Spread layers of white bread with butter, then with grated cheese. Cover with a top slice and press down hard. Place in oven and toast. These are delicious with tea.

Mrs. J. H Black

CHEESE SANDWICH HOT

Slice bread very thin and cut round with a large biscuit cutter. Put a thick layer of grated cheese between the two forms, sprinkle with salt and a dash of cayenne pepper and press the round pieces of bread well together. Fry them to a delicate brown on each side in equal parts of hot lard and butter, and serve very hot

Mrs. C. L. Davidson.

CHEESE AND PINEAPPLE SANDWICH

2 T melted butter   ¼ C pineapple
½ C cheese   1 T lemon juice

Chop pineapple and mash with cheese, cover with lemon juice and mix with melted butter Spread between slices of bread

CHEESE AND STRAWBERRY SANDWICH

Spread pimento cheese between square slices of buttered whole wheat bread, cut a round hole in each corner of the top slice of bread, and put a large preserved strawberry in each hole. Serve on lettuce leaf.

CHERRY AND PECAN SANDWICH

Maraschino cherries and pecans with lemon juice to soften, spread well on graham bread makes a good sandwich.

CHICKEN SANDWICH

1 C chicken	1 t capers
6 stuffed olives	½ C mayonnaise
1 T parsley	

Chop chicken, parsley, olives, and capers fine; add mayonnaise, mix well and serve between thin white bread.

CLUB SANDWICH

1 C cold sliced chicken	3 lettuce leaves
2 tomatoes	½ C mayonnaise
1 large dill pickle	9 slices toast
6 slices bacon	

Toast bread, butter each slice well; place on it first a layer of chicken, then bacon and pickle. Cover with toast and on this second layer place lettuce leaf, sliced tomato and mayonnaise. Top with toast. Should be made quickly and served at once. Ham may be added.

Mrs. Chester Long

COTTAGE CHEESE AND JELLY SANDWICH

Spread equal parts of cottage cheese and tart jelly between layers of buttered whole wheat bread.

CRACKER SANDWICH

Spread cracker wafers with cheese and put in the oven 2 min. Do not let the cheese cook or it will become tough.

CHICKEN AND NUT SANDWICHES

Remove the crusts from the four sides of a loaf of bread, at least twenty-four hours old; then cut in four slices lengthwise. Spread three of the slices sparingly with butter which has been worked until creamy, and put layers together, using between, two spreadings of chicken filling and one spreading of nut filling For the chicken filling, chop finely remnants of boiled or roast fowl, and moisten with mayonnaise dressing For the nut filling, chop English walnuts or Pecan nut meats and moisten with mayonnaise dressing.. Fold in cheese cloth, press under a light weight, and when serving time is near at hand cut in slices and arrange on a sandwich plate in crisp lettuce leaves.

Mrs. L. C. Jackson

CUCUMBER SANDWICH

Cut cucumber very thin and let stand 1 hr in French dressing. Drain, butter sandwiches of wheat bread, spread the cucumber on top and add a little chopped parsley.

DREAM CAKES OR HOT SANDWICHES

Slice bread very thin and cut round with a large biscuit cutter. Put a thick layer of grated cheese between the two forms, sprinkle with salt and a dash of cayenne pepper and press the round pieces of bread well together. Fry them to a delicate brown on each side in equal parts of hot lard and butter, and serve very hot

Mrs. Davidson.

FIG PASTE

½ lb figs
½ lb B. sugar
Juice of 1 lemon

¼ lb. raisins
¼ t salt

Chop until fine and spread between brown bread.

FILLING FOR SANDWICH

1 C pecans
1 C B sugar
1 C raisins

3 apples
½ t salt
1 lemon

Chop all very fine, use juice of lemon and rind of lemon grated. More lemon juice may be used if desired .

FINGER SANDWICH

Spread Tuna or Salmon with lemon juice, or lettuce and minced dill pickles; between slices of white bread Cut 4 inches long and 1 inch wide.

FRESH CRISP LETTUCE SANDWICH

Fresh crisp lettuce leaves laid between very thin slices of creamed buttered bread, are fine with lemonade in summer.

FRIED EGG SANDWICH

6 eggs   12 slices bread

Fry bacon or bake in oven and fry eggs in the grease. Place eggs and bacon between buttered bread, salt and pepper.

GINGER AND NUT SANDWICH

Preserved ginger sliced thin and nuts chopped fine, marinating the nuts with olive oil and salt, makes a good filling

GRAPE MARMALADE AND NUT SANDWICH

Spread grape marmalade and minced English walnuts equal parts, between slices of white bread

HAM AND EGG SANDWICH

1 C cold ham
1 T melted butter
1 t mustard

2 hard boiled eggs
1 T lemon juice
¼ t salt

Mince ham and eggs, add butter, lemon juice, mustard and salt. Do not butter bread.

POTTED HAM SANDWICH

Mix finely chopped pickles with mustard, and add to potted ham. Spread between bread.

LETTUCE SANDWICH

1 head of lettuce
2 T dill pickles

1 t capers
4 stuffed olives

Wash and chill lettuce. Chop other ingredients fine, shred lettuce with scissors. Toss together and keep on ice 2 hrs. Butter sandwiches and spread with above filling. Serve immediately.

LUNCHEON SANDWICH

Mince fine any cold boiled or roasted chicken, also mince fine some well roasted peanuts or almonds. Trim crusts from thin slices of breast and cut in any desired shape Butter and then put in a layer of chicken, spread a little mayonnaise dressing over it, then a layer of minced nuts. These are delicious and are fine for luncheon or tea.

Mrs. C. L. Davidson

MACEDOINE SANDWICH

1 layer of white bread
1 layer of graham bread

1 layer of white bread
1 layer of rye bread

Alternate. Use nut filling and cut down in slices.

MEAT SANDWICHES

Meat sandwiches are made after the same recipe. The meat should be chopped fine, nicely seasoned, and flavorings added to blend with meat. For instance, season mutton with a little mint or capers, salt and pepper. To chopped beef, add tomato catsup in proportions of 2 T to each ½ pt. of chopped meat; add also salt, pepper and just a suspicion of onion. To chicken add salt, pepper, thick sweet cream and a little finely chopped celery Spread these mixtures between thin slices of bread and butter Cut into fancy shapes and serve.

Mrs. C. L. Davidson

NEW SANDWICH

Chop Canton preserved ginger very fine, adding a little of the syrup to moisten when chopped. Cut white bread in fancy shapes, spread with sweet butter, then with the ginger mixture. Place another piece of bread on top of the lower slice, press together and serve. Serve for afternoon tea.

NUT BUTTER

Nut butter may be made at home from Peanuts, Almonds, Pecans or Brazil Nuts. Blanch the nuts then place in double boiler and cook them 3 hrs   Remove while hot and grind   If too thick to spread, a little water may be rubbed in with the nuts, or if used at once cream is better. Salt may be added Brazil nuts need no cooking; after removing the woody skins they should be ground at once and salted.

OLIVE SQUARES

2 doz. green olives   ½ C celery (cut fine)
1 C mayonnaise   1 t catsup

Separate the olives from the seeds, cut or chop fine, mix with the catsup, celery and mayonnaise, and use for the filling for dainty 3 in. square sandwiches.

Mrs. Robt. B. Campbell.

PATRIOT SANDWICH

6 slices of white bread   6 olives
1 pimento

Spread bread with creamed butter, 3 slices of bread to each sandwich. On the bottom layer spread red pimento and on the upper layer spread chopped olives. Cut an in wide and 3 in. long. Instead of pimento and olive, green and red peppers can be used alternately.

PICNIC APPETIZERS

For picnics wrap sandwiches in a damp cloth and they will arrive as fresh as when they were made. Nothing is more refreshing than a fruit or vegetable salad or cocktail   This may be made, then packed into hollowed-out oranges, apples or tomatoes, the top fastened on with a bit of gelatine. Crisp celery stuffed with cheese is also delicious   Hard-baked rolls may be hollowed out for chicken or salmon salad. Tin cracker boxes are just the thing for baking picnic cakes in. Do not take the cake from the box, ice it and put the cover on and it will carry beautifully   Another good cake to take on picnics is made by lining pattypans with pie crust and then baking gingerbread in them. They do not crumble as plain cup cakes do. The pie crust keeps them whole   A spoonful of jelly may be put into the pans before the batter is added.

PIMENTO CHEESE AND NUT SANDWICH

1 C pimento cheese   6 olives
½ C English walnuts   Chop all fine and mix

RIBBON SANDWICH

Use vegetable coloring, red and green. Butter white bread, mix cream cheese with coloring, and spread one layer with red cheese, another with green and so alternating until 6 slices are put together. Cut down crosswise into slices, showing the alternate colors.

ROLLED SANDWICH

Rolled sandwiches are attractive. These require soft fresh bread, cut very thin, spread with a paste filling and creamed butter. Roll each slice and secure with a tooth pick.

SARDINE SANDWICH

1 can sardines   ½ t mustard
2 hard boiled eggs   ¼ t lemon juice

Chop sardines, mince egg. Mix and add mustard and lemon juice.

Mrs. Chester Long

SORRENTO SANDWICH

1 C chicken livers   ½ C mayonnaise
1 C olives

Chop and mix well.

SPANISH FILLING

1 neufchatel cheese   8 stuffed olives
½ t dry mustard   Cream butter to spread bread

Chop olives fine, mix all into a paste and spread bread with the mixture.

SUGAR AND CINNAMON SANDWICH

Cut bread very thin, toast, butter generously, cover with sugar and cinnamon, heat in oven for a few min. and serve with tea or cocoa.

Mrs. J. H. Black.

TARTAR SANDWICH

Spread whole wheat or graham bread with tartar sauce, put together with lettuce leaf and minced celery.

TOASTED SANDWICH

Toast bread on one side. Butter untoasted side, spread generously with "nippy" cheese, lay on slices of bacon, cut thin according to size of bread, and toast under blazer. Serve at once.

Mrs. J. H. Black

TONGUE SANDWICH

1 C cold tongue   Mayonnaise
1 T parsley or 1 T water cress

Mince tongue and parsley. Add mayonnaise dressing and spread between bread

WELCH RAREBIT SANDWICH

Spread welch rarebit between buttered slices of fresh bread and roll.

C. C.

Ham, cold beef, tongue, pressed chicken, fried steak, canned meats, beef loaf, tuna, salmon and sardines, all make good substantial sandwiches.

DRINKS

DRINKS

Cafe au Lait
Chocolate   Mrs G. M. Whitney
Cold Lemon Soup   Mrs. P. C. Lewis
Currant Punch
Demi Tasse
Egg Lemonade
Hot Spiced Grape Juice   Agnes Long
Iced Chocolate   Mrs. Harold D. McEwen
Iced Coffee
Iced Tea
Kansas Julip   Mrs. Chester Long
Lemonade
Lemon Foam
Lemon Juice with Sugar
Lime Punch
Mint
Mint Punch
Mint Water
Orangeade
Orange Eggnog
Percolated Coffee
Pineapple Lemonade
Raspberry Bombe Glace
Strawberry Cocktail   Mrs Chester Long
Summer Drinks
Tea-cup
Tea-Pot
Tea punch
Temperance Punch
Vanilla Punch

CAFE AU LAIT

Cafe au Lait is equal parts of coffee and boiled milk served together.

CHOCOLATE

1 qt. milk	3 T sugar
2 oz. chocolate	2 T hot water
1 T cornstarch	

Mix the starch with a little of the milk and sugar. Cook untill smooth and glossy. This serves 6 people.

Mrs. Geo. M. Whitney

1½ t grated chocolate to the cup.
1 t cocoa to the cup.

Cocoa is improved by adding cinnamon or a few drops of vanilla to it.

COLD LEMON SOUP

3 qt. water	juice of 1 doz. lemons
1½ lbs. sugar	2 T arrow root

Put the thin yellow rind in the water and sugar and boil 10 min., then strain. When luke warm add the strained lemon juice. Add the arrow root dissolved in a little cold water to the boiled water and sugar. Add the lemon juice

Mrs. P. C. Lewis.

CURRANT PUNCH

With a wooden spoon crush one quart of red currants, add one pound of loaf sugar and 2 T of strong fresh ground ginger. Let this stand over night. Strain, and add the juice of 1 lemon and 1 qt. of cold water.

DEMI TASSE

Demi Tasse is a small cup of black coffee served after dinner

EGG LEMONADE

2 lemons	4 T sugar
1 pt. boiling water	1 egg

Sweeten lemon juice, add boiling water, and when ready to serve add stiffly beaten egg and beat again.

HOT SPICED GRAPE JUICE

1 qt. grape juice	1 stick cinnamon
1 qt water	1 lemon, juice
1 C sugar	1 orange, juice
1 T whole cloves	

Mix in order given, bring to boil, simmer until thoroughly spiced. Serve hot with thin slice of orange Spices should be tied in thin cheese cloth bag.

Agnes Long.

ICED CHOCOLATE

5 T chocolate grated   1 qt. milk
½ C sugar   1 t flavoring

Mix ingredients with one half of milk and cook until thoroughly mixed. When cool add the other half of the milk. If not smooth use egg beater.

Mrs. Harold D. McEwen.

ICED COFFEE

Make coffee as strong as is liked. 1 T coffee to the cup. Cool and pour in tall glasses, using 3 T of rich cream to each glass. Sugar to taste and fill with shaved ice.

ICED TEA

1 t tea to the cup. Pour boiling water over, let stand until cool, and serve in tea glasses with sugar and a slice of lemon split and struck on the glass.

KANSAS JULIP

6 T sugar   1 lemon rind
18 mint leaves   5 C ice water
1 C lemon juice

Soak mint, sugar and lemon juice 1 hr. leaving in 1 lemon rind sliced into cubes, add water and shake in lemonade shaker. Wet edges of tall glasses and dip in sugar, fill glasses ¼ full of shaved ice. Pour in mixture and serve at once.

Mrs. Chester Long.

LEMONADE

6 lemons   15 t sugar
10 C water

Squeeze juice from lemons and cut rinds into bits and cover both with sugar. Let stand 1 hr. then add ice water and let stand 1 hr., shaking or stirring well This may be strained, squeezing out rinds, or may be served with the rinds left in. Do not let stand longer than 2 hrs or it becomes bitter. Serve with mint spray or cherry on top. Mint lemonade is made by boiling 4 T mint in ½C water and adding to above when cool.

LEMON FOAM

3 qts. water   3 lemons
1 oz. cream tartar   ½ C sugar or more

Pour boiling water over cream of tartar, stir in lemon juice and ½ of the rind cut in thin strips, add sugar, stir well, and let cool. Strain and serve with ice

LEMONADE JUICE WITH SUGAR

Squeeze out the juice of lemons and to every quart of juice allow 6 lbs. sugar. To the stiffly beaten whites of 2 eggs add gradually a quart of water, pour over the sugar in a porcelain kettle, stir well until all is dissolved, then place over the fire and boil, skimming off the scum as it rises. When there is no more scum add the strained lemon juice and boil about ten minutes, remove from the fire and let cool. Clean your bottles well, rinsing with alcohol, pour in your lemon juice and seal tightly. Will keep indefinitely.

LIME PUNCH

Take ½ C lime juice and mix with 2½ C of sugar syrup; add 2 C of pineapple juice and ¾ C of orange juice. When ready to serve, put in glasses half filled with crushed ice and add a cherry.

MINT

3 mint leaves to 1 C of tea
4 mint leaves to 1 glass of lemonade, orangeade, or limeade.

MINT PUNCH

Take 10 sprigs of fresh mint and remove all the bruised leaves. Shake a cupful of crushed ice and ½C of sugar until the sugar is dissolved, add the mint, pouring over it 1 T of lemon juice; put in a cupful of currant juice and water to make a quart of liquid. Add more water if desired weaker.

MINT WATER

1 C mint leaves   1 pt. of hot water

Wash, clean and chop fine the mint leaves, pack in cup, cover with water allowing to steep 30 min., strain and use for flavor. Will flavor apple jelly.

ORANGEADE

6 oranges   12 t sugar
2 lemons

Squeeze juice of lemons and oranges. Cut rind of oranges in small pieces, cover with sugar and let stand 1 hr. Add juices, shake well and strain. Dip the wet rim of tall glasses in sugar giving a frosted look, and pile high with crushed ice.

ORANGE EGG NOG

5 eggs   4 oranges (large)
6 t sugar

Beat eggs, whites and yolks separately until as stiff as possible. Add sugar and cut orange into small cubes, mix together and serve in 6 portions in glasses. Must be ice cold. Any other fruit may be used.

PERCOLATED COFFEE

1¼ T coffee for each cup.

PINEAPPLE LEMONADE

1 C sugar
3 C water
1 C pineapple juice

3 lemons
1 C orange juice

Boil pineapple and sugar in water 10 min. Strain. When cool add other juices.

RASPBERRY BOMBE GLACE

Mash a quart of red raspberries, either fresh or preserved, add half a C of pineapple juice or grated pineapple, 1 C sugar, and 1 C of water. Cook for 10 min., remove from fire, add the juice of an orange. Press thru a sieve and add 1 pt. of water. Serve with shaved ice.

STRAWBERRY COCKTAIL

Slice berries, cover with orange juice and let stand 2 hrs. in ice box. Serve in punch glasses adding shaved ice and ½ t sugar to each glass.

Mrs. Chester Long.

SUMMER DRINKS

Fruit juices contain valuable mineral salts and can be canned at home and mixed with sweetening, making a most delicious pure drink. Sugar should preferably be melted. Use 1 C sugar to 1 C water, boil 3 min. and can to use when needed.

Cold chocolate with plenty of cream, sugar, and chopped ice.

Loganberry juice, peach juice, grape juice, pear juice, orange, lemon, strawberry, and pineapple juice or combinations of these make most delicious cool drinks.

Ice should be shaved or broken in very small pieces for all cold drinks.

Lemonade or any fruit drink is improved by being shaken vigorously in a lemonade shaker.

(CUP OF) TEA

1 C water
½ t tea

Tea ball

Do not use water that has boiled. Use fresh water and do not let it boil over 2 min. Having placed the tea in the tea ball, place the tea ball in a tea cup, and pour over it the boiling water. Let stand until as strong as desired. Serve with lemon bits and orange strips and lump sugar.

(POT OF) TEA—2 CUPS

3 C water   1½ t tea

Have tea pot dry and hot, put in tea, in 2 min., add fresh boiling water and let stand 3 to 5 min. according to the strength desired. Strain into cups.

The best tea comes from China, Japan, Ceylon and the West Indies.

TEA PUNCH

Pour boiling sweetened lemonade on tea leaves. Let stand till cool. Strain and serve in tall glasses, with triangle of sliced lemon and a sprig of mint. Sweeten to taste and serve with shaved ice.

TEMPERANCE PUNCH

1 lb. raspberries	Bit of lemon rind
1 lb. currants (or other fruit)	8 lemons (juice)
4 qt water	6 oranges (juices)
4 C sugar	1 qt. finely crushed ice
4 C water	1 lb cherries (candied)

Mash raspberries and currants to a pulp; add 4 qts of water; let it stand covered for 2 or 3 hrs; boil granulated sugar and the 4 cups of water, dropping in a bit of lemon rind, for 10 min When cold add juice of lemons and oranges, strain both mixtures and pour together, keep cold and add finely crushed ice when ready to serve; one pound of candied cherries may be added.

VANILLA PUNCH

¼ C boiling water	2 T sugar
1 egg	4 T milk
10 drops vanilla	5 drops mint

Add sugar to well beaten egg, then add boiling water, then the milk and vanilla. Shake thoroly and add mint.

CANDY

CANDY

Butter-Scotch	Mrs. B. H Campbell
Candy	C C.
Caramel Candy	Mrs. Lewelling
Caramels	Mrs. R. L. Millison
Cracker-Jack	C. C.
Cream Candy	Mrs. F. A. Amsden
Divinity Candy	Mrs. Phil Buck
Divinity Loaf	Mrs. F. G. Smyth
Fondant	Mrs. B. H. Campbell
Fudges	C. C.
Ice Cream Candy	C. C.
Maple Loaf	Mrs. J. H. Black
Mint Leaves, Candied	Mrs J. H. Black
Nugat, French	Mrs. W E. Stanley
Patience Candy	Mrs. F. G. Smyth
Smith College Fudge	Mrs. Harry Dockum

BUTTER-SCOTCH

1 C sugar
1 C Karo Corn Syrup
1 C butter

3 t vinegar
1/3 t soda
½ nutmeg, grated

Mix and boil until when tested in cold water it will be brittle and snap against the side of the cup. Pour into buttered pans and before it is too hard, score it into squares with a sharp knife.

Mrs. B H. Campbell

CANDY

2 C sugar
½ C water

½ C water
1 egg (white)

Boil sugar, syrup, and water until it hardens on the edge of the pan. Add the beaten white of egg and whip until very stiff. Add nuts if desired.

CARAMEL CANDY

1½ C granulated sugar
½ C butter
½ C syrup

½ C milk
1 C nuts

Boil. Just before taking from the fire, add one cup chopped nuts.

Mrs Gov. Lewelling.

CARAMELS

1½ C sugar
½ C corn syrup
1 C butter

½ C milk
1 t vanilla

Cook until when dropped in ice water it becomes hard. Pour in a buttered shallow pan and cut in squares.

Mrs. Ralph L. Millison.

CRACKER JACK

4 qts. popped corn
2 C hulled peanuts
1 C sugar

1 C molasses
2 T butter

Boil sugar, butter and molasses together until syrup will hair, pour over popcorn and peanuts, mix all together, and form into balls.

CREAM CANDY

3 lb. sugar, gr
1 lb. nuts or fruit

1 lb Karo Syrup
1½ pt. heavy cream

Stir one way, and, all the time while cooking, until dropped in cold water forming a ball. Take from fire and stir until cool

Mrs F A. Amsden.

DIVINITY CANDY

1½ pt. cream
6 C granulated sugar
1 lb. dark Karo Syrup
1 C Engish Walnuts

1 C Pecans
1 slice candied pineapple
1/3 can candied cherries
(Both fruits cut in pieces)

Boil cream, sugar and syrup together on low fire until it begins to boil, then on a hot fire until it forms a soft ball when dropped in cold water. (Fifteen or twenty minutes). Remove from fire and stir constantly until creamy. Add nuts and candied fruits and pour in bread pan (buttered) to form a loaf.

Mrs. Phil Buck.

DIVINITY LOAF

6 C sugar
3 C cream

2 C golden drip syrup
3 C walnuts

Cook, sugar, cream and syrup until it tests a soft ball, stirring all the time. Remove from stove and let stand until it cools a little, then stir hard until it begins to thicken, add broken nuts, and put in a bread tin that has previously been rinsed with cold water, do not grease tin.

Mrs. F. G. Smyth.

FONDANT

3 C sugar
1-3 C glucose
1½ C water

1 t vanilla
1 t butter

Cook until it will soft ball in cold water, then add vanilla and butter.

Mrs. B. H Campbell.

FUDGES

2 C sugar
1 C milk

2 T butter
2 sq. chocolate

Boil till it will make a soft ball in water. Beat till stiff.

ICE CREAM CANDY

3 C light B. sugar
¼ C butter

½ t cream tartar
1 t lemon extract

Boil together sugar, butter, and cream tarter till it threads, leave till cool, add lemon while pulling.

C. C.

MAPLE LOAF

3 pt. granulated sugar
1 pt. golden syrup

1½ pt. cream
1½ lbs. nuts

Boil without stirring until it will form a soft ball   Cool a little and stir until it creams. Put in nuts broken in fine pieces just before pouring into mold.

Mrs. J. H. Black.

CANDIED MINT LEAVES

1 C sugar   2 C mint leaves
½ C water

Boil sugar and water without stirring until it spins a thread when dropping from spoon. Add mint leaves, boil slowly for five minutes. Remove from fire, stir with fork until sugar crystallizes.

Mrs. J. H. Black.

FRENCH NUGAT

Part 1
2 C sugar   1 C boiling water

Part 2
1 C sugar   1 t vanilla
1 C rock candy syrup   3 egg-whites

Put Part 1 on first. Boil each until it balls in cold water. Beat egg-whites and beat into Part 2. Now beat this into Part 1 Add vanilla and nuts. Put a buttered paper in pan, and cut nugat into squares.

Mrs. W. E. Stanley.

PATIENCE CANDY

3 C sugar   1 pt. milk
¾ lb. walnuts in the shell   Butter size of walnut

Take one cup of sugar and melt it (using an aluminum kettle) until this is rich brown. Add one cup milk and stir until the melted sugar is dissolved. Then add rest of sugar and milk and butter. Cook and stir until it forms a soft ball, in water test. Have nuts broken and in a deep bowl, turn candy over the hulled nuts and let stand a few minutes, then beat as long as possible, putting it in a pan to mold.

Mrs. F. G. Smyth.

SMITH COLLEGE FUDGE

2 C B. sugar   Butter size of an egg
1 C G. sugar   Iron spoonful Karo syrup
2 sq. bitter chocolate   1 C sour cream
2 t vanilla

Cook until it makes a soft ball in ice water.

Mrs. Harry Dockum.

RECIPES BY
Famous Women

THESE RECIPES WERE COLLECTED FROM
HER FRIENDS BY MRS. CHESTER I. LONG
BEFORE HER DEATH.

A RECIPE FOR A HOME—FOR THE BEGINNER'S CLASS

The beginner's classes are *home*-loving lasses,
And here is a way to make it:
Take a pound of *Sense*, and a pound of *Skill*,
A pinch of *Pride*, and as much *Goodwill;*
Put in *Honest Work* to taste
Contentment, to make a good rich paste,
And in *Love's* oven bake it.

To do to a turn,
With no scorch nor burn,
All the years of a life must be given;
With *Unselfishness* make a dainty frost
Where *Forgiveness* flavor is never lost—
Then your Home will have the worth
That adds to the very best things of Earth,
The sweetness and joy of heaven.

Margaret Hill McCarter.

RECIPES BY FAMOUS WOMEN

Rhubrab Marmalade with Almonds	Mrs. Theodore Roosevelt, Oyster Bay, N. Y.
Mushrooms	Mrs. William Howard Taft.
War Cake	Mrs. Brand Whitlock
	Miss Mable Boardman
Oyster Cocktail	Mrs. Charles F. Scott
Gingerbread	Mrs. Charles F. Scott
Ragout of Duck	Mrs. Phillip P. Campbell
Peanut Butter Fudge	Mrs. T. N. Tincher
Date Bars	Mrs. T. N. Tincher
Pumpkin Pie	Mrs. W. E. Hoch
Graham Bread	Mrs. S. J. C. Crawford
Drop Cakes	Mrs. S. J. C. Crawford
Suet or Plum Pudding	Mrs. L. U. Humphrey
Corn Bread	Mrs. Guy T. Helvering
Sponge Cake	Mrs. John J. Ingalls
Hard Sugar Ginger Bread	Senator Ingall's Mother
Famous Blackberry Jam	Mrs. John J. Ingalls
Snowball Pudding	Mrs. William Jennings Bryan
Mustard Pickle	Mrs. George H. Hodges
Conserve of Red Raspberries	Miss Mary Best
Nutted Cream	Mrs. W. J. Bailey
Chicken Turbit	Mrs. Arthur Capper
Bunting Hash	Mrs. Jouett Shouse
Delicious Sweet Potatoes	Mrs. J. N. Tincher
Pimento Cheese Filling	Mrs. J. N. Tincher
Pineapple Sherbet	Mrs. Phillip P. Campbell
Fried Peaches	Mrs. William A. Johnston
Beet Relish	Mrs. William A. Johnston
Cocoanut Pudding	Mrs. Charles Curtis
Potato Cakes	Mrs. Phillip P. Campbell
Scotch Shortbread	Miss Mary Best
Pork Cake	Mrs. John R. Connelly

RHUBARB MARMALADE WITH ALMONDS

1 qt. finely cut rhubarb
2 C granulated sugar
¼ C water

2 T shelled and blanched Jordan almonds

Wash and dry the rhubarb (do not skin), cut in very small pieces; put in agate or porcelain-lined kettle, cover with the sugar, add the water; place over slow fire 5 min., stir until sugar is dissolved, then boil rapidly for 5 min., reduce the heat and boil 40 min. very slowly. Be sure to remove all scum as it arises. Add the almonds which have been blanched and sliced very fine, boil 5 min. longer. Sterilize the glasses or jars. Put the marmalade in at once and cover. When cold put in cool, dark place for winter use. This amount makes 3 glasses. For 12 glasses use:

4 qts. of rhubarb
8 C sugar (4 lbs.)
1 C water

1 C shelled and blanched almonds

Mrs. Theodore Roosevelt,
Oyster Bay, N. Y.

MUSHROOMS

1 lb. of mushroms
1 t butter
1 C cream

6 slices of toast
Salt
Pepper

The mushroom bells are made of fireproof glass. One lb. of large fresh mushrooms, peel and remove stems. Saute the mushrooms in butter, salt and pepper 1 min. Add the cup of cream, and simmer 10 min. Put the toast, which has been toasted on 1 side, in the "nappes" which come with the bells. Cover with the mushrooms, pour the liquid over, put on the covers, bake from 15 to 20 min. Serve without removing the bells

Mrs. William Howard Taft

WAR CAKE

2 C hot water
2 T lard (can use ½ Crisco and ½ oil)
1 pkg. seedless raisins (cut once)

2 C B. sugar
1 t salt
1 t cloves
1 t cinnamon

Boil all these ingredients 5 min. after they begin to bubble. When cold add 1 t soda dissolved in 1 t of hot water and 3 C sifted flour. Bake in 2 loaves 45 min in slow oven. This cake is better when a few days old.

Mrs. Brand Whitlock.
Miss Mable Boardman.

OYSTER COCKTAIL

5 to 7 raw oysters or clams for each service
1 T tomato catsup
1 t horseradish
1 t tarragon vinegar

1 t Worcestershire sauce
1 t lemon juice
4 drops Tabasco sauce
¼ t salt

Mix all the seasonings thoroughly, add the bivalves and set in the ice box to become thoroughly chilled and blended before serving

Mrs. Charles F. Scott

GINGERBREAD

1 C New Orleans Molasses
1 C B. sugar
½ C butter
1 C buttermilk
3 eggs
2½ C pastry flour

2 t ginger
½ t cinnamon
¼ t nutmeg
¼ t salt
1 t soda

Mix sugar and butter, molasses and spices, cook until nearly to the candying point. Beat in soda and cool. Add buttermilk and egg-yolks, beaten light, then flour and lastly the well beaten whites. Bake in a moderate oven. It kills the flavor to hurry it. Serve hot with hard sauce.

Mrs. Charles F Scott

RAGOUT OF DUCK

1 pair of ducks
2 T flour
2 T butter
1 T onion juice

1 bay leaf
1 pt stock or boiling water
1 t lemon juice
6 mushrooms

Prepare ducks for basking and place them in a pan. Put thin slices of bacon over breasts and add ½ C water and salt and bake until tender, but not too done, about 1 hr. Take from the oven and carve. Put butter in a saucepan. Cook until brown, add flour, stir until smooth. Then add stock or boiling water stirring continually until it boils. Then add onion juice, lemon juice, bay leaf, salt and pepper and mushrooms chopped fine. Add ducks, and all juice from plate upon which they were carved. Cover and simmer gently about 20 min. Take from the fire and serve on heated dish with border of toasted bread cut in triangles. Garnish with parsley.

Mrs. Phillip P. Campbell

PEANUT BUTTER FUDGE

2-3 C sweet milk   3 T peanut butter
2 C sugar

Put over fire and boil until it will make a soft ball in water. Remove and stir until creamy. Pour into buttered pans to cool.

Mrs. J. N. Tincher

DATE BARS

1 C sugar   1 C flour
3 eggs   1 t B. P.
1 C chopped English walnuts   ¼ t salt
1 lb. dates

Beat egg-yolks, combine with sugar, stir until creamy. Mix together, flour, baking powder and salt; add nuts and dates stoned and quartered. Beat egg-whites stiff and add alternately with the flour mixture to the yolks and sugar. Bake in a sheet in pan in a moderate oven for about 30 min. Remove from the pan, cut into bars, roll in powdered sugar, or ice with orange or chocolate frosting and decorate with nut meats or with stoned dates.

Mrs. J. N. Tincher

PUMPKIN PIE

1 can of pumpkin   ¼ t salt
1½ C sugar   1 pt. milk
1 T butter   1 C cream
1 t ginger   4 eggs
1 t cinnamon

Put pumpkin in a stew pan and let cook slowly for ½ hr., or until it is quite dry. To this add the sugar, butter, ginger, cinnamon and salt Then add the milk and cream and the well beaten eggs. Stir all together thoroughly. Put in pans lined with good pastry, bake to a nice brown. Serve cold with a large spoon of whipped cream on each piece. This will make 2 pies.

Mrs. E. W. Hoch.

GRAHAM BREAD

2 C flour   1 egg
2 C graham   3 t B. P.
½ C sugar   ¼ t salt
½ C molasses

Melt the molasses and add the sugar, then egg, then dry ingredients sifted together. Bake as for cake. Serve either hot or cold.

Mrs. S. J. C. Crawford

DROP CAKES

1 egg   ¼ t nutmeg
½ C milk   1 t B. P
1 T sugar   Flour to make a stiff batter
¼ t salt

Drop in fat and fry As you take them out drop them into a plate of pulverized sugar and roll once They look like snow balls. If they should soak fat, add another egg and more flour.

Mrs. S. J. C. Crawford

SUET OR PLUM PUDDING

1 C suet   2½ C flour
1 C molasses   1 C or more of raisins
1 t soda in molasses   1 T cinnamon
1 C sweet milk   ½ t cloves

Steam 3 or 4 hrs. in greased baking powder cans filled ½ full

Mrs. L. U. Humphrey

CORN BREAD

1 egg   2 T sugar
1½ C milk   3 t B P
1 C flour   1 t salt
2 C corn meal   3 T melted butter

Mix flour, meal, sugar, salt and B P , stir into beaten egg and milk, add melted butter and stir until smooth. This recipe should be appreciated by all the people of the state where corn is King.

Mrs. Guy T. Helvering

SPONGE CAKE

12 eggs   2 t cream of tartar
1 lb of granulated sugar   ¾ t salt
½ lb of flour

Sift flour with the cream of tartar and salt 3 times. Separate the eggs, beat yolks thoroughly and add sugar gradually. Add then the well beaten whites and lastly the flour. Bake in a *slow* oven 50 min Ice with a lemon icing

Mrs John J Ingalls

HARD SUGAR GINGER BREAD

3 C granulated sugar   1 t soda
2 C butter   2 T ginger
1 C sour milk

Enough flour to roll out like biscuit dough. Cut in strips 8 in by 2 Mark with the back of knife Bake in moderate oven

Senator Ingall's Mother

FAMOUS BLACKBERRY JAM

2 gal. blackberries   1 qt. sugar
1 pt. water

Take 2 gal. of blackberries, pick over and wash carefully. Cover with a pint of water and cook until soft. Put pulp and juice through a wire sieve. Take 1 qt. of the strained juice and pulp, put in a granite kettle and place on stove. When it boils add 1 qt. of heated granulated white sugar; boil steadily until it jellies. It can be easily tested by dropping a little on a cold saucer. Pour in glasses and seal. Fruit must not be quite ripe. Wild berries are the best. Never make more than a qt. at a time.

Mrs John J. Ingalls

SNOWBALL PUDDING

Pare and core 6 apples, steam them, run through colander, add 1 C sugar, let stand till cold, then beat whites of 3 eggs stiff. Stir all together and serve with whipped cream.

Mrs. William Jennings Bryan

MUSTARD PICKLE

1 small head cauliflower   2 qt. cucumber
2 qt small onions   1 pt. small pickles
2 qt. sliced green tomatoes

Cut in half the whole small pickles. Cut the cucumbers, then cut in chunks.

6 green peppers ground   1 or 2 sweet red mangoes cut in
                                  strips

Soak all in weak brine and scald.

Mustard paste:

2-3 C flour   2 t cinnamon
3 T ground mustard   2 t cloves
1½ T tumeric   Some nutmeg and celery seed
3 C B. sugar

Mix dry ingredients, add 2 qt. of vinegar (diluted if very strong). Cook well and pour over pickle after it has been well drained. Cook slowly about 30 min. Stir often.

Mrs. George H. Hodges

CONSERVE OF RED RASPBERRIES

1 lb. red raspberries   1½ lb. sugar

To each lb. of red raspberries allow 1½ lb. of sugar. Put raspberries into pan, mash until perfectly smooth, then add sugar. Place on stove and let remain until scum rises with a few bubbles, do not allow to boil beyond 1 min. When the process is finished seal and keep in cool place. This jam keeps perfectly. It looks and tasts like fresh crushed fruit. Served with thick cream (not whipped) it is delicious

Miss Mary Best

NUTTED CREAM

¼ box Knox gelatine   1 pt. cream
½ C cold water   1 C chopped pecans
¾ C powdered sugar

Cover ¼ box of Knox's gelatine with ½ C of cold water and let soak ½ hr. Whip 1 pt. cream stiff. Add ¾ C powdered sugar, 1 C chopped pecans, and 1 t vanilla. Pour 3 or 4 T of water over gelatine and set over kettle of boiling water until it is thoroughly dissolved. When entirely cool and before the gelatine begins to set pour into mixture and stir well until it starts to thicken. Keep covered till served.

Mrs. W. J. Bailey

CHICKEN TURBIT

3 chickens   2 T flour
1 can mushrooms   1 pt cream
2 T melted butter   1 pt. stock

Melt butter in skillet, add flour, mix well, add the cream and the stock. Stir till it thickens. Boil the chickens and cut. Mix all together and bake in the oven with bread crumbs on top

Mrs. Arthur Capper.

BUNTING HASH

Buy steak cut from the round about an inch thick Cut into pieces about an inch long and half an inch wide. Stew in butter without browning in a covered pan until tender. Be careful not to allow meat to fry. When cooked thoroughly pour into the vessel sufficient milk for gravy. Thicken, and season with salt and pepper. Serve on toast.

Mrs. Jouett Shouse.

DELICIOUS SWEET POTATOES

3 C mashed potatoes   ¼ C broken pecan meats or
½ C sugar   walnut meats
¼ C butter   Few grains of cinnamon or
¼ C raisins   nutmeg
1-3 t salt   ¼ lb. marshmallows

Peel and cut potatoes in small pieces and boil as Irish potatoes. 3 moderately sized large sweet potatoes will be ample for the amount specified. When mashed add the sugar, butter, salt and spice, beat until light and puffy, then stir in the raisins and the nuts. Pile in a buttered baking dish, dot with the marshmallows and brown.

Mrs J. N Tincher

PIMENTO CHEESE FILLING

½ C vinegar
1 T butter
1 well beaten egg
1 t cornstarch

½ t salt
¼ T sugar
1 lb cheese
1 small can pimentos

Make the salad dressing and while hot add the cheese and pimentos which have been run through the food chopper.

Mrs. J. N. Tincher

PINEAPPLE SHERBET

1 qt granulated sugar
1 large can grated pineapple

4 lemons
3 egg-whites

Make a thick syrup and pour it boiling hot, over the pineapple. Add juice and pulp of the lemons. After the syrup has been allowed to cool put into a gallon freezer, stir in the stiffly beaten whites of eggs and fill with water to within one quart of the top. This will serve 20 persons.

Mrs. Phillip P. Campbell.

FRIED PEACHES

Select large free-stone peaches, divide in halves, but do not peel. Have a spoonful of melted butter in skillet and place peaches open side down. Cook over slow fire until tender. Then turn them, fill seed cavities with sugar, cover again and cook until sugar is in a syrup. Serve hot. This is a nice breakfast or luncheon dish in warm weather.

Mrs. William A Johnston.

BEET RELISH

3 or 4 medium sized beets
3 onions

2 stalks of celery
2 green peppers (mangoes)

Grind coarse or chop, add salt to taste and cover the whole with sweetened vinegar.

Mrs. William A. Johnston.

COCOANUT PUDDING

2 eggs
1 C sugar
1 pt. milk
¼ lb. cocoanut

5 T bread crumbs
1 C raisins, seeded
¼ C melted butter

Cream sugar with yolks of eggs, beat in the beaten whites, add milk and cocoanut, bread crumbs and raisins, beat together and add butter last. Bake until browned. Serve not too cold.

Mrs. Charles Curtis

POTATO CAKE

1 C butter	4 eggs
2 C sugar	1 C raisins
3 C flour	1 C grated chocolate
½ C milk	½ C pecan meats
1 C mashed potatoes	1-3 t cinnamon
2 t B. P	1-3 t cloves
1 t salt	1-3 t nutmeg

Cream butter and sugar. Add yolks of eggs beaten, then add milk. Sift flour, baking powder and spices together Add these, then chocolate, then pecans and raisins well floured, potatoes beaten light and cold, and lastly the whites of eggs well beaten. Bake in layers and put together with either white or chocolate frosting.

Mrs. Phillip P. Campbell

SCOTCH SHORTBREAD

2 lb. flour	1 ounce of sweet almonds
1 lb. butter	Candied peel
½ lb powdered sugar	

Beat the butter to a cream, gradually dredge in the flour, and sugar, add almonds which should be blanched and cut in pieces Work paste until very smooth and divide in 6 pieces. Put each cake on separate sheet of white paper, pat out square until 1 in. thick, pinch edges, and ornament with strips of candied peel. Bake in moderate oven 30 or 40 min. This Scotch cake will keep as long as the family does not know of its whereabouts. Caraway seeds are often used in Scotland instead of almonds Both may be omitted

Miss Mary Best

PORK CAKE

1 lb fat pork, ground	1 t cinnamon
1 pt. boiling water poured over fat	1 t ginger
	1 t lemon extract
2 C sugar	2 C flour
3 eggs well beaten	1 t soda

Stir the above ingredients into a dough. Then add the following mixture:

2 C flour	2 C raisins
1¼ t B. P.	1 C currants

Bake about 40 min.

Mrs John R. Connelly

THINGS YOU SHOULD KNOW

Making the tea for ice tea in the morning, and letting it cool for dinner or lunch saves ice.

Soda should be mixed with the dry flour, never stirred into liquid as much of the rising quality is lost in the wetting.

Soda or B. P. mixtures should never be allowed to stand in a warm place, but should be put in oven at once.

Sometimes cake falling may be avoided by putting a piece of paper over the top of the cake at first.

Fruit cake recipes call for dried currants these are hard and lack flavor, try using an equal measure of chopped prunes. They hold moisture and impart a delicious flavor.

So many left over bits of meats or vegetables may be combined with cream sauce and served on stale bread toasted.

Use lemon juice in salads and you have a more delicate salad than useing vinegar.

"The Dinner never should await the guests; but the guests the dinner."

Crisco burns at a lower temperature than butter. Does not absorb odors.

Carron Oil, which is half Linseed oil and half lime water, is a wonderful remedy for burns. Pour on burn at once, saturate gauze with the oil, cover burn, and rap in cotton. Do not place the cotton next the burn, keep well saturated, several days, no scars will result and there are no bad effects.

Rose Jar. Gather leaves put in bread tray and salt, leave for one week tossing and mixing daily, until dry; about 5 to 7 days. Pack away in stone jar for 6 weeks to ripen when it may be put into rose jar. This will be fragrant many years and is lovely placed in a linen closet or dresser drawers.

½ ounce violet sachet	½ ounce of Rose
½ ounce of heliotrope	1 T cloves
1 T Cinnamon	1 T allspice

WASHING FLUID

1 can of lye	2 ozs. of lump amonia
2 ozs. of salts tartar	1 lb. of borax in lump
2½ gallons water	

Use one cup in a boiler of water, with soap cut fine.

TO REMOVE MILDEW

1 bar laundry soap	5 cents gloss starch
1 qt. soft water	3 lemons
1 C salt	Kansas sunshine

Cut laundry soap fine, and boil in the water, add salt, starch and lemon juice, dip and wet garment in this thoroughly and expose to sun until the mildew disappears, mixture should be like soft soap.

A SPECIFIC FOR POISON OAK OR IVY

A solution of Chinosol is a specific for poison oak or Ivy One tablet dissolved in a quart of water. The tablets come 12 in a package. Put it on a piece of cotton and apply.

TO REMOVE SPOTS

Five cents worth Oxalic acid, dissolved in half pint water. Rub on spots over old soft cloth, when dim, rinse spots with fresh water.

TO PACK EGGS

Put 1 quart liquid glass in stone jar with 12 quarts water Add fresh eggs as you get them. Infertile eggs best

To spread butter when hard have some boiling water handy and dip the point of the knife into it each time This will enable you to butter the thinnest bread without spoiling the slice.

If a little salt be sprinkled over dishes on which eggs have been served the dishes will wash easily.

When preparing a chicken try rubbing inside with a piece of lemon, and you will find it very good, as it whitens the flesh and makes it more tender.

To remove old putty from window after the glass has been taken out, pass a hot soldering iron or poker over it. This softens it and it is easily removed

Pop overs, puffs, omeletes and custards cooked too fast will fall apart.

Salt will remove egg stain from silver when applied dry with a soft cloth

Squeaking doors should be oiled on the hinges.

If the white porcelean of the sink becomes stained, wet it and sprinkle cloride of lime into it. Let stand about half an hour and it will become white

Open a can on the side. It is easier.

Cookies split in the center and burst when baked too quickly on top.

Boiling the burners on the gas stove in soap suds once in a while keeps them free from gummy substances and permits the supply of gas to flow more freely.

Making out a menu for breakfasts and dinners every day for a week saves much wear and tear on the home maker's thought machine. Lunch can be a time to use left overs.

If you feel very tired and drowsy, dash very cold water in your face.

An insipid pudding should have a strongly flavored sauce, and vice versa

Never allow meat to stand in water. The water drains out the juice.

Every good housewife knows the importance of having novelty in the meals.

Salt should never remain in anything rubber. It causes the rubber to rot.

Prunes cooked without adding sugar are more wholesome and better flavored.

Spinach is in a class by itself because of its large amount of iron.

To clean furs, moisten some bran with hot water; rub fur with it, and dry with a flannel, then rub with a piece of muslin and some dry bran.

If you rinse a plate with cold water before breaking the eggs on it, add to them a pinch of salt and then stand where there is a current of air and you will have no difficulty in beating them to a froth.

If you wish a beautifully browned pie crust, brush with cream or milk when ready for oven.

The finger marks on a door can be removed by a clean flannel cloth dipped in kerosene oil; afterward wipe with a cloth wrung out in hot water in order to take the smell away.

To prevent cakes, pies and other pastry from burning on the bottom, sprinkle the bottom of the oven with fine, dry salt, and your cake or pies will bake perfectly.

Fried things are more indigestible, because the fat reaches a higher temperature which dissolves into fatty acids.

When you are digging in the garden you will be discouraged to find how the dirt clings under your nails. Try rubbing soap under the nails before you go out to work. It will form a fine protection against dirt and will not be hard to remove when the digging is done.

Don't make the mistake of using your table or bed linen in rotation, one after the other. Use a few changes until they are worn out, then take the next best and add new ones to your store. In this way you will not be embarrassed by finding everything in holes at once. The same thing refers to personal underclothes.

Dampen clothes with a whisk broom, it is far better than the hand and easier.

Never pour grease down a drain. If you have not a sink strainer to catch the grease try laying a piece of paper over the drain before pouring out greasy water. The paper will catch the grease and can be burned.

Too much starch will cause linen to crack in the folds.

When ironing linen, move the iron with the threads, never diagonally.

To keep curtains from blowing, cover small tailor's weights with goods of the color of the curtains and sew to the lower corners

If bottles of medicine are to be carried when traveling, dip the tops in melted paraffine to prevent leaking. Do not cork too tightly or the cork will "work up."

Never allow milk to remain uncovered.

Wood ashes make a good polish for tinware.

Minced olives in potato salad are an improvement.

Heat sugar and milk first when making doughnuts.

Onions peeled under water will prevent your eyes from watering.

Cream doubles its bulk in whipping. It must be cold and 24 hours old to whip.

Cold butter is more digestible than warm, because the heat dissolves the butter into fatty acids which are indigestible.

A small child should have a small quantity of orange juice a day.

To remove coffee stains from silk, pour pure glycerine on the stain, put in bath towel rub with a soft cloth, and repeat the operation, sponge in soft water in fine white soap, until all disappears

Rub the top of a drawer or the hinges of a door with soap if they creak.

Paint brushes make by far the most convenient and satisfactory dusters for crevices, woodwork and carved surfaces. A housekeeper will find several sizes worth having in the house.

Tack Indian Head bordered with rick rack back of the stove and the table in the kitchen to protect the walls.

Soapstone set over a low gas flame will cook food much better than setting food over a high gas flame. Any kind of food requiring long cooking can be done much more economically in this way. Meat is especially good.

A soapstone griddle does not require greasing It is designed for the purpose of doing away with all disagreeable smell of grease and smoke. See that it is perfectly smooth and thoroughly heated before pouring on the batter When once heated to proper degree it can easily be kept at uniform heat. If too cold the cakes will stick Have a clean oven cloth or large paint brush and brush off the griddle after each baking. But it must never be greased.

To give castor oil put the dose in orange juice with the tiniest bit of soda stirred in to make it foam.

Furs and woolens may be kept free from moths, if they are well cleaned before putting away. Then line a box with newspaper so there are no cracks for moths to enter, sprinkle either tobacco, camphor or moth balls in with the clothes or furs. Cover well with newspaper and no moths will enter.

Rugs should be well cleaned, rolled with newspapers in between each layer; and moth balls. The ends should be tied in newspapers also.

The ink on the newspaper is an enemy of the moth. Mice will not enter a drawer where there is camphor.

Rub spots with yolk of eggs before washing.

Put tough meat in vinegar before cooking.

Rubbing with chloroform will remove paint from goods. Kerosene oil or gasoline cleans silks

When flat irons stick or become rusty rub them on cedar when hot.

Tar may be removed from cloth with turpentine.

Machine grease may be removed by rubbing the spot with pure lard, or spot may be saturated with turpentine

Place a pitcher of cold water in a room and it will absorb all the impurities in a few hours It will purify the room but the water will be entirely unfit for use

To set colors in wash goods soak before washing in 1 T oxgall to 1 gal of water.

Salt should always be eaten with nuts to aid digestion.

A fireless cooker and a steam cooker are great accessories to the kitchen equipment. A good steam cooker will cook 6 different things at once on one gas burner and no mixing of flavor.

Vinegar added to rhubarb jam gives it a spicy flavor.

Ink from carpets may be removed by wetting in milk after all has been taken up by blotting paper that is possible.

Suit cases that look dingy may be brightened by rubbing with oil.

Brooms dipped for 2 minutes in boiling soap suds once a week and then plunged in cold water last longer and are tougher.

Marble statuary may be washed with soft water and ivory soap, rinsed with clear water and dried with a soft cloth.

One T grated horseradish in a pan of milk will keep it sweet longer.

Never put cake in the refrigerator, it makes it tough.

Angel Food cake is the only cake improved by keeping in refrigerator, in oil paper

A heated knife will cut warm bread or cake without crumbling.

In making ginger cookies try mixing batter with cold coffee instead of water.

If cream does not whip try adding 2 drops of lemon juice and whip again

In making cake if oven gets too hot set a pan of cold water in it.

To get the meats of pecan nuts whole soak the pecans over night in water, next morning crack them on the end The meat will come out without breaking.

A slice of lemon skin eaten with sugar or salt will kill the odor of onion on the breath.

An egg well beaten added to rhubarb pies, will thicken the rhubarb and improve the taste.

To get rid of red ants wash the shelves clean and while damp rub fine salt on them quite thickly. Let it remain on for a time and the ants will disappear.

A glass of vinegar put into the water in which salt fish is soaking will draw out most of the salt.

In mixing liquids with solids add the liquid to the solid by degrees. They will blend more readily.

To prevent milk or cream from curdling when used in combination with tomato, add a bit of bicarbonate of soda before mixing.

If you use too much salt by mistake add a trifle of sugar or of vinegar, according to dish. This will counteract the salty taste

Melons may be chilled in midsummer by wrapping them about with a burlap sack, saturating this with water and keeping it wet and placing it in the direct rays of the sun for a time Evaporation does the work.

Before tacking down linoleum, let it lie in place and be walked on a few days   This will make it be perfectly smooth

Milk or cream which is just turning sour may be sweetened with a little soda stirred into it

Soap should be unrapped and put in a dry place to harden and it will last longer.

Lemon juice and salt will remove iron rust. Put on the garment and place in hot sun. Mildew also can be removed in this way.

Kerosene will soften leather

Melted paraffine poured on top of the jelly prevents mold

Flowers will keep fresh 24 hours by wetting and covering with paper to keep out air, place in cool place.

Nickel may be cleaned with kerosene and whiting

Bitter butter is the result of cream standing too long.

Paint on glass may be removed with strong hot vinegar.

Drain pipes should have lime water or lye water poured into them occasionally.

Sand put in bottles with soap suds and shaken will clean them

Glass measuring cup is best, for you can see through exactly.

Do not salt milk until it boils or it may curdle

Use a fork in mixing flour and milk for a thickening, also a pinch of salt helps to dissolve lumps.

PRESERVING OLIVES

After opening a bottle of olives, if the remainder are not required for immediate use, pour off the liquid and cover with olive oil   This will keep the olives good and fresh for several weeks

SUNKIST ORANGES

Soak oranges in boiled water 1 hour   The skin will come off easily, and the pulp will be sweeter—serve cold Grapefruit may be done the same way.

TO CLEAN WHITE FEATHERS

1 pt. gasoline   1 C corn starch

Wash feathers; then stroke until dry

TO TAKE STAINS OUT OF WHITE TAFFETA

Sponge first with alcohol and warm water to remove the fatty particles. Rub dry with soft linen and sponge with peroxide of hydrogen to bleach the stain Should a trace remain, rub flour well into the spot. Leave for a day and brush.

FURNITURE OIL AND CLEANER

1 qt. soft water	1 qt olive oil or raw oil
1 qt. cider vinegar	1 qt. alcohol

TO TAKE WHITE SPOTS FROM POLISHED WOOD

Rub with the meat of English walnuts.
Rub with sweet oil and camphor.
Rub with essence of or oil of peppermint.
If cookies stick, put sugar on the board.

TO FRY OYSTERS

Fry in half lard and half butter.

TO REMOVE WHITE SPOTS FROM WOOD

1 oz. Wood Alcohol   1 oz. Banana Oil
Rub quickly with the grain of the wood.

WEIGHTS AND MEASURES

SUGAR AND FRUIT

2 Tablespoons ....1 oz.
2 Level coffee cups of granulated...1 lb.
2 Level coffee cups of powdered ....1 lb.
2 Cups of raisins ....1 lb.

FLOUR AND MEAL

3½ Cupfuls corn meal ....1 lb.
2 Cupfuls unsifted or 1 qt. sifted flour ....1 lb.

BUTTER AND EGGS

1 Tablespoonful soft butter ....1 oz.
2 Teacups packed soft butter ....1 lb.
1½ Cups firm butter ....1 lb.
8 Large or 10 medium sized eggs ....1 lb.

MEASURING HINTS

A cup of liquid means all the cup will hold.
A spoonful of liquid is all a spoon will hold.
Salt, flour, seasonings, spices, butter and all solids are measured level.

To measure a level spoonful, dip the spoon in dry material taking up a heaping spoonful, then level it off even with the edge of the spoon with a knife

To measure a part of a spoonful, cut lengthwise of spoon for the half, and crosswise for quarters.

A tablespoonful of butter melted should be measured before melting.

A tablespoonful of melted butter should be measured after melting

Measure a cupful of cream whipped before it is whipped.

Measure a cupful of whipped cream after it is whipped.

Always sift flour, salt, baking powder, sugar and soda before measuring.

TABLE OF PROPORTIONS

2 rounding or 4 even teaspoonfuls of baking powder to 1 qt. of flour.

1 t of flavoring extract to 1 qt of custard

1 t of soda to 1 pt. sour milk.

1 t mixed herbs to 1 qt. soup stock.

1 t soda to 1 C molasses.

$\frac{1}{4}$ t extract of beef to 1 C hot water.

1 t salt to 1 qt. of soup stock or 2 quarts of flour.

1 T chopped vegetables each to 1 qt. soup stock.

$\frac{1}{2}$ t soda to pt. buttermilk 1 day old.

$\frac{3}{4}$ t soda to pt. buttermilk 2 days old.

1 t soda to pt. buttermilk 3 days old.

BAKING POWDER MIXTURES (Plus Variations)

	1 1 (Pour Batter) (Griddle Cakes)	1 2 (Drop Batter) (Muffins)	1 3 (Soft Dough) (Biscuits)	1 4 (Hard Dough) (Rolled Cookies)
Liquid	1 Cup	1 Cup	1 Cup	1 Cup
Flour	1 Cup	2 Cups	3 Cups	4 Cups
Leavening agent	1½ t B. P	3 t B. P.	4½ t B. P.	6 t B. P.
Salt	¼ t	½ t	¾ t	1 t
Stiffening	1 egg	2 eggs		4 eggs
Shortening	1-2 T	2 T	6 T	1 Cup
Sweetening	?	1 T	2 t (?)	1½ C (?)
Flavoring—				

N. B.—Nuts, dates, currants, raisins, etc., are usually used rather than flavoring.

QUANTITIES FOR SERVING

Chicken Salad—A 4 lb. chicken to a qt. of salad.

10 lbs. of chicken serve 25 people.

Jelly Molds—1 qt. to 8 people.

Boullion—1 qt. to 8 people.

Ice Cream, Mousse—1 qt. to 8 people.

Lemonade or Fruit Punch—10 qts. to 50 people.

Tea—1 gal. to 50 people

Coffee—32 cups to a gallon.

Chocolate—27 cups to a gallon, use half lb. chocolate.

Whipped Cream—1 qt. will make 25 spoonsful.

Loaf Sugar—1 lb. to 25 people.

Sugar for Berries—1 lb. for 25 people.

Wafers—3 boxes to 50 people.

Large cake cuts in 24 small slices.

Bonbons—1 lb. serves 16 people

Salted Nuts—1½ lbs. for 25 people.

Tibals and Patties—1 qt makes 25.

Croquetts—1½ qts. make 25.

Potato Chips—2 lbs. serve 25.

Oysters—4-10 for 1 person.

Welsh Rarebit—3 lbs. of cheese for 15.

Chicken or Turkey Dressed—25 lbs. for 48 people.

Two whole sandwiches serve 3 people.

24 sandwiches to a loaf.

1 lb. butter to 2 loaves.

1 C paste and butter to 1 loaf.

1 pt. other fillings to 1 loaf.

LAWN SUGGESTIONS

A bushel of lawn grass weighs about 20 lbs.

A qt of seeds is sufficent to cover 300 square feet—15 by 20 feet.

Grass seed germinate in from 14 to 18 days.

Do not sow grass seed during hot, dry weather, particularly in July and August.

Lawns that are frequently watered need more fertilizer than those that are not, as the water washes away much plant food.

INDEX

CPSIA information can be obtained
at www.ICGtesting.com
Printed in the USA
LVHW081414151118
597254LV00011B/96/P